The Case against Punishment

The Case against Punishment

Retribution, Crime Prevention, and the Law

Deirdre Golash

NEW YORK UNIVERSITY PRESS

New York and London

NEW YORK UNIVERSITY PRESS
New York and London
www.nyupress.org

Library of Congress Cataloging-in-Publication Data
Golash, Deirdre.
The case against punishment :
retribution, crime prevention, and the law / Deirdre Golash.
p. cm.
Includes bibliographical references and index.
ISBN 0-8147-3158-9 (cloth : alk. paper)
1. Punishment.   I. Title.
HV8693.G65   2004
364.6--dc22   2004015007

New York University Press books are printed on acid-free paper,
and their binding materials are chosen for strength and durability.

Manufactured in the United States of America

10 9 8 7 6 5 4 3 2 1

For my grandchildren
Assata, Tatiana, Soraya, Dante, and Raymi

Contents

Acknowledgments

I wish to thank all of the many people who have provided help and support during the writing of this book. I am particularly grateful to Jim Doyle, David Fagelson, Brian Forst, Rob Johnson, Barbara Koziak, Alan Levine, Jim Lynch, Stephen Mathis, Philip Montague, Stephen Nathanson, Liam O'Melinn, Patrick Stone, Laurence Thomas, Roslyn Weiss, and William Wilcox, all of whom provided written comments at various stages; to Eric Forste, who read the whole manuscript; and to two of my research assistants, Corae Briscoe and Mary Velasco, as well as my son Justin, who were all of great help in preparing the final manuscript. I am also indebted to the friends and colleagues, too numerous to name, who provided informal comments at the various conferences where I have presented predecessor papers, particularly those at AMINTAPHIL meetings, and to my students, who have always been my first audience. I regret that I have not been able to respond to all of the points raised by these various critics, who are not responsible for my remaining errors. Finally, I owe a special debt of gratitude to my husband, Michael, for his unfailing encouragement and support.

1

An Institution in Search of a Moral Grounding

As one reads history . . . one is absolutely sickened not by the crimes the wicked have committed, but by the punishments the good have inflicted.
—Oscar Wilde, "The Soul of Man under Socialism," 1891

I. Introduction

Punishment, at its core, is the deliberate infliction of harm in response to wrongdoing. As an institution, it is so deeply rooted in history that it is difficult even to imagine a society without it. We have grown up with it, and it seems natural and inevitable to us. At the same time, there is no denying that it is a human creation; we must accept responsibility, collectively and individually, for the harm that we do in punishing: the deprivation of life, liberty, or property, or the infliction of physical pain. We ought not to impose such harm on anyone unless we have a very good reason for doing so. This remark may seem trivially true, but the history of humankind is littered with examples of the deliberate infliction of harm by well-intentioned persons in the vain pursuit of ends which that harm did not further, or in the successful pursuit of questionable ends. These benefactors of humanity sacrificed their fellows to appease mythical gods and tortured them to save their souls from a mythical hell, broke and bound the feet of children to promote their eventual marriageability, beat slow schoolchildren to promote learning and respect for teachers, subjected the sick to leeches to rid them of excess blood, and put suspects to the rack and the thumbscrew in the service of truth. They schooled themselves to feel no pity—to renounce human compassion in the service of a higher end. The deliberate doing of harm in the mistaken belief that it promotes some greater good is the essence of tragedy. We would do well to ask whether the goods we seek in harming offenders are worthwhile, and whether the means we choose will indeed secure them.

In the pages that follow, I shall be arguing for the abolition of punishment, insofar as it involves depriving people of things to which they have a right (typically, life, liberty, or property), either simply in order to deprive them of those things (as retribution), or in order to secure some further end (such as deterrence or incapacitation) to which the deprivation of these rights is essential. I shall distinguish punishment from other practices, such as blaming or formal condemnation (and collateral consequences such as difficulty in obtaining employment), which do not deprive the offender of anything to which he has a right; and from harm-shifting interventions that prevent (through direct intervention) or reverse (through compensation) harm to victims at the offender's expense. I begin with a brief description of the actual harms that are done by punishment.

II. Harms Done by Punishment

Today, the most common punishments in the Western world are deprivation of liberty or property; only the United States still imposes the death penalty. The debate over the death penalty has made imprisonment look benign, but the harm done by incarceration is not trivial. Imprisonment means, at minimum, the loss of liberty and autonomy, as well as many material comforts, personal security, and access to heterosexual relations. These deprivations, according to Gresham Sykes (who first identified them) "together dealt 'a profound hurt' that went to 'the very foundations of the prisoner's being.'"[1] But these are only the minimum harms, suffered by the least vulnerable inmates in the best-run prisons. Most prisons are run badly, and in some, conditions are more squalid than in the worst of slums. In the District of Columbia jail, for example, inmates must wash their clothes and sheets in cell toilets because the laundry machines are broken. Vermin and insects infest the building, in which air vents are clogged with decades' accumulation of dust and grime.[2] But even inmates in prisons where conditions are sanitary must still face the numbing boredom and emptiness of prison life—a vast desert of wasted days in which little in the way of meaningful activity is possible.

For the more vulnerable, and for those confined in worse prisons, imprisonment often means exposure to predators and an extreme loss of personal security. The rate of victimization — assault, robbery, extortion—of prisoners is much higher than that of the general population. Some studies have reported that more than 10 percent of the prison population has suffered forcible rape, with a much larger number having succumbed to pressure to engage in sex.[3] Even more disturbingly, as the prevalence of this form of violence has made its way into the popular imagination, it has become common to hear it referred to as part of the punishment or as a deterrent factor. Although most jokes about rape are excluded from the public forum as in grossly bad taste, a soft drink company recently saw fit to make light of prison rape in a television commercial.[4]

In recent years, sentencing has become harsher, and more and more individuals have been imprisoned. Worldwide, some 8.5 million persons are incarcerated. After staying relatively constant since World War II, the number of persons imprisoned in the United States increased fourfold between 1980 and 2000. Most of this increase resulted from a crackdown on drug offenders. Today, the United States is second only to Russia in per capita incarceration rate (690 per 100,000 as compared to Russia's 730), while two-thirds of countries have rates below 150 per 100,000.[5]

Increased harshness has resulted in a new coterie of prisoners who began as juvenile offenders and have spent most of their lives in prison. It is no exaggeration to say that punishment has destroyed the souls of these offenders. Jack Abbott, physically beaten and sexually abused in a series of foster homes as a child, was first committed to a juvenile institution at the age of nine. After his release at eighteen he soon found himself back in prison for writing bad checks. He killed another inmate for informing on him and got more time. Later, he managed to escape, robbed a bank, and was sent back with another nineteen years to serve. At the age of forty-five, he described himself as follows:

> When I walk past a glass window in the corridor and happen to see my reflection, I get angry on impulse. I feel shame and hatred at such times. When I'm forced by circumstances to be in a crowd of prisoners, it's all I can do to refrain from attack. I feel such hostility, such hatred, I can't help this anger. All these years I have felt it. Paranoid. I can control it. I never seek a confrontation. I have to intentionally gauge my voice in a conversation to cover up the anger I feel, the chaos and pain just beneath the surface of what we commonly recognize as reality.[6]

Of his relations with fellow prisoners, he wrote:

> You don't comfort one another; you humor one another. You extend
> that confusion about this reality of one another by lying to one another.
> You can't stand the sight of each other and yet you are doomed to stand
> and face one another every moment of every day for years without end.
> You must bathe together, defecate and urinate together, eat and sleep to-
> gether, talk together, work together.[7]

After his release, Abbott killed a waiter in a restaurant for insulting
him and was sent back to prison, where he committed suicide in 2002.[8]
He was an irredeemably violent and destructive man, filled with hate and
fear—much of which must be attributed to his almost lifelong imprisonment. Today, there are more such prisoners than ever.[9]

Those we punish have by and large failed to meet the challenges that
life has presented them. It is not surprising that they include a large proportion of those who have faced more significant obstacles to success.
The probability that a black man born in the United States will be imprisoned at some time in his life is more than five times that for a white
man. Prisoners are overwhelmingly drawn from the lower rungs of the so-
cioeconomic ladder. Throughout the world, it is those in marginalized
groups who find themselves imprisoned. Also overrepresented in the
prison population are persons with little education, mental illness or retardation, and a history of abuse as a child. In punishing, then, we tend
to harm those who already bear great burdens.

III. Justifying the Harm of Punishment

These harms, one might think, though regrettable, are not inflicted for no
reason; they are necessary, just, right, and proper. At least, this must be
true of the minimum harms, if not of the uglier real ones. Philosophers
have made many sophisticated arguments to show that this is so. For the
most part, these arguments fall under one of three broad positions: that
the harm of punishment is outweighed by some greater good; that harming offenders is good in itself; and that punishment is not properly considered a harm to the offender.

Three basic purposes correspond to these three basic forms of justification. To the idea that harming the offender is good corresponds the pur-

pose of giving offenders what they deserve. To the idea that punishment does more good than harm corresponds the purpose of preventing crime. And to the idea that punishment benefits the offender corresponds the purpose of making the offender a better person. Optimists see a happy confluence of these purposes in an institution that simultaneously serves all three. But the appropriateness of punishment to each of these ends has been called into serious question at some period during the history of the institution. If punishment had been thought to serve only one of these ends—no matter which—doubts about its appropriateness would probably have been sufficient to topple the institution. The survival of punishment as a legitimate institution has been facilitated because the continuous defense of any one purpose has not been necessary; when doubts became too strong, it has always been possible to turn attention to one of the other purposes instead. In this chapter I present a brief account of the intellectual history of punishment and suggest that we would do well to give more attention to our uneasiness with each of these purposes—to ask forthrightly whether any of them, seen in light of its weaknesses, is sufficient to support an institution that does so much harm.

The idea that harming offenders is good in itself may be the oldest idea associated with punishment. If this had been thought to be the only underpinning of the institution, it might have been eliminated by Christians, who thought that vengeance was best left to God, or in the early twentieth century, when the consensus among philosophers was that retribution was barbaric and pointless. If instead punishment had been consistently seen simply as a regrettable necessity to promote the good of society, it would have had difficulty withstanding the late twentieth century recognition both of the practical elusiveness of deterrent and rehabilitative goals and of the questionable morality of using individuals to promote social ends. And if we had consistently thought of punishment as something we do to benefit offenders, the stark reality that it typically does the opposite would eventually have forced itself on our attention. Instead, as successive generations have inherited the institution of punishment and found the old rationale wanting, they have found new reasons—or revived older ones—for continuing it.

How did punishment begin? Although it is more prominent in some early civilizations than in others, the idea of justice as served by punishment appears to be as old as civilization itself. Correspondingly, though, the development of civilization is also correlated both with questioning of how and whether justice is so served and with a sense that there must be limits on the scope of punishment. The history of punishment is in some respects like the history of war; it seems to accompany the human condition almost universally, to enjoy periods of glorification, to be commonly regarded as justified in many instances, and yet to run counter to our ultimate vision of what human society should be.

Indeed, it appears likely that punishment in its earliest forms was not distinguishable from warfare. Both, perhaps, arose from the instinct to strike out at those seen as injuring one's interests, either from simple anger or from a desire for self-protection. Blood feuds, in which the family of the aggrieved person inflicts an equivalent or greater injury on the offender and his family, are found in a number of early societies; it is hard to know whether these are better described as punishment or as warfare. Later societies found cause to reflect on the justification and limits of harm to enemies, on both the individual and the social scale.

In the *Iliad* (c. 800 B.C.), justice is presented as pure vengeance, as when Agamemnon urges Menelaus not to take pity on his Trojan captives:

> This is no time for giving quarter. Has, then, your house fared so well at the hands of the Trojans? Let us not spare a single one of them—not even the child unborn and in its mother's womb; let not a man of them be left alive, but let all in Ilius perish, unheeded and forgotten.
>
> Thus did he speak, and his brother was persuaded by him, for his words were just.[10]

Justice is not limited by personal responsibility or proportionality to the original offense; it is enough that the person on whom vengeance is taken is on the side of the enemy. Agamemnon explicitly rejects any bounds to his vengeance; the wrong done by the Trojans, in his eyes, justifies their annihilation.[11]

In contrast, in Aeschylus's fifth-century retelling of Agamemnon's story in *The Oresteia*, the Furies, representing the ancient demand for vengeance, seek the death of Orestes for the murder of his mother. Orestes, following the demands of honor as urged by Apollo, had killed his mother to avenge her murdering his father, Agamemnon. The Furies are eventually soothed and persuaded to let him live. The taming of the Furies—following a process in which Orestes is judged by the citizens of Athens—can be seen as representing the sublimation of vengeful emotions into the service of the social ends of justice. Rather than glorifying vengeance, Aeschylus presents it as tragic when carried to extremes. The

Furies are brought under control, promised respect, but forced to recognize mitigating factors and to bow to the judgment of the citizens.

In *The Oresteia*, the value of deterrence is also made explicit, as the Furies appeal to the necessity to punish wrongdoers so that the innocent can live without fear:

> So when a terrible disaster strikes
> let no one make the old appeal,
> "Justice, you Furies—hear me,
> you powers on your thrones!"
> It may well happen soon—
> a father in despair, a mother
> in some new catastrophe,
> may scream out for pity,
> now the house of justice falls.
>
> Sometimes what's terrible can work
> to bring about what's good.
> Such terror needs to sit on guard,
> to check the passionate heart.
> There is a benefit for men
> to learn control through suffering.
> For where is there a man or city—
> both alike in this regard—
> who still respects what's just
> without a heart attuned to fear?[12]

Up to this point, we have seen the infliction of harm in response to wrongdoing as an expression of vengeance, followed by the idea that there should be limits to vengeance, and a hint of deterrent purposes. Harming wrongdoers is justified (to the extent that it is seen as requiring justification) by ideas roughly corresponding to desert and deterrence. But the first sophisticated philosophical defense of punishment rejects the idea that punishment harms the wrongdoer. Plato takes the novel position that the just man should harm no one, thus immediately raising the issue of how punishment is to be justified. His solution to this problem is that punishment is not a harm, but a good, for the person who suffers it.[13] Plato's argument for this surprising proposition is simple: the good of the soul is more important than the good of the body; the commission of crimes indicates disorder in the soul; and the infliction of just punishment imparts justice to the soul. Comparing punishment to medical treatment, Plato argues that the most wretched of men is he who does wrong and is not punished.[14] Thus, punishment is imposed primarily for the sake of the wrongdoer.[15] The "incurable" wrongdoer, however, should be executed as an example to others.[16]

Thus, by 400 B.C., the basic ideas of punishment as vengeance, as deterrence, and as a benefit to the offender are already in place. Precursors of these ideas can be found even earlier. The idea of a disrupted cosmic order is reflected in the Egyptian concept of *ma'at* and in the Hebrew concept of blood guilt; in both cases, order is to be restored through punishment. These two cultures also share the idea of a vengeful God, although that idea is much more prominent for the Hebrews. Explicit references to punishment as deterring and as instructive for the offender are found in the literature of ancient Egypt. Although there is little in the way of formal justification for punishment practices in antiquity, recognition of the value of limiting punishment is already present.

Neither the Egyptians nor the Hebrews saw themselves as merely containing vengeance, however. Harming offenders was part and parcel of an ongoing effort to maintain a cosmic balance and prevent the coming of chaos. The Egyptians' worldview was shaped by their dependence on the annual flooding of the Nile.[17] As the river flooded, washing the rich alluvial soil over the riverbanks, one could be confident that the crops would grow and life would continue for another year. Those who lived on its banks asked no more than that life should continue as before, continually returning to the point of renewal. They feared only that some untoward event would disrupt the orderly sequence of life and plunge Egypt into the primeval chaos that, according to legend, had existed before the coming of order. One part of the preservation of this order was to live one's life according to the principles of *ma'at*, or justice.[18] Illustrations in the Egyptian Coffin Texts, dating back to the end of the Old Kingdom (2800–2200 B.C.)[19] show the heart of the deceased being weighed against a feather representing Ma'at, the goddess of justice. Transgressions against ma'at—ranging from being overly talkative to murder and blasphemy—would make the heart heavy. The monster Ammut waits nearby to consume the heart found wanting; but if the heart passes the test, the dead person is admitted to a pleasant afterlife. Death—the loss of the afterlife—is the consequence of failing to live a good life. In that the Egyptians of that period saw punishment as the natural and expected response to wrongdoing, it may be that they saw punishment as restoring the cosmic order that it disrupted.

A similar concept is evident in the ancient Hebrew belief that the "blood guilt" resulting from homicide could be expiated only by the shedding of the blood of the offender: "For blood pollutes the land, and no expiation can be made for the land, for the blood that is shed in it, except by the blood of him who shed it."[20] The Hebrews feared that wrongfully spilled blood would collect in the altar of God, creating a point of entry for demons. Animal sacrifices could wash out the guilt of lesser offenses, but only human blood could wash out that of murder. Like the Egyptians, the Hebrews believed that the sacrifice of the offender would restore the lost order and protect them from chaos.

For both systems of thought, the vengeful impulse is closely tied to justice. The Old Testament presents God as vengeful and his vengeance as justified. Sinners, such as those of Sodom and Gomorrah, are justly destroyed; Lot's wife is turned into a pillar of salt merely for looking back in contravention of God's instructions; most of the human race is wiped out in the Great Flood. *The Teaching for Merikare* (a pharaoh of the First Intermediate Kingdom) admonishes:

> Do justice, that you may live long on earth. Calm the weeper, do not oppress the widow, do not oust a man from his father's property, do not degrade magnates from their seats. Beware of punishing wrongfully; do not kill, for it will not profit you, but punish with beatings and with imprisonment, for thus this land will be set in order, excepting only the rebel who has conspired, for God knows those who are disaffected, and God will smite down his evil doing with blood.[21]

Evil for evil is clearly a well-established idea in the earliest civilizations. Note, however, that neither the Egyptian nor the Hebrew tradition prescribes the kind of limitless vengeance urged in the *Iliad*. The famous passage from Leviticus, "breach for breach, eye for eye, tooth for tooth; as he has caused a blemish in a man, so shall it be rendered unto him,"[22] often quoted as an example of barbaric harshness, may actually represent an attempt to limit the consequences of wrongdoing.[23] The earlier blood feud knew no limits; clans simply retaliated against each other, inflicting what injury they could.[24] The same desire for limits may have motivated the best-known provisions of the Code of Hammurabi (c. 1800 B.C.), in which matching retaliatory harm is exacted.[25]

The first glimmerings of concern for the harm inflicted on offenders by punishment and its analogues can thus be found in antiquity. While there is little indication in any of these contexts that punishment itself was regarded as problematic, there is the idea that there must be a limit to what can be done in response to wrongdoing, and that the limit is in some way related to the nature of the wrong. The wrongdoer is not merely an enemy, to be harmed in any way possible, but a person whose own interests must be considered.

At this early point in the history of punishment theory, we have seen punishment presented as benefiting the cosmic order, the victim (or the victim's family), society, and the wrongdoer. While the subsequent history offers many refinements and variations of these views (and formidable objections to each), these early portrayals contain the seeds of everything that is to follow.

The question of how it can be right to harm another has particular significance for Christians, who believe, with Plato, that the good man inflicts no suffering, even on his enemies, and who set great store in the idea of forgiveness. The New Testament preaches the reserving of retribution to God: "Beloved, never avenge yourselves, but leave it to the wrath of God; for it is written, 'Vengeance is mine, I will repay, saith the Lord'";[26] "Judge not, lest ye be judged."[27] Moreover, this passage from Matthew explicitly rejects the "like for like" version of punishment of Leviticus:

> 38: Ye have heard that it hath been said, An eye for an eye, and a tooth for a tooth:
> 39: But I say unto you, That ye resist not evil: but whosoever shall smite thee on thy right cheek, turn to him the other also.
> 40: And if any man will sue thee at the law, and take away thy coat, let him have thy cloak also.
> 41: And whosoever shall compel thee to go a mile, go with him twain.
> 42: Give to him that asketh thee, and from him that would borrow of thee turn not thou away.
> 43: Ye have heard that it hath been said, Thou shalt love thy neighbour, and hate thine enemy.
> 44: But I say unto you, Love your enemies, bless them that curse you, do good to them that hate you, and pray for them which despitefully use you, and persecute you;

45: That ye may be the children of your Father which is in heaven: for he maketh his sun to rise on the evil and on the good, and sendeth rain on the just and on the unjust.[28]

The infliction of retributive punishment by human beings is rejected here; if the institution had been founded on retribution as its sole basis, the rise of Christianity might have seen its end. But Christians had other purposes in mind for secular punishment. Augustine squarely rejects revenge and retribution, but argues that secular punishment is necessary both to provide an example to others, and to induce repentance so that the offender may be spared divine punishment.[29] Aquinas argues that secular punishment is necessary for two reasons: to restrain the wicked from evil by force and fear, and to compel the evilly disposed to learn virtue.[30] Vengeance and retribution may be left to God, but secular punishment is justified for the good of society and for the good of the offender.

The good of the offender as a reason to punish turned out to be a particularly pernicious factor when combined with the Christian emphasis on the importance of salvation. The excesses of the Inquisition are familiar to everyone. But they are rooted in a much earlier belief that, in compelling the conversion of heretics, the Church did them a service. Augustine, having overcome his earlier compunctions on the subject, writes:

When . . . wholesome instruction is added to means of inspiring salutary fear, so that not only the light of truth may dispel the darkness of error, but the force of fear may at the same time break the bonds of evil custom, we are made glad, as I have said, by the salvation of many, who with us bless God, and render thanks to Him.[31]

The Middle Ages were dominated by such thinking. Every evil in the world, from crop failure to the Black Death, was attributed to the sinful nature of man, who could never be chaste enough or humble enough to satisfy God. Under the strain of these beliefs, many people imposed extreme suffering on themselves in an attempt to appease God, from the hair shirts of penitents to the iron-tipped whips of the flagellants. Imposing punishment on those most exposed to moral condemnation was all too naturally seen as an appropriate measure to induce the repentance that would save their everlasting souls. It was not an age that encouraged doubts about the roots of crime in moral wickedness or the efficacy of violence as a route to moral improvement.[32] The emphasis in penal practice was on the infliction of pain and humiliation in public, through measures such as the pillory, branding, flogging, and drawing and quartering—death being an insufficient punishment for some crimes.[33]

Enlightenment thinkers, in keeping with Christianity, repudiated retribution, but also saw more clearly the broader question of the justifiability of punishment for other purposes. Hobbes asks directly "by what door the right or authority of punishing . . . came in?"[34] His answer is that in the state of nature everyone has the right to kill or hurt others for his own preservation (or indeed to obtain anything he wants, as "every man has the right to everything"); with the forming of the social contract, the citizens lay down their own right to punish, leaving the sovereign alone with that right. Interestingly, Hobbes seeks to limit the sovereign's right to punish to acts that are against previously announced laws and to punishment proportional to the crime, although no such limits are present in the state of nature.[35] The aim of punishment, he says, "is not revenge, but terror"; consequently, punishment requires both the intention and the possibility "of disposing the delinquent (or, by his example, other men) to obey the laws."[36]

Locke, too, grounds the right to punish in the social contract, beginning from the right of all to punish in the state of nature, which is entrusted to the sovereign upon the making of the social contract. Punishment, he says, must be limited to the purposes of "reparation and restraint."[37] Further, "Each transgression may be punished to that degree and with so much severity as will suffice to make it an ill bargain to the offender, give him cause to repent, and terrify others from doing the like."[38]

Beccaria (1764) similarly blended individual rights and utilitarian reasoning to conclude that punishments must be limited to those that served useful social ends:

> The purpose of punishment . . . is nothing other than to dissuade the criminal from doing fresh harm to his compatriots and to keep other people from doing the same. Therefore, punishments and the method of inflicting them should be chosen that, mindful of the proportion between crime and punishment, will make the most effective and lasting impression on men's minds and inflict the least torment on the body of the criminal.[39]

All of these writers recognized that the social good could not be promoted by random or excessive punishment. Thus, the ideal punishment was the one that produced the most social benefit at the least cost to the offender. This articulation of the reasoning supporting limits on punishment invalidated in principle any punishment that did not provide a favorable balance of benefit over cost. Each squarely rejected the idea that harming the offender is good in itself.

This line of reasoning is made more explicit by Jeremy Bentham (1789), who begins his discussion of punishment with the observation that "all punishment is mischief: all punishment in itself is evil. Upon the principle of utility, if it ought at all to be admitted, it ought only to be admitted in as far as it promises to exclude some greater evil."[40] He goes on to list specific instances in which punishment fails to be justified, that is, where it is groundless, unprofitable, ineffective, or unnecessary. Bentham sought, in practice as well as in theory, to eliminate those punishments that were predicated simply on harming the offender. In his lifetime, repugnance against harm for harm's sake obtained some popular hold; efforts were made to institute punishments that could be justified by their good effects rather than their bad ones.

The eighteenth-century British prison was rife with disease and hunger, especially bad for those who, with their families in tow, were imprisoned for debt and could not pay for food. Following the end of transportation to the American colonies after 1776, excess prisoners were confined to ships moored at the docks. Prison reform in the late eighteenth and early nineteenth centuries, spurred by John Howard's 1777 report on scandalous conditions in the prisons of England, was in large part an effort to bring rationality to prison practice in order to direct it more effectively to the goals of reform and deterrence. In the United States, punishment before 1800 still relied for the most part on beatings, public humiliation, and the gallows. A wave of criminal law reform after independence resulted in the wholesale replacement of capital punishment with long prison terms. But the newly built prisons were as disorderly and ill-run as their British counterparts, and hopes that democracy and legal reform would eliminate crime were soon seen to be ill-founded. By the 1850's the efficacy of reform was widely doubted, though some still hoped for deterrent effects.[41]

Meanwhile, retributivism had found new advocates in Europe in Kant and Hegel. Although Kant wrote little specifically on the issue of punishment, his views are of enduring significance in punishment theory, most especially because of his unequivocal rejection of the serving of social ends as a justification for punishment:

> Judicial punishment can never be used merely as a means to promote
> some other good for the criminal himself or for civil society, but instead
> it must in all cases be imposed on him only on the ground that he has
> committed a crime; for a human being can never be manipulated merely
> as a means to the purposes of someone else.[42]

The grounding of this rejection in his powerful conception of persons
as equal rational beings whose autonomy must be respected has made it
one of the most formidable obstacles to any persuasive justification of
punishment.

Kant explicitly rejects practicality in favor of the maintaining of cosmic order; if a society disbands, it must first execute "the last murderer
remaining in prison" to avoid complicity in his crime.[43] "If legal justice
perishes," he claims, "it is no longer worth while for men to remain
alive on this earth."[44] The apparent basis of this claim is that legal justice (*Gerechtigkeit*) represents the ability of men to be, and to treat others as, ends in themselves, and thus to transcend the purpose of animals.
Because, on Kant's view, rationality requires that we act justly, our failure to do so puts us on a level with nonrational animals, so that there is
no (special) purpose in our continued existence. Kant, too, grounds the
justice of punishment in the social contract, arguing that, though we
punish the offender against his will, he has consented to the punishment
because he has (or may be deemed as a rational being to have) consented
to the laws. On Kant's view, personal autonomy is achieved only when
one is ruled by reason; he sees desires as "external" influences that prevent us from acting according to the dictates of rationality. Only the person who is able to ignore these influences and to act from purely rational motives achieves full autonomy. A rational being considers the interests of all rational beings as deserving of equal consideration; thus, no
person may be used merely as a means to accomplish the ends of another. Compassion for the wrongdoer is ruled out of order along with
the desire for vengeance: the rational (and thus the moral) person strictly
ignores emotional motivations. The theme of retribution, long muted by
the willingness of Christians to leave the meting out of just deserts to
God, again became a significant strand of the justification of punishment.

In contrast, the first arguments for the abolition of punishment entirely
rejected the retributive idea. Robert Owen argued in 1813 that bad moral
character was formed by circumstances, not by the offender, and that for

society to punish the thieves it had manufactured was unjust. He argues, in words not inapposite today:

> Can we for a moment hesitate to decide, that if some of those men whom the laws dispensed by the present Judges have doomed to suffer capital punishments, had been born, trained and circumstanced as these Judges were born, trained and circumstanced, that some of those who had so suffered would have been the identical individuals who would have passed the same awful sentences on the present highly esteemed dignitaries of the law.[45]

Others who continued to accept punishment also questioned retributivism in the strongest terms. Bentham's intellectual successor, John Stuart Mill, wrote in 1867:

> If, indeed, punishment is inflicted for any other reason than in order to operate on the will; if its purpose be other than that of improving the culprit himself, or securing the just rights of others against unjust violation, then, I admit, the case is totally altered. If any one thinks that there is justice in the infliction of purposeless suffering; that there is a natural affinity between the two ideas of guilt and punishment, which makes it intrinsically fitting that wherever there has been guilt, pain should be inflicted by way of retribution; I acknowledge that I can find no argument to justify punishment inflicted on this principle.[46]

By this time, then, not only the principal strands of the justification of punishment but also the principal objections to each had already been laid out. Punishment might be defended on either retributive or utilitarian grounds; correspondingly, it might be criticized from the other point of view. While one set of criticisms required the elimination of all punishments that did not further the social good, the other set required the elimination of all punishments that furthered the social good at the expense of individual autonomy. To the extent that these developments had any effect on policy, however, it was on the question of how, rather than whether, to punish; the institution of punishment itself lumbered on unscathed.

A new wave of prison reform in the nineteenth century focused on isolating the prisoner from the influence of his fellows while requiring him to work. The emphasis was on reform of moral character. In the United

States, efforts to reform prisoners through silent penitence resulted in the pitiless infliction of physical and mental suffering. A rule of total silence was enforced in many prisons, driving many of the prisoners insane. The rule was enforced through such methods as flogging, the ball and chain, or an iron gag held in place by twisting the arms behind the back and tying it to the wrists with a few inches of rope.[47] Similar ideas were implemented in Britain, where the regime of penal servitude was so strict that it drove many to insanity or suicide. Particularly pernicious was the substitution of grueling, unproductive work—such as the treadmill, the crank, or the capstan—for meaningful tasks. These Sisyphean labors were often such as to leave the prisoner in constant pain, if not to kill him outright. The prison diet was itself punitive: not merely pathetically inadequate, but deliberately prepared to be as repulsive as possible. Ironically, the rejection of harm for harm's sake seemed only to make colder the cruelties of the penal system. Nor did it achieve its aims; the Wines and Dwight report on prisons in the United States and Canada spurred the National Congress on Penitential and Reformatory Discipline to declare in 1870 that "neither in the United States nor in Europe . . . has the problem of reforming the criminal yet been resolved."[48]

But such practical failures were of little concern to retributivists such as F. H. Bradley and James Fitzjames Stephen, who urged the attention of their countrymen to the ideas of Kant and Hegel, then current in Europe. Bradley argued that the retributivist view was more in accord with the view of "the vulgar man," and attributed to that man a view strikingly similar to Hegel's well-known, if little-understood, position that punishment "annuls the crime":[49]

> Punishment is the denial of wrong by the assertion of right, and the wrong exists in the self, or will, of the criminal; . . . he has asserted . . . his wrongful will, the incarnate denial of right; and in denying that assertion, and annihilating, whether wholly or partially, that incarnation by fine, imprisonment, or even by death, we annihilate the wrong and manifest the right; and since this . . . was an end in itself, so punishment is also an end in itself.[50]

Retributivists of this period were concerned to disassociate themselves from the discredited thirst for private vengeance and retaliation, yet offered little beyond such appeals to intuition to establish that punishment was indeed good in itself. Their emphasis on guilt as a necessary precondition for punishment, though, brought attention to a weakness of utilitarian theory: that under the right empirical conditions, it would justify punishment of the innocent. Bradley sarcastically observes:

> We need not ask how it is that, if 99 men are of opinion that it is more convenient, for both the 99 and the 100th, or for the 100th without the 99, or the 99 without the 100th, that he, the 100th, should cease to exist—that *therefore* it is right for their opinion to be conveyed to him by the hanging of him, whatever may be his opinion on the subject. The discussion of this question we leave to utilitarian philosophers.[51]

Interestingly, Bradley was later among the advocates of social Darwinism, and suggested that criminals, whom he described as "diseased" and "unfit," and even their children, should be put to death under a principle of "moral surgery"; while declining to abandon retribution, he argued that it must be "secondary and subject to the chief end of the general welfare."[52] This was the apogee of the idea that the harm done by punishment is counterbalanced by the good that it does.

In 1918, Bosanquet writes of "the growing repugnance to punishment," citing as causes of that repugnance ill-treatment of prisoners and the idea that moral badness is a disease that should be subject to curative treatment, while retribution is "a survival from primitive retaliation." Bosanquet, like Bradley, urged the "annulment of the crime" as the proper basis of punishment, criticizing the reformative model as leading to excesses:

> You want to annul the bad will, and in doing so, to help the offender against it so far as within reasonable limits you can. But to bind a man under the jurisdiction of some official expert in morals—say a gaol chaplain—till the latter should be satisfied of his reformation, would be a tyranny to which I find it hard to conceive a parallel.[53]

Nevertheless, Bosanquet did not base his views on the idea that harming offenders was good. Rather, he thought that the significant function of punishment was the emphatic expression of disapproval, and even suggested that, for the educated, punishment lay primarily in public trial and condemnation.[54] Although he rejected both reform and deterrence as the principal aim of punishment, demanding that the limits of punishment must be set by the nature of the crime, he too saw punishment as promoting the social good. Mabbott, the only other prominent proponent of retributivism in the first half of the twentieth century, also declined to advocate evil for evil: instead, he argued that the concept of a rule required that its violation be punished, quite apart from any consideration of whether the act was morally wrong.[55] For this he was aptly criticized by M. R. Glover, who pointed out that he was confusing logic with morality.[56]

Distaste for retributive sentiments and the perception that they were philosophically ill-founded would have made it difficult for a system of punishment based entirely in retribution to survive the first half of the twentieth century. Attitudes at midcentury were typified by Barbara Wootton, who argued that moral responsibility for crime was illusory, and Karl Menninger, who wrote, "The great secret, the deeply buried mystery of the apparent public apathy to crime and to proposals for better controlling crime, lies in the persistent, intrusive wish for vengeance."[57]

But critics of retribution like Menninger and Wootton sought, not to abolish the penal system, but to remodel it along rehabilitative lines. The hope of providing humane and constructive treatment for offenders had a powerful hold on the public imagination. After World War II, the rehabilitative model became the dominant public policy in the United States. Treatment personnel were added to the prison staff; efforts were made to ameliorate prison conditions; and successful rehabilitation became a basis for early parole.[58]

As attention turned to rehabilitation, the Kantian concern about using persons as mere means had not been forgotten. Both John Rawls[59] and H. L. A. Hart[60] endeavored to escape these difficulties by proposing to separate the question of the overall aim of the institution from that of the particular purpose to be served by punishment in a specific case. They suggested that, while the institution of punishment might be justified on utilitarian grounds, punishment of a specific individual could be justified only on the ground of personal guilt. Retributivists and utilitarians could be seen as answering different questions, rather than as disagreeing on the answer to the single question, "Why punish?" Although this approach avoided the principal criticism of utilitarianism (that it was consistent with punishing the innocent) as well as the principal criticism of retributivism (that it required the pointless infliction of pain), it had the disadvantage of requiring it to be true both that harming the offender is good and that the good done by the overall institution outweighs the harm.

But a hundred years after the Wines and Dwight report, Robert Martinson's famous study again concluded that, despite advances in scientific knowledge, prisons by and large did not successfully rehabilitate offenders, even in the rare instances in which the institution fully conformed to the therapeutic model, and did not serve deterrent ends either.[61] With this new evidence, it became increasingly difficult for proponents to claim that punishment was either a good for the offender or that it did more good than harm. As most philosophers had already rejected as indefensible the idea that harming the offender was good in itself, this second round of disillusionment with rehabilitation and deterrence might logically have led to a rejection of the institution of punishment in all its forms. Instead, utilitarian justifications fell into the background, and the old idea of retribution was revived.

The contemporary debate began to take shape with the publication of Herbert Morris's "Persons and Punishment." Sharply criticizing the logic of "therapy" for criminal offenders, Morris breathed new life into the concept of retribution by suggesting that punishment could be viewed as respecting the choices of offenders, given a fair set of rules and a voluntary decision to break them. He argued that, unlike rehabilitation, which seeks to mold a person to the liking of society, retributive punishment respects the offender's choice to disobey and leaves him free to make the same choice again, with the understanding that he will again pay the consequences. Holding people responsible for their acts—viewing them as the product of choices that could have been otherwise—is essential if we are to treat offenders as persons rather than as objects to be manipulated. The purpose of punishment, on this view, is to restore the proper balance of benefits and burdens disrupted by the criminal offense. This appeal to Kantian autonomy revived the notion that punishment could be justified even though it harmed the offender and had no (separate) good consequences; harm to the offender could be seen as restoring the social order and as an appropriate, respectful response to his conduct.

But, given the already greater weight of social burdens borne by the typical criminal offender—poverty, substandard schooling, inadequate medical care, and so on—the idea that he must be punished to "restore the balance" or to "pay his debt to society" can seem farcical. In "Marxism and Retribution," Jeffrie Murphy details the ironies of a society that, while everywhere praising the merits of acquisitiveness and the prestige of material wealth, makes plain to certain segments of society that there is no legitimate path for them to that destination. Murphy goes on to argue that, given the social situation of most criminal offenders, "it is hard to see what these persons are supposed to reciprocate for."[62] Others have questioned whether, for most of us, refraining from most kinds of crime could appropriately be characterized as a "burden" at all.[63] Most of us, after all, do not daily restrain ourselves from murder, mayhem, or even armed robbery; rather, we would find it a crushing burden to be required to carry out such acts. Certainly, if application of the theory were limited to those cases in which the rules are fair, the burdens of compliance are evenly distributed, and the choice to break them is truly voluntary, the prison population would take on an entirely different character.

While some writers, particularly those advocating an economic analysis of law, continued to defend utilitarian views,[64] the combination of Morris's attack and Rawls's Kantian critique of utilitarianism in his influential *Theory of Justice* pushed utilitarian views decisively into the background. A spate of followers picked up on Morris's theme, and the idea of desert, not merely as a limit, but as a complete justification for harming the offender, found its way into the public forum under the rubric of "just deserts."[65] Concerns about the fairness of the rules and the voluntariness of violation were, of course, lost in the translation to political rhetoric. The political appeal of just deserts was supplemented by a new focus on what punishment of offenders could do for victims. Among philosophers, the long-held aversion to vengeful emotions received new attention, and it was suggested that the satisfaction of victims' anger might be a legitimate purpose of retributive punishment.[66]

Interestingly, Herbert Morris, in later work, turned away from the idea of harm for harm's sake, favoring instead a "paternalistic" view of punishment. His and other theories of the early 1980's sought to justify punishment on the ground that it was for the moral good (though immediate harm) of the offender.[67] This move, while it did not avoid the overriding issue of the fairness of the rules, combined the attractions of rehabilitative theory with the attractions of respect for the offender. Because punishment is for the moral good of the offender, it is not necessary to show that it is for the overall benefit of society; indeed, it need not actually accomplish moral change as long as it is "directed at" such change. The central problem with these theories is that they have to show, not merely that moral change is desirable, nor that punishment is a way of achieving it, but both that punishment is a necessary path to moral change and that its imposition is justified even when such change is not forthcoming.

We see the germ of a move back to the idea that punishment benefits society in the self-defense theories proposed by Philip Montague[68] and Daniel Farrell.[69] These theories seek to establish that deterrence does not impermissibly use offenders as means to the greater good of society, but instead counts as self-defense, shifting harms from innocents to those who have made harm inevitable. True self-defense consists of harm to an attacker that is necessary to avert an attack not yet completed. Punishment, if it prevents any harms at all, cannot be said to prevent the harm for which it is inflicted; thus, the challenge for these theories is to show that we are defending ourselves against the persons punished, rather than using them to deter others.

Thus, today, each of the principal strands of the justification of punishment has its adherents, and each its bitter opponents. Too often, the question of justification is phrased as one of which of them is correct, rather than whether any of them is. The indefinite prolongation of the debate over the theoretical grounding of punishment in a sense permits an indefinite suspension of judgment that enables the institution to persist and to expand, amid confusion over what it is supposed to be doing. We are building, from the crushed spirits of society's despised, a bridge of dubious quality to a disputed destination.

In the chapters that follow, I shall examine the weaknesses of the most influential justifications and suggest that it is time to end our suspension of judgment and adopt instead a course of action based on the assumption that punishment cannot, after all, be justified.

2

Does Punishment
Do More Good than Harm?

I. Introduction

For the utilitarian, a social practice is justified insofar as it tends to produce more good than harm. A practice that produces the same benefit with less harm is morally preferable, and one that produces more harm than good is unjustified. The harms done by punishment would be justified, on utilitarian reasoning, provided that those harms are necessary to produce a greater good by averting a sufficient number of crimes. Given perfect information, the utilitarian would first rule out any penal policy that caused more suffering (through punishment) than it prevented (through crime prevention). She would then choose, from among those that prevented more harm than they produced, the policy that promised the greatest net harm prevention. On standard deterrent assumptions, this is unlikely to be the same as the policy that promises the greatest possible reduction in crime, because the degree of harshness necessary to deter the least deterrable would likely make the total harm caused by punishment greater than the harm prevented. Crime rates were at an all-time low in Nazi Germany, for example, but there is little doubt that Hitler's reign of terror produced more harm than it prevented. The policy promising the greatest net harm reduction might thus be one that provided a modest amount of crime prevention at a low cost in harm to offenders. The utilitarian would also want to know what measures other than punishment might achieve similar reductions in crime, and would prefer those measures over punishment to the extent that they caused less harm while providing the same benefit. Finally, the utilitarian would ask whether the dollars to be spent on crime prevention could provide more benefit if spent elsewhere—perhaps on the prevention of disease or accidents.

Punishment is thought to prevent crime through deterrence, rehabilitation, and incapacitation. Although the efficacy of these mechanisms continues to be in dispute among criminologists, there is a small but respectable literature supporting the general idea that the crime-preventive benefits of incarceration outweigh its social costs.[1] It may seem that this literature supports the view that punishment can be justified from a utilitarian point of view. But the criminologists who perform these cost-benefit calculations often assume that effects on offenders need not be considered, and thus that punitive policies are justified if the value of their crime-preventive effects is greater than their cost in tax dollars.[2] If punishment is to be justified in utilitarian terms, however—as providing more benefits than harms—we cannot pick and choose among the harms done, counting some and not others. As Bentham says:

> [A]ll punishment is mischief: all punishment in itself is evil. Upon the principle of utility, if it ought at all to be admitted, it ought only to be admitted in as far as it promises to exclude some greater evil.[3]

Utilitarianism determines the moral worth of actions solely on the basis of the good or harm that they do. So leaving harm to offenders out of account in determining penal policy can itself be right (or permissible) only if *that* action can somehow be shown to do more good than harm when everyone's interests—including those of offenders—are considered.

Thus, if we show that punishment does more good than harm, not counting harm to offenders, we have failed to provide a utilitarian justification for the practice. Criminological studies that take this approach must therefore be understood, not as employing a utilitarian analysis, but rather as assuming a retributive justification, and simply asking whether the otherwise justified practice of punishment is producing the desirable side-effect of preventing crime, and if so, at what dollar cost. Such an inquiry might conclude that the social value of the crime-preventive effects of a particular penal practice is greater than its dollar cost, but the result can have bearing on the justification of that practice from a utilitarian point of view only after all harms, including harms to offenders, are included in the calculation. From a retributive perspective, of course, the cost-benefit calculation has no relevance to the question of justification.

In this chapter I shall first undertake a utilitarian analysis of the practice of punishment in light of the current state of empirical knowledge about its effects. My first concern here is to cast doubt upon the idea that punishment does indeed produce more good than harm, and to show what additional findings would be needed to support such an outcome. I shall also indicate ways in which penal practice might be changed to satisfy the requirements of utilitarian thinking. In the final section I argue that, even in the instances in which meeting these requirements does not itself require obviously unacceptable practices, well-known weaknesses in utilitarian reasoning preclude the justification of punishment on utilitarian grounds.

II. Crime-Preventive Effects of Punishment

Deterrent and incapacitative effects are often taken for granted. One assumes that negative consequences will reduce undesired behavior, and that imprisonment of an offender will reduce crime by the number of crimes she would otherwise have committed during the period covered by her incarceration. But there are problems with both assumptions.

A. Deterrence

It seems obvious that the threat of punishment deters crime. Everyone has had the experience of observing parking signs despite inconvenience in order to avoid a ticket, or resisting the temptation to evade taxes for fear of criminal sanctions. But most of us have also had the experience of parking illegally despite the probability of getting a ticket, and we are not surprised to learn that taxpayers are much more likely to lie about cash income than about dividend or interest income.[4] In short, the threat of negative consequences is often a factor in our behavior, but it often fails to be a decisive factor. Sometimes the negative consequences are overwhelmed by other considerations: positive reasons for doing the action or other reasons to refrain. For example, criminal penalties for child abuse are irrelevant for most parents, who value the welfare of their children as highly as their own—and they are equally irrelevant for those who are unable to control their abusive behavior. Even where people can control their behavior and the threatened consequences are important to them, they may choose to commit crimes for immediate benefit despite those risks in much the same way as many people choose to smoke cigarettes, drink alcohol, and forgo exercise. Moreover, it is not unlikely that such failures of rational calculation are more common among those likely to commit crimes. Individuals who have cognitive problems such as mental illness or retardation, or emotional difficulties such as poor impulse control, or who simply have learned through unfortunate experience that the future is unpredictable, are certainly overrepresented in the prison population.

Most people have other reasons—such as reasons of conscience and effects on reputation—to refrain from committing serious crimes. People who lack such reasons—who instead expect criminal behavior to enhance their reputations, or who are not deterred by pangs of conscience—may well be less responsive to punitive measures as well. Indeed, the kinds of street shootings that were so distressingly prevalent in inner cities in the 1990's seem to exemplify the irrelevance of deterrence: young men who were not deterred from such killings by the immediate threat of deadly retaliation by the friends of the victim would hardly be deterred by the comparatively remote threat of imprisonment or even death at the hands of the criminal justice system.[5]

Given the factors that may militate against effective deterrence, we cannot know a priori whether punishment has any net deterrent effect at all. Even if we did know this much, to make a utilitarian evaluation of deterrence, we would need also to know how large an effect it is, compared to the costs exacted, in order to tell whether the pain that it prevents is more or less than the pain that it causes. We must turn to empirical evidence to make this calculation. The empirical evidence for deterrent effects of punishment is mixed. Actual measurement of deterrent effects is inherently difficult because it requires the measurement of events that did not occur—crimes that would have been committed had they not been deterred by the threat of punishment.[6]

What is the empirical evidence for deterrent effects? Field studies have shown some short-term effects for police crackdowns on offenses such as drug dealing, disorderly conduct, and drunk driving.[7] These studies don't separate the effects of arrest from those of trial or punishment, so we don't know how much of the deterrent effect is attributable to sanctions. The long-term effects of such policies, as well as their generalizability to serious crime and more typical offenders, also remain in question. Few studies have documented deterrent effects directly resulting from sanctions, though one study does show that mandatory penalties for gun offenses have been shown to decrease gun homicides.[8] There are even some studies showing that measures aimed at deterring crime have had the opposite effect.[9]

Perceptual studies in experimental settings have shown that subjects report a decreased likelihood of offending (for drunk driving and date rape) with an increased perception of risk of apprehension. The middle-class subjects of one experimental study of tax evasion reported that they would not engage in behavior carrying *any* risk of criminal sanction—even though the same subjects were quite willing to risk civil penalties for sufficient gain. The author of the study attributed this difference to the public nature of criminal proceedings and the consequent attachment of social stigma; that is, the subjects feared detection and publicity, rather than the sanction itself.[10]

Studies that have documented deterrent effects have often lumped together the effects of detection, apprehension, arrest, conviction, punishment, and collateral effects (such as effects on employability). Some have suggested that the major part of the deterrent effect may come from the collateral effects, rather than from the punishment itself.[11] As these collateral effects can be obtained without actually imposing punishment (that is, by arrest, trial, conviction, and attendant public knowledge), it is crucial for the utilitarian analysis to separate the effects of punishment itself from these other effects.

For a proper utilitarian analysis of deterrence, we would have to know not simply whether punishment ever has any deterrent effects—no doubt it does—but also, at the very least, whether the crimes prevented by the threat of some specific punishment would have caused more or less pain than that caused by the imposition of that punishment on those who were not deterred. While it is perhaps obvious that the inconvenience of drunk-driving arrests for a few dozen people causes less pain than would be occasioned by the loss of someone's life in an accident, we can by no means always assume that the costs imposed by punishment are less than the costs saved from the crimes deterred. Assume, for example, that the threat of a death sentence will deter ten of the fifty potential murders in a given year, while the rest remain undeterred. Should we manage to catch only half of the forty undeterred murderers, we would have to take twenty lives in order to save ten. We can, of course, make up numbers that produce the opposite result: the death sentence deters forty of the fifty potential murders, so if we catch half the ten murderers, we save forty lives by taking five. What we can't do is to assume that the benefits of deterrence outweigh its costs, without empirical evidence.

The point is not limited to the death penalty. For example, suppose that the pain of a nose-breaking punch is equivalent to the pain of six months in jail. If we can deter one in nine such punches with the threat of three months' imprisonment, and catch half the offenders, we will wind up imposing four three-month sentences to deter one punch—a bad bargain from the utilitarian point of view. But if we can deter eight in nine, on the same assumptions, we come out far ahead, imposing the pain of only half that of a punch in the nose to deter eight actual punches. It should be clear that to do the utilitarian analysis we need to know what the actual numbers are, at least with sufficient precision to know which way the calculation will go; it is not enough simply to establish "some" deterrent effect. The death penalty that deters only one in five murders, or only one in one hundred, has such an effect, as does the prison sentence that deters only one in nine punches. Politicians periodically announce that we "need more" deterrence of some particular crime, and that penalties will therefore be increased. Utilitarians would want to know *how much* (if any) more deterrence the increased penalty will bring, and how this benefit will compare with the increased costs that it will impose, both on offenders and on taxpayers. The same argument would hold if we sought to replace incarceration with a different penalty, such as corporal punishment.[12]

The case is somewhat different for penalties that do not have a net social cost, such as fines and (conceivably) community service. If we impose a fine heavy enough to have the same deterrent effect as some specific term of imprisonment, the benefits of deterring crime are added to the benefits of using the offender's funds or services for other purposes, while the negative effects on the offender are (by hypothesis) the same. Thus, utilitarians will prefer the imposition of a fine or community service to imprisonment where the deterrent effect is the same. Note that this harm would have to be equivalent to the harm done by imprisonment to have the same deterrent effect—so in discussing fines and community service as alternatives to imprisonment, we are not necessarily discussing minor harms.

To the extent that the offender has funds (or labor power) beyond his needs and tends to make wasteful use of the surplus, we ought to be able to produce more social good by appropriating that surplus than by allowing the offender to keep it—perhaps simply by redistributing it to more needy others. At least, we ought to be able to break even, with the cost to the offender balanced by the gain to others. If so, the addition of any amount of deterrent effect would be sufficient to tip the balance and provide a utilitarian justification for fines. Fines are not extensively used in practice because so many offenders are impoverished and unable to pay. Some may think that we have criminal sanctions, rather than purely civil ones, for precisely this reason. David Friedman points out that more offenders would find themselves able to raise the money for fines if threatened with a sufficiently drastic alternative sanction.[13] We would then, of course, have to impose that drastic alternative on those who were truly unable to raise the funds. Many nonutilitarians would find this unfair (a problem discussed in section IV below). For utilitarians, it would mean only that we would have to add in a bigger negative value for those who could not pay than for those who could—the good done through deterrence might still outweigh those harms. Again, though, we cannot know whether this would be the case without more information about the relationship between the expected harshness of the alternative sanction and the frequency with which we would be able to collect fines and so avoid imposing it. This question is not very different from that of the magnitude of the deterrent effects of imprisonment, although it is somewhat simpler because of the (presumable) greater certainty of imposition (in case of default on the fine) and better information about actual compliance.

Advocates of community service as an alternative sanction tend to stress its rehabilitative and constructive effects rather than its deterrent ones; certainly, it would be difficult to find much consistency in its deterrent effects, given the varying types of service and varying attitudes of offenders. Community service would be less reliable than fines in generating as much social good as the offender's chosen use of her resources, and would generate more administrative costs. The history of prison labor is a cautionary tale for those who seek to make productive use of the time of the bulk of criminal offenders. Such efforts have typically succeeded more in their punitiveness than in their profitability. Although there might be fewer actually unable to perform any such work than those unable to pay fines, the levels of competence likely to be found among offenders are not high to start with. Forced labor requires either intensive supervision or harsh sanctions, and the production level from such quintessentially alienated labor is likely to be even lower than the capacity for work would indicate. Thus, although extracting some productive work from offenders would reduce the social cost of punishment, that gain might be overbalanced by the additional costs of extraction. Again, more information is needed before we can evaluate the possibility of justifying such measures in utilitarian terms.

It is well to keep in mind, in discussing the necessity of deterring crime, that we cannot yet even be sure that deterrence is possible beyond the narrow range of offenses and offenders for which it has been demonstrated. The lack of evidence might mean that such effects do not exist, or may simply be a result of methodological problems: it is notoriously difficult to tease out the effects of changes in penal policy from those of contemporaneous changes, such as changes in the percentage of young men (who commit the lion's share of all crimes) in the population.[14] In either case, utilitarian analysis of the benefits of deterrence is precluded; we simply cannot say whether the deterrent effects of punishment as currently practiced outweigh its costs to offenders and society, given that we do not know the extent of those effects. And there is no straightforward way in which we can change current practice and be assured of producing a system of punishment justified in utilitarian terms.

B. Incapacitation

It may seem that, while deterrent effects are difficult to pin down, there can be no doubt that imprisonment at least has incapacitative effects. But some of those imprisoned would not have committed any additional crimes if left free,[15] and some will simply be replaced by others who will commit the same crimes (for example, a drug dealer whose role in drug distribution is taken over by someone else). Still others may make up for lost time by committing more crimes after release than they would have if not imprisoned, because they have learned additional criminal skills, lost employment prospects, or acquired more resentful attitudes while imprisoned. And some offenders may be able to continue their criminal activities while incarcerated—by directing the activities of associates—or simply shift their victimization efforts on to their fellow inmates.[16]

Despite these difficulties, there is some evidence that incarceration can have incapacitative effects. The Rand study of selective incapacitation in 1982 estimated that incapacitation effects prevented two crimes per man-year of incarceration at a cost of $16,000 each.[17] A more recent study by Steven Levitt comparing crime rates before and after court edicts to reduce prison overcrowding suggests that each man-year of incarceration prevented one assault, one robbery, three burglaries, and nine larcenies, as well as fractions of the more serious crimes of rape and murder (.05 and .004, respectively).[18] Although these estimates substantially exceed the results produced by other recent studies,[19] they are solidly founded.

Unlike most others who have sought to measure the downward influence of sentencing on the crime rate, Levitt succeeded in constructing a study that avoided what criminologists call the "simultaneity problem." That is, it is to be expected not only that longer sentences reduce the crime rate, but also that a higher crime rate results in shorter sentences, because a higher crime rate will increase the number of arrests, and the prosecutor, unable to try many more cases than usual, will settle more cases through plea bargains. Thus, a showing that shorter sentences are correlated with higher crime rates (or that longer sentences are correlated with lower crime rates) is inherently ambiguous: we don't know whether the primary effect is that of crime rates on sentencing, or that of sentencing on crime rates. Levitt's study avoided the simultaneity problem by selecting differences in time served that did not result from prosecutorial decisions—he studied the variations in crime rates following court-ordered early release of prisoners to relieve overcrowding. While these results are far from definitive—the effects noted may not persist long for each offender[20] or be generalizable to other times and places[21]—they are sufficiently well founded to serve as a valid basis for considering what else would have to be true, assuming general incapacitative effects of this magnitude, in order for the current punishment regime to be justified on utilitarian grounds.

Levitt estimates the saved "social cost" of the prevented crimes at about $50,000 ($20,000–$80,000), based on jury awards for similar harms in civil cases.[22] Because Levitt's estimate of the cost of imprisonment is limited to its dollar cost to taxpayers, he concludes that the social benefits are greater than, or at least comparable to, the social costs (given a dollar cost for incarceration of about $30,000). His calculation, however, does not count either the costs of incarceration to offenders or the benefits of crime to offenders.[23] The "social cost" of crime is not just its cost to the victim, but rather its cost to the victim minus its benefit to the offender. Some may find it objectionable to count benefits of crime, or costs to offenders of punishment. These are objections to utilitarianism itself, however. The measure of the wrongness of crime, for utilitarians, is its effect on total happiness, not just its effect on the victim. Similarly, the test of the rightness of punishment is its effect on total happiness, not just its effect on the happiness of potential victims.

In the case of property offenses, it is likely that the cost to victims is substantially counterbalanced by gains to offenders. If a thief steals $100 from me, I am $100 poorer, but he is $100 richer. If I am wealthier than the thief, the money will actually be worth more to him than to me. Thefts of cash from the rich by the poor don't necessarily reduce total social happiness. Much theft of property is inefficient, however, in the sense that it causes more loss to the victim than gain to the thief. A thief will not pause to consider whether she needs all of the extra options on a car she is stealing, or whether a Datsun would serve her needs as well as a Cadillac, because these extras don't cost her any more. In addition, a thief who steals property in order to sell it will realize only a fraction of its market value. So the cost of these crimes to victims is unlikely to be fully counterbalanced by gains to offenders, but is certain to be partly offset by such gains—gains that must be included in the utilitarian calculation.

Even without reducing Levitt's estimate of total social cost to account for gains to offenders, it is improbable that the benefits produced by a year's incarceration would offset its costs, when costs to offenders are included. In order for those costs to be less than the total benefits, we would have to estimate the cost of incarceration to the offender at less than $20,000 per year (if we take $50,000 as the actual figure for social benefits through crime reduction). But it is improbable that anyone would consider $20,000 to be adequate compensation for being imprisoned for a year. In quantitative terms, this cost is approximately equivalent to being the victim of two average assaults, according to Levitt's schema.[24] Even not counting the cost of lost liberty, victimization rates within prison walls are sufficiently high to make clear that the average prisoner's loss of well-being is greater than that. To put the point another way, many of the crimes that offenders would otherwise commit may simply be relocated to the interior of the prison, where they are extremely unlikely to find their way into official statistics. One victimization survey found that 69 percent of prisoners in a state prison for young offenders had experienced at least ten of the fourteen surveyed forms of victimization during their current prison term.[25] Effects of incarceration on the families of offenders, and on the communities from which they are drawn, must also be considered.[26] Thus, even given the significant crime reduction effect documented by Levitt, it is improbable that the higher incarceration rate that would have prevented these crimes could have been justified on utilitarian grounds.

Levitt's study looks at the marginal prisoner—the type of prisoner who is released to relieve overcrowding—rather than the average one. It seems likely that such offenders commit fewer crimes than the average, so that the crime-preventive function of incarceration generally would be greater than its effect at the margin. Self-reports of criminal activity during the year before arrest show that the average (mean) number of crimes committed in that year is about 150,[27] although the median is about 15, close to the number shown prevented in Levitt's results. (The average is much higher than the median because of extremely high rates reported by those at the top of the distribution.)[28] This average set also includes a much higher proportion of crimes that cause reduction in the quality of life for the victim, which is much less likely to be counterbalanced by gains to the offender than loss of property.

It seems initially that these figures would show it to be substantially more plausible that imprisonment prevents more harm than it causes. But this appearance depends on the questionable assumption that each year's incarceration prevents, on average, a set of crimes equivalent to the average of those reported as having been committed in the year before arrest. First, some have questioned the accuracy of the extremely high crime rates (more than ten times the median) typically reported by the top 10 percent in such surveys (and the allegations of the bottom 10 percent, who claimed to have committed no crimes).[29] Second, we must ask about the effect of incarceration on lifetime rates of offending, rather than just at its effect on the years spent in prison. If a year's imprisonment simply postpones a year's worth of crime to a later year, there is no incapacitation benefit. Worse yet, that year's imprisonment may increase the propensity of the individual to offend, increasing his lifetime rate. Locking up offenders for life (which will seem like the logical conclusion to some) is likely to substantially reduce the per year benefit, to the extent that offenders age out of their crime-prone years. Al Blumstein has estimated that the average length of a criminal "career" (index crimes committed in adulthood) is less than six years, so that the average number of crimes per year of adulthood would be a fraction of those committed in the year before imprisonment.[30] Others have found that chronic offenders do not commit crimes at a steady rate, but rather in spurts, with the four years immediately preceding imprisonment representing a high point.[31] Further, for some types of crimes, the incarcerated offender will simply be replaced by someone else who takes over his "job." We thus can't assume on the basis of these self-reports that the benefits of incapacitation are substantially higher for the average offender than those shown for marginal offenders in Levitt's study, although it is probable that they are somewhat higher.

Are the benefits of incapacitation sufficient to outweigh the harms that imprisonment causes? To know the answer to this question, we would need to know at least the following: (1) how much harm is done to the average prisoner over his term of imprisonment, measured in the same terms as the harm prevented; (2) how much harm (or good) is done, on average, to his family by his absence; (3) what the effect of imprisonment is on the average lifetime rate of offending, including offenses committed while imprisoned. If the answers to these questions showed that punishment (as currently practiced) does do more good than harm, the next level of analysis would involve categorization of offenses and offenders to determine whether the good outweighs the harm within each category.

It is possible, of course, that the benefits of incapacitation could be made greater, or that its costs to inmates could be made lower. We could take steps to reduce risks to inmates, for example, or otherwise to improve the conditions of life in prison. Or we could try to limit the use of imprisonment to the top 6 to 10 percent of chronic offenders (who, according to self-reports, commit ten times their share of crime) so that the benefits of incapacitation would be greater. From a utilitarian point of view, incapacitating just this subset of high-rate offenders looks very attractive; with fewer persons imprisoned, the harm done would be less, and many more crimes would be prevented for each man-year of imprisonment. The immediate question is whether it is possible to identify this subset, as the self-report method would obviously not be accurate if used in the context of sentencing decisions.[32]

To date, the best efforts to predict dangerous or criminal activity by individuals have had limited success. Studies of factors such as prior criminal record, employment record, drug use, and so on, have successfully identified at best half of those who later proved "dangerous," while incorrectly identifying as dangerous many who proved not to be.[33] Clinical studies involving in-depth interviews and individual evaluation have fared no better.[34] We can increase the likelihood of correctly identifying dangerous persons as dangerous (true positives) by using a less restrictive criterion—for example, we can identify as "dangerous" all those with any prior criminal record. But this criterion will be even more inaccurate; the price of capturing more of the dangerous individuals will be an even greater increase in the number of nondangerous individuals identified as dangerous (false positives)—much as if we assumed that all U.S. visitors from the Middle East were terrorists. We could, of course, correctly identify all of the dangerous persons simply by assuming that everyone in the sample is dangerous—or we could correctly identify all of the nondangerous persons by making the opposite assumption. The filter we use is useful only insofar as it lets through all and only those who will in fact prove to be dangerous.

Moreover, because of the low prevalence of "dangerous" persons in the population, the increase in false positives that results from the use of a less restrictive criterion will be several times greater than the increase in true positives. Suppose (implausibly) that 1 percent of young men with military backgrounds entering the United States from the Middle East were terrorists, and 0.1 percent of all adult visitors from the Middle East were terrorists, some of the latter being older, or female, or lacking military backgrounds. If we picked out all young men from military backgrounds entering the country from the Middle East, we would incorrectly identify ninety-nine people as terrorists for every person correctly identified as a terrorist. At the same time, we would miss those Middle Eastern terrorists who were not young men with military backgrounds. But if we used the less restrictive criterion of being an adult visitor from the Middle East in order to catch the others, we would incorrectly identify 999 people as terrorists for every correctly identified terrorist.

Given the low prevalence of "dangerousness" in the population, the prediction that will attach correct labels to the maximum number of persons is the prediction that no one is dangerous; the percentage of incorrect predictions will then be the same as the prevalence of dangerousness—if only 1 percent of the population is dangerous, only 1 percent of the predictions will be wrong.

The utilitarian's choice of filter would depend on the relationship between the costs of unnecessarily imprisoning nondangerous persons improperly identified as dangerous (false positives) and the costs of the crimes committed by dangerous persons released because they have been improperly identified as nondangerous (false negatives). If the cost per wrong identification is equal (regardless of whether it is false positive or false negative), we should, as utilitarians, minimize wrong identifications—which means assuming that no one is dangerous. The best that has been done so far is one false negative and eight false positives for every true positive.[35] We would have to imprison all of the nine predicted to be dangerous (the one true positive and the eight false) to prevent the crimes of the one person correctly identified as dangerous. For this move to be superior in utilitarian terms to the assumption that no one is dangerous, the saved cost of the prevented crimes would have to be more than nine times the cost of a year's imprisonment to the inmate and society.

It is improbable that further scientific developments will improve significantly on these figures. We might look forward to such developments if it were simply a question of finding some biological or psychological marker for "dangerousness." But "dangerousness," in the sense of a propensity to commit crimes (or some subset, such as violent crimes), is not a characteristic that inheres in individuals, and, indeed could not be. Crime is an artifact of law, not a natural category, and most types of acts—even violent ones—may be either legal or illegal, depending on the context. Laws may or may not prohibit the sale of particular drugs, forcible sex, sodomy, abortion, torture, killing, child abuse, slavery, appropriation of the property of others, or various types of fraud and exploitation.

It is marginally conceivable that there could be an identifiable inherent tendency in some people to respect authority, but if so, we would not want to incapacitate all those who lack it. Deference to authority on the part of the entire population at liberty has unacceptable implications for the power of those in authority (not to mention that those at the top level of authority would presumably fail the test as well). Individuals may have personality traits such as aggressiveness, a short temper, or poor impulse control, but such characteristics are consistent with law-abiding behavior in many sets of circumstances. We don't know what situations a given individual will face in the future, nor do we know what stabilizing (or destabilizing) factors will enter her life, or whether she will encounter personal tragedy or undergo religious conversion. Because we don't and can't know these things, the best we will ever be able to do is to say that a population made up of individuals with a given set of characteristics—not an individual with those characteristics—will commit more crimes than a comparable population lacking such characteristics. But it will always be true that if we detain all of those having such characteristics, we are detaining many people who would not otherwise have committed crimes, as well as letting go free some who will commit crimes.

It is possible that we can find surrogates for situational factors and thus increase predictive strength. Even today, we could improve the predictive power of the filter by focusing on what criminologists call "extra-legal" factors, such as race, gender, and even zip code. The authors of a recent study of juvenile delinquents in Philadelphia conclude:

There is considerable evidence to support the hypothesis that location can serve to ameliorate or intensify the existing risk factors toward chronic offending. Zip code 19144 (Germantown) had no juveniles, even those classified as high risk, that went on to become chronic delinquent offenders. Zip code 19133 (North Philadelphia—primarily a Latino section) also had very low rates for the high-risk group. In contrast, zip codes 19132 (Strawberry Mansion, Stanton in North Philadelphia—mostly African American) and 19143 (Kingsessing and Cobbs Creek in West Philadelphia—mostly African American) had very high proportions of high-risk juveniles who did become chronic delinquents.[36]

One neighborhood had 50 percent high-rate chronic delinquents, as compared to an overall average of 8 percent among the delinquents studied.[37] We could thus improve "dangerousness" predictions substantially by adding a multiplier for zip code. Indeed, it is also likely that we could achieve some success in dangerousness predictions simply by combining age, gender, and zip code—without reference to prior adjudication as a delinquent. What the zip code captures here is, of course, the social circumstances of the individual—some information about the situations he is likely to encounter, the quality of his schooling, and his general life prospects.

Many people would, of course, consider the use of such extra-legal factors in sentencing profoundly unfair. But unfairness—like anything else—matters to utilitarians only to the extent that it can be expressed in terms of bad consequences. We cannot be sure a priori that the consequences of such practices—perhaps in terms of deteriorating race relations—would be bad enough to outweigh the positive effects of increased crime prevention. This is an aspect of the failure of utilitarianism to account for unfair distribution of penalties, discussed in section IV below. As such, the prospects for improving dangerousness predictions by appeal to extra-legal factors may be better regarded as a reason for rejecting the utilitarian approach altogether than as a hopeful sign that the benefits of punishment can be made to exceed its costs.

Another way we could get more information for dangerousness predictions would be to keep track of each individual's personal relationships. A stormy relationship with members of one's family, for example, might be an indicator of greater dangerousness given certain personality traits. Perhaps we could technologically capture an individual's internal emotional state, thoughts, or attitudes, as well as her plans, and so form a complete picture of the likelihood that she will endanger others, and even of which others she will endanger. There may be good consequential reasons for not amassing this level of information about individuals, but supposing these objections are overcome, the information could not be used to justify long-term incapacitation. Given information at this level of specificity, we would be able to prevent the dangerous interaction without a blanket restriction on freedom.

Despite the evidence that imprisonment has significant incapacitative effects, then, there is also a good case to be made that those effects are currently bought at too high a price to satisfy the utilitarian criterion of promoting the greatest good of the greatest number. It is possible, however, that given better prisons, more information about individuals, and restriction of imprisonment to a smaller group, the benefits of incapacitation could be greater than the harms that it does.

C. Rehabilitation

Rehabilitation as a strategy for reducing crime suffered a body blow with Martinson's 1974 conclusion, after a thorough review of rehabilitation programs, that "nothing works."[38] But since then, research has shown positive results for a number of rehabilitation programs. Recidivism rates for juveniles have been reduced by 2 percent for programs using family counseling and by 36 percent for programs focusing on securing employment. Behavioral programs studied were also quite effective, reducing recidivism by 24 percent. In general, current treatment programs probably reduce recidivism rates by about one-fifth for juveniles and one-tenth for adults.[39]

Effects of this size may well be sufficient to make rehabilitation efforts cost-effective in the sense that they produce results worth spending money on. If we take imprisonment as given, adding rehabilitation is likely to be a net improvement. If we want to use rehabilitative success as a justification for imprisonment, however, we must take a different perspective. The crime-preventive effects of successful rehabilitation programs can justify the imprisonment of offenders only to the extent that imprisonment is necessary to their success. For example, educational or vocational programs can be offered either inside or outside prisons, but participation rates may be higher in prison. Only the positive effects of the increased participation rate on the crime rate and the life prospects of offenders could then be counted as benefits to be weighed against the costs of imprisonment to offenders and society. Similarly, if drugs are less available in prison (although this is not always the case), drug treatment programs may enjoy more success in that environment; the difference between success rates inside and outside prisons would then be considered a benefit of imprisonment to be weighed against its costs.

The current state of affairs, according to a recent meta-analysis of more than four hundred studies of correctional treatment, appears to be the opposite: treatment programs are in general less effective in institutions than in the community.[40] As long as this continues to be the case, there is no possibility that imprisonment can be justified on the ground that it does enough good via rehabilitation to outweigh the harm; it seems instead to impair rehabilitative efforts that might otherwise enjoy more success.

Voluntary rehabilitation programs are unproblematic, because they do not deprive their subjects of liberty. Forced rehabilitation outside prisons (for example, drug treatment programs) raises somewhat different issues. Such programs have had some success, and it is more likely that the benefit produced can outweigh the harm done by this smaller restriction of the offender's liberty, at least in some circumstances.

However, as with deterrence and incapacitation, the possibility that future research may show greater effectiveness within institutions for at least some types of rehabilitative programs cannot be ruled out. It may be easier to show that the benefits gained from forced rehabilitation outside the prison setting outweigh the harm caused by the deprivation of liberty thus entailed, although the success rate of voluntary programs can generally be expected to be higher. It is also quite plausible that further research to identify successful methods and more widespread implementation of those methods will at least improve the overall effectiveness of forced rehabilitative programs. Whether success rates inside prison will ever be higher than those outside prison is another matter.

III. Consideration of Alternatives

It thus seems unlikely that the current system of punishment can be justified on utilitarian grounds, but possible that, given advances in knowledge and improvement of prison conditions, some system of punishment could be so justified. But even if punishment prevents more harm than it causes (or can be reformed to do so), that is still not the end of the inquiry. The utilitarian will also want to know whether the same benefit can be gained at a lower cost. Here, it is instructive to consider the multiple points at which interventions might reduce crime.

Punishment (instrumentally conceived) seeks to affect the motivation or opportunity of potential offenders to commit crimes. Their motivation to do so can instead be affected before it is formed by socialization, corrected after it is formed by psychological interventions such as drug treatment programs, or outweighed by motivation toward positive goals such as employment and community standing. Opportunities for crime can be reduced by protective measures such as locks, personal alarms, and security gates, or by environmental design conducive to community supervision. For punishment to be justified in utilitarian terms, it must be true not only that punishment prevents more harm than it causes, but also that it cannot be replaced by other measures that do as much good and less harm. Interventions such as voluntary drug treatment programs or parenting support begin with the advantage that they do not in themselves cause any harm beyond the expenditure of public funds; thus, to achieve a similar net social saving, they do not even need to be as effective as punishment to be preferred on utilitarian grounds. Some studies have shown that such interventions, on a small scale, are more effective than punishment in preventing particular types of crime.[41]

Child abuse and neglect are commonly agreed to be significant factors in later criminal behavior. In a 1999 study, more than half of those serving sentences for violent offenses reported a history of abuse (compared to about one-tenth of the general population).[42] Such abuse, in turn, often reflects severe psychological and social stresses on the abusing parent. Alleviating these stresses, while at the same time providing help with constructive child-raising techniques, could significantly reduce the amount of child abuse and consequent criminal involvement.[43] It is likely that the expenditure of public funds on such a program, rather than on punishment, would by itself provide a sufficient increase in the general welfare to compare favorably with punishment from a utilitarian point of view.[44]

Moving out from the family to the community, one of the most striking features of crime incidence statistics is the extreme variation in crime rates among communities in the same city and even among communities having the same demographic characteristics. Sampson and Wilson suggest that it is the convergence of a number of social factors in these neighborhoods that fosters the susceptibility of youths who grow up there to adopt a criminal lifestyle.[45] Among the factors they identify are the loss of employment opportunities, transience of residency, prevalence of single-parent households, undermining of local institutions such as churches, and consequent concentration of poorly supervised youths who find a paucity of positive models for their behavior. A focus on providing more resources to such neighborhoods to improve employment prospects and to provide support for single parents so that they would be able to devote their energies to giving children the supervision they need and to rebuilding local institutions would be a constructive alternative to incarcerating a large percentage of the young men who live in these communities.

The utilitarian would also want to consider the possibility that change in larger structural factors could affect the crime rate without introducing new harms. Messner and Rosenfeld locate the cause of high levels of serious crime in the United States compared to other countries in the cultural overemphasis on material wealth coupled with lack of structural support for the institutions of education, family, and polity.[46] Expanding on Robert Merton's anomie theory, they argue that the consistent cultural emphasis on material wealth and on attaining one's goals, together with a lack of regard for restraint (and active admiration for unconventionality) in the methods used, creates a climate in which those who are blocked from legitimate avenues to wealth will readily choose illegitimate ones. On this view, income inequality is not an accident, but a necessity:

> [T]he basic logic of this cultural ethos actually presupposes high levels of inequality. A competitive allocation of monetary rewards requires both winners and losers, and winning and losing have meaning only when rewards are distributed unequally. The motivation to endure the competitive struggle is not maintained easily if the monetary difference between winning and losing is inconsequential.[47]

On the short end of economic inequality, young men who see no prospect of material success through legitimate means seek that prize through illegitimate ones, of which the drug market is the prime example. Violence often results as the only effective means of enforcing contractual obligations in the extra-legal context. But even at the high end, the emphasis on the goal rather than the means by which it is reached takes its toll, as we have learned through wave after wave of financial scandals in which highly placed professionals sought to boost their competitive gains through unscrupulous tactics.

At the same time, the focus on material wealth has made the workplace and economic arena the primary social structure to which other structures—through which regard for other values might be fostered—are consistently subordinated. The needs of family are generally expected to be subordinated to the needs of the workplace: as they point out, many people have difficulty "finding time" for family activities, yet few have difficulty "finding time" for work. Having children is seen as self-indulgence—foolish for the poor, and optional for the well-off—rather than as an essential contribution to the continuation of society. Increasingly, young people postpone family formation until they are economically secure, with the result that more young adults are independent of their family of origin without a new family of their own to exert a stabilizing influence. The high rate of divorce leaves many children in weaker, single-parent families. Worse, the legitimacy of parental authority in poor families is undermined by children's perception that the parents are unable to provide them with culturally prized (though often laughably inessential) goods. Educational institutions face increasing demands to provide immediate work-related training rather than broader knowledge: students are often scornful of learning that has no evident application in the world of work.

In other industrialized nations, families are routinely supported through public day care, monetary subsidies, and extensive paid parental leave. The values of education and participation in public life receive a greater share of cultural support than they do in the United States. If Messner and Rosenfeld are correct, the potential for reducing the rate of violent crime in the United States through structural and cultural change far exceeds the wildest dreams of current crime control policy. With rates of violent crime approximately 40 percent higher than those of other industrialized democracies, and a rate of homicide three or four times that of these countries,[48] there is a lot of room for improvement, even while staying within the limits of comparable economic and political structures. Going further afield, Japan has an overall rate of crime that is microscopic by U.S. standards, with 2.2 reported robberies and less than one homicide per 100,000 population.[49]

Regardless of whether the Messner and Rosenfeld analysis is correct, the connection between income inequality and various social ills, among which violent crime is prominent, cannot be gainsaid. Comparative studies including many nations have shown a correlation between income inequality and a welter of social ills, prominent among which are crimes of violence.[50] It is plausible that income inequality (as opposed to absolute poverty, which does not have these effects) alienates those members of society who see others enjoying much greater material comfort and fail to find a satisfying explanation of why they have less. Groups thus alienated may reject the larger society's code of conduct, as well as harboring anger and resentment that can spill over into violent behavior. Reduction of income inequality is therefore another alternative that a utilitarian would consider, particularly in view of the probability that highly unequal distributions do not themselves maximize the utility to be gained from material goods.[51]

The importance of family attachments to social stability and as a foil to the temptations of crime is also well recognized. The utilitarian would also consider the option of providing material support to struggling families so that parents can provide children with the emotional support they need.

Finally, to complete the utilitarian analysis, the expenditure of public funds on crime prevention must be compared to other possible uses of those funds. They could, for example, be diverted to the prevention of other causes of bodily harm and property loss such as automobile accidents, suicide, and illness,[52] or to the furtherance of positive goods such as education or better nutrition. Optimally, the utilitarian would expend funds on any of these social goods only up to the point where the funds can produce more benefits elsewhere.[53] Given the grounds for doubt that punishment is producing any net benefit at all, it would be likely to compete poorly with any of these alternatives.

What then, do we know? We know, with undeniable certainty, that punishment is causing a large amount of harm to a large (and growing) number of people. To set against this, we know that at least some crime is being prevented in this way, and we know that there is some possibility that the harm we are causing is less than the harm prevented. But we also know that there is a significant possibility that the harm we are certainly causing is greater than the harm we are preventing. And we know that there is some possibility that we could achieve comparable crime-preventive effects through nonharmful alternative approaches. A utilitarian, I think, would immediately move to decrease expenditures on punishment and use the funds to pursue alternatives, keeping a close eye in the meantime on the development of further evidence about the many things we do not know.

I have argued that it is not probable, although it is possible, that the combined deterrent, incapacitative, and rehabilitative effects of punishment as currently practiced in the United States are sufficient to recommend it on utilitarian grounds. Although there are a number of ways in which the balance could be made more favorable while retaining the institution of punishment, it is not clear that the institution so reformed could successfully compete on utilitarian grounds with other ways of reducing crime that do not involve harm to offenders. Specifically, in order to be justified on utilitarian grounds, punishment would have to be shown to be substantially *more* effective than equally costly nonharmful alternatives in preventing crime to counterbalance the negative effects that it has on offenders.[54]

IV. Theoretical Objections

Let us assume, then, that the above stipulations are met, and that it is empirically demonstrated that punishment does more good than harm, at a lower overall social cost than other alternatives that would achieve the same result. Although I have argued that such an outcome is unlikely, it is clearly within the realm of possibility. It will then be the utilitarian's task to determine what penalty structure promotes the greatest overall good, and it is here that the familiar theoretical weaknesses of utilitarianism can most clearly be seen.

Given perfect information, the calculation of optimal penalty structure might have almost any result. For example, it may well be true that massive penalties for minor crimes by juveniles would prevent their going on to lives of crime, obviating the need for any penalties for more serious crimes. More plausibly still, we might achieve the optimum balance by vicarious punishment—punishing the families of offenders rather than the offenders themselves. Or we might find, as suggested above, that incapacitating a dangerous group that cannot be clearly identified in advance requires also incapacitating a large number of nondangerous persons. Worse yet, if we were able to make more accurate predictions of future criminality, the utilitarian approach would require that we incapacitate many persons who have, as yet, committed no crime.[55] In short, the burden of producing the social good of crime prevention might fall heavily on some subgroup of the population, and there is no reason in (utilitarian) principle why that subgroup must correspond to the subgroup responsible for the crimes. Utilitarianism is thus consistent with punishment of the innocent, in that it does not make guilt a necessary condition of punishment. Guilt will be necessary for punishment only if punishing the guilty produces more social good than punishing the innocent. Although there are reasons for thinking that this will often be the case—because deterrent and incapacitative effects to some degree depend on guilt—there is no guarantee that it will always be so. Because utilitarianism aggregates goods and ills across persons, it necessarily admits the possibility that severe harm to a small group may be justified by a widespread, if minor, benefit to a large number of others.

Rawls has argued that a permission to punish innocents, given sufficiently positive consequences, could not be incorporated into the social institution of punishment without undermining its aims.[56] People would never know, and so would always wonder, whether a given individual had been punished for her guilt or simply for the greater social good; consequently, they would feel insecure in their own liberty, and deterrent effects would be undermined. This argument works well for instances such as condemning an innocent person to avoid a riot—a practice that could not openly be sanctioned while maintaining the legitimacy of the institution. It works less well for cases such as vicarious punishment or overly broad incapacitation. People might be willing to trade some measure of personal security against punishment for the crimes of their own children to increase their security against victimization by other people's children; at least, it is not facially obvious that the open adoption of vicarious punishment would undermine the institution. Equally, adoption of a strategy of overly broad incapacitation could be publicly announced and understood as a preventive measure without compromising the institution itself. Public willingness to accept such measures, particularly when they are directed primarily at marginalized groups, is evident in the aftermath of the September 11, 2001, attacks on the United States. Even if such strategies turn out to be ruled out on utilitarian grounds, they will be ruled out for their total social effects, and not on the straightforward basis that the innocent may not be punished.

The criticism goes deeper than this, however. As Jeffrie Murphy has pointed out, even considering only the punishment of the guilty, if we punish them to serve the greater social good, we are still harming some individuals to serve the ends of others (in Kantian terms, we are using them as mere means to society's ends).[57] And, if it is wrong to punish the innocent to serve the greater social good, why is it not also wrong to punish the guilty for that purpose? On reflection, it appears that everything that is wrong with punishing the innocent to serve the social good is also wrong with punishing the guilty for that same purpose.[58] We do not generally think, for example, that it is justifiable to use the morally worse members of our society to serve the interests of the morally better. Faced with a choice between lives (for example, where only one organ is available for transplant), we might conceivably take into account, as one factor, the moral worth of individuals; but even this much is distasteful. Certainly it is true that such a consideration would not be dispositive in every case. Either the greater social good is a sufficient reason for harming individuals, or it is not. If achieving that good is not sufficient to justify imposing harms on the innocent, then how can it justify anything, including imposing harms on the guilty?

It may seem that we regularly impose harms on individuals, even innocent ones, in order to achieve the greater social good. For example, we accept the deaths of hundreds of people every year in automobile accidents in order to facilitate the convenience of the rest. Bridges are built despite our knowledge that construction accidents happen. We operate stock markets and allow other forms of business competition in which, in order for there to be winners, there must also be losers. A rule that we may never sacrifice anyone for the greater good would paralyze all these and many other large-scale endeavors. Yet we would not want to adopt a rule that permitted the deliberate withholding of effective treatment from some individuals in order to observe the natural history of a disease (as in the infamous Tuskegee syphilis experiment). There is a significant difference (roughly captured in the Catholic doctrine of double effect) between acts that deliberately target some individuals for harm in order to bring about a desired end and those that result in foreseeable, but unintended, harm. Punishment for crime-preventive purposes is like the withholding of effective treatment, and unlike the building of bridges, in that the harming of those punished is integral to the achievement of its aims. The underlying concern here is that we have a moral duty to treat every individual with the respect due to a person, rather than to use them as mere instruments to our own ends.[59] This is the same concern that prevents us from killing off the less productive members of society to benefit the rest. The problem of using a person as mere means to the ends of others is particularly acute where the method through which she is to serve others' ends involves only harm to her.

There are more sophisticated versions of utilitarianism that seek to meet these criticisms. For example, preference-utilitarianism defines the good to be maximized as the satisfaction of preferences. By ruling out certain types of preferences (for example, preferences founded on false information) from consideration, it is possible to avoid some of the undesirable implications of classical utilitarianism. Proponents of this view argue that it respects persons, in that it gives the preferences of each person equal weight.[60] But as long as the preferences of the many can outweigh the preferences of the few, the fundamental objection to aggregating goods across persons is not met.[61] There seems to be no principled way to rule out preferences for discriminatory treatment of certain ethnic groups, for example. As Robert Nozick has pointed out, even a principle that rights violations are to be minimized—which would lie beyond the bounds of utilitarianism proper—is quite different from conceiving of rights as side constraints, violation of which is not permitted in the pursuit of any end.[62]

Although few have suggested in recent years that these well-known criticisms of utilitarianism can be met, Ferdinand Schoeman has argued that preventive detention might be justified on the same grounds as quarantine. Specifically, he argues that if we could know to a moral certainty that a particular individual posed a threat to life and limb, we would be justified in detaining him to the degree and for the length of time necessary to prevent him from doing so, or until the probability that he would harm another diminished to a tolerable level. Here, it may be argued, is a case in which it is justifiable to impose deliberate, rather than merely foreseeable, harm (loss of liberty) on some individuals in order to benefit others. Unlike punishment for deterrent purposes, but like punishment for incapacitative purposes, it is necessary only that the individuals in question be separated from the rest of the population for the aims of the policy to be achieved; but this separation cannot be attained without restriction of liberty.

I have argued above that it is improbable that we will ever develop the capability to state to a "moral certainty" that a particular individual is dangerous, simply because dangerousness does not inhere in individuals. Note that the Wenk study cited above, even though it can be characterized as 50 percent accurate (because it captures 50 percent of the dangerous), can only tell us that one of nine people satisfying the identifying criteria will actually be dangerous.[63] Schoeman argues that we would not hesitate to quarantine an individual who had a 50 percent chance of infecting others and a 50 percent chance of killing infected persons. But there are many differences between the prospect of epidemic and the possibility of crime, quite apart from the problem of identifying the dangerous. First, contamination of another person typically does not just make that person ill, but also makes that person a carrier of illness, whereas being a victim of crime does not typically also make the victim into an offender. Second, quarantine of infected persons in an area where the illness is not already endemic can completely stop its spread, but incapacitation of those identified as criminally inclined cannot stop crime. Third, the period of danger from infection is typically measured in days, while the period of danger from crime is typically measured in years. Fourth, in today's world, quarantine is rare, so that the risk to any individual of being quarantined is small. Fifth (in part for the reasons mentioned), most individuals voluntarily accept quarantine once notified of the danger that they pose to others. I think that we would hesitate—and it would be wrong—routinely to impose quarantine for a period of years on large numbers of unwilling individuals who were or might be carriers of some illness that would not spread geometrically if uncontained, where we could hope to identify only a fraction of the carriers. Indeed, the history of quarantine is studded with periodic rebellion, as well as not incidentally having been associated with stigmatization of quarantined persons and the ethnic groups to which many of them belonged.[64] Thus, while Schoeman's suggestion that we may incapacitate the dangerous on the same basis as that on which we quarantine may be sound, this comparison may tell as much about the limits of quarantine as about the justifiability of preventive detention.

V. Conclusion

We have seen that, notwithstanding the apparently favorable results of some cost-benefit calculations, it is unlikely that punishment as presently practiced in the United States can be said to do more good than harm. From a utilitarian perspective, the correct approach would be to pursue nonharmful methods of discouraging crime, perhaps supplemented by less harmful forms of imprisonment concentrated on a smaller prison population. The deeper problem, however, is that utilitarianism is inherently flawed: it requires that we use individuals as mere means to the good of others, provided only that the total good outweighs the total harm. Punishment, conceived simply as the doing of harm to some in order to prevent harm to others, is as morally suspect as quiet euthanasia of the unsightly homeless.

3

Preserving the Moral Order

> And if any of you would punish in the name of righteousness and
> lay the ax unto the evil tree, let him see to its roots;
> And verily he will find the roots of the good and the bad, the fruit-
> ful and the fruitless, all entwined together in the silent heart of the
> earth.   —Kahlil Gibran, *The Prophet*, 1923

At the heart of retributivism is the contention that it is the wrongness of
the criminal act that justifies the imposition of punishment on the offender. Yet punishment itself consists in the performance of a parallel act
against the offender. Thus showing that the harmful acts that are crimes
have a moral value precisely opposite to that of the harmful acts that are
punishments is the central task of retributive theory. It is not enough to
show that some crimes involve acts unacceptable in any context, such as
rape and torture. In addition, the retributivist must demonstrate that the
rightness of punishment derives directly from the wrongness of crime—
that it is right to kill the murderer, or to deprive the kidnapper of liberty,
because it was wrong for the murderer to kill, or for the kidnapper to deprive her victim of liberty. Not every punishment corresponds so directly
to the crime in question, but every punishment inflicts upon the offender
some harm that, if it were not a response to crime, would itself be a crime.

Contemporary arguments for retribution most often take a Kantian
view, appealing to the notion that commission of a crime entails consent
to punishment. Before addressing those arguments in chapter 4, I consider a second strand of retributive theory, which holds that it is necessary to respond to wrongful acts by retributive punishment, because
only in that way can the moral order be preserved and defended. This
line of thought focuses on the moral stance taken by the state in punishing. In this chapter I consider three versions of this view: Hegel's view

that punishment annuls the crime, Hampton's interpretation of Hegel to mean that punishment vindicates the rights of the victim, and the view of Walter Berns and others that punishment is a necessary expression of the justified anger of the community.

I. Hegel

One of the central problems for any retributive theory is that it must explain why it is right to do to the offender things that it would be wrong for him to do to others—to deprive him of life, liberty, or property. It is not enough to show that some crimes involve acts unacceptable in any context, such as rape and torture. Punishment necessarily involves acts that are ordinarily unacceptable—specifically, acts that in another context would themselves be crimes. The retributivist must be able to show not only that kidnapping is wrong while punishment by imprisonment is right, but also that there is an intimate connection between these two judgments, that is, that imprisonment is right *because* kidnapping is wrong.

Hegel addresses directly the apparently paradoxical nature of retributivism:

> [I]f crime and its annulment . . . are treated as if they were unqualified evils, it must, of course, seem quite unreasonable to will an evil merely because "another evil is there already." To give punishment this superficial character of an evil is . . . the fundamental presupposition of those [theories] which regard it as a preventive, a deterrent, a threat, reformative &c., and what on those theories is supposed to result from punishment is treated equally superficially as a good. But . . . the precise point at issue is wrong and the righting of it. . . . [C]rime is to be annulled, not because it is the producing of an evil, but because it is an infringement of the right as right.[1]

What is wrong with crime is not its consequences, but its intrinsic nature as wrong. From that point of view, punishment shares with crime only the incidental feature of producing harm; in its essential nature, punishment is the righting of a wrong, and thus correctly described as opposite to crime.

Hegel further points out that the same evils may be produced by accident: people die in accidents as well as from murder. What distinguishes crime is that it is done intentionally, and thus reflects on the will of the offender.

> The sole positive existence which the injury possesses is that it is the particular will of the criminal. Hence to injure [or penalize] this particular will as a will determinately existent is to annul the crime, which otherwise would be held valid, and to restore the right.[2]

But although this makes clear how crime (or rather moral wrong) is distinguished from mere harm, it is less clear how punishment—another intentional infliction of harm—can serve to annul the crime. As J. L. Mackie notes, future events never cause past events not to have happened.[3] For some crimes (especially property crimes), the damage done to the victim can be fully "undone" by compensation; for others, such as homicide or maiming, the damage will never be undone. But Hegel's focus is not on undoing the harm: he concedes that compensation may undo it. What he is concerned to annul is only the bad will of the offender.

Hegel is clearly correct in saying that the crime is a crime only because of the offender's intent. But in what sense does "penalizing his will" (presumably by doing something to him that he does not want done) serve to annul that intent? Importantly, Hegel does not mean here that the offender must be reformed, made into a person who will not will to do wrong in the future; nor does he mean that others are to be frightened out of committing similar crimes. Rather, it is only the specific crime that is to be annulled by penalizing the will that created it. The crime is to be annulled, not because it does harm or may be repeated, but because it is wrong.

Rights, according to Hegel, can only be understood by reference to coercion; that is, rights are defined as those things that may justifiably be defended by the use of coercion. A wrong act is a transgression of the right, the trammeling of another's freedom. Mere harms can be cured by the payment of damages; but a deliberately willed wrong—a crime—must be annulled through the use of coercion.

Assuming that Hegel is correct that rights can only be defined by reference to coercion, and that the use of coercion in defense of rights is thus definitionally justified, it remains possible that coercion may be used only to *prevent* rights violations, rather than to respond to them after the fact.[4] The key to Hegel's justification of punishment is therefore the sense in which post hoc coercion can be said to annul the crime.

Coercion "taken abstractly," Hegel says, is wrong because "it is an expression of a will which annuls the expression or determinate existence of a will,"[5] that is, coercion is wrong because it thwarts the will of another. A kidnapping, for example, annuls the will of the victim, treating it as nonexistent. This act is wrong because it annuls a will that is blameless, and therefore ought not to be annulled. The coercion later exercised against the offender annuls his will; that second act of coercion is right because it annuls a will that is wrong.[6]

This argument clearly shows the justifiability of direct preventive measures such as intervening in the kidnapping to prevent the offender from completing it. Using coercion to annul his will to kidnap someone (by preventing him from doing so) is in this sense obviously right—a use of coercion to defend the rights of the victim. It is more problematic, however, to say that using coercion against him after the fact, after the kidnapping is over and cannot be undone, is an annulment of his will to kidnap. The use of coercive punishment does annul the will of the offender: he wills to be free, but he is confined. But such annulling bears only a tenuous relationship to his will to kidnap (which, indeed, may no longer exist at all). There is no obvious sense in which this use of coercion (taken in abstraction from its possible effects on behavior) is a literal defense of the rights of others.

II. Punishment as Vindicating Victims

For this kind of reason, Hegel's view of punishment as annulling crime has more often been understood as a metaphorical annulment—an announcement that the crime is wrong. In *Forgiveness and Mercy*, Jean Hampton elaborates on this idea, arguing that crime can be understood to be annulled through punishment where the state acts as an agent of the victim.[7] I shall argue that punishment cannot be so understood, whether the state is seen as acting as the victim's agent or on its own behalf.

Hampton argues that the criminal act demeans its victim: the offender fails to realize that the treatment accorded the victim is inconsistent with her value. The purpose of punishment, she argues, is to reassert their equality and to nullify the evidence of the offender's superiority provided by the crime.

In her eyes, the offender is a "malicious hater" who seeks a competitive victory over her victim, while the victim who seeks retribution can be understood as seeking to nullify that victory, rather than to triumph over the offender. I shall argue that this distinction fails. Hampton's argument leads instead to the conclusion that, just as the offender seeks a competitive victory over her victim, punishment represents a competitive victory over the offender. The statement made by retributive punishment is that the offender is of lower value than the victim; the statement that the two are of equal value would be made by requiring compensation rather than punishment.

A person who curses another literally speaks an untruth about the person's moral value, as is evident in Jack Katz's eloquent description:

> [Cursing] is a direct and effective way of doing just what it appears to do: symbolically transforming the offending party into an ontologically lower status. As in a cartoon, a wife becomes a barking dog. An acquaintance loses his recognizable personal appearance and becomes nothing more than an anus penetrated at will by anonymous others. A person who a moment ago was a friend with a recognizably human name now has become fecal material animated in fellatio.[8]

How can the victim (or her agent) nullify the evidence of her value provided by the curser and show her true value? She may hold her head high and to show her true value through her conduct. Thus the curser is made to look foolish as his lie is exposed. Alternatively, the victim may show that she does not care about the opinion of the curser by failing to react with anger, grief, or shame. Least effective of all is an attempt by the victim to bring the curser low by responding with an equally foul vilification. Should this effort succeed, it hardly elevates the (original) victim; rather, it seems to reduce her to the same status as the (original) offender. I shall argue that punishment similarly fails to affirm the victim's value.

It is easy to see how the crime can be understood as evidence of the offender's superiority over the victim. If Badman kidnaps Heiress and holds her for ransom, he thus reveals his belief that his desire for the money is more important than Heiress's right to liberty (and her parents' right to their money).[9] As rights are much more important than simple desires, the only way that his desires can override Heiress's rights is if he is a much more valuable person than she.[10] Badman's crime can therefore be understood as a claim that he is more valuable than Heiress. But how does punishment refute such evidence of superiority? Hampton suggests that by depriving Badman of his own liberty as punishment, we show that Badman is *not* more valuable than his victim: what Badman can do to Heiress, we can do to him, on her behalf. We thus nullify the evidence for his false claim of superiority. But if Badman's crime is evidence that he is more valuable than his victim, then isn't the state's deprivation of Badman's liberty on her behalf simply evidence that she is more valuable than Badman—a claim as inconsistent with the equal value of persons as the original crime?

To avoid this result, Hampton says that the retribution-seeking victim is not looking for a competitive victory over the offender; that would be the strategy of the malicious hater, who is open to moral criticism. The motives of offender and victim are crucial to the kinds of claims their actions are taken as making, so that even though their overt actions are the same, the meanings of their actions may be quite different.

The malicious hater, according to Hampton, seeks to harm her victim in order to demonstrate her superiority over him. This, we may assume, is the strategy followed by the offender. The crime demeans the victim in the sense of according her treatment that is too low for her. The offender may also seek to diminish the victim, that is, to lower the victim's own estimate of her value, or to degrade her, that is, actually to change her value. Retributive punishment, on the other hand, seeks only to accord the offender the treatment he deserves, and thus to give him the treatment that is in accordance with his true value. Thus, Hampton says, the victim who seeks retribution does not seek to demean the offender but only to diminish him, that is, to deflate his overblown sense of his own value by giving him the treatment that is appropriate for him. Hampton contrasts such a victim with a vengeful victim who seeks to show that the offender is of lower value than she is, arguing that such a victim is indeed a malicious hater whose efforts to bring the offender low are not to be respected.

If, however, all persons are of equal value, and kidnapping (depriving the victim of her liberty) is treatment that is too low for a person of that value, it seems to follow that depriving the offender of his liberty similarly represents treatment that is too low for persons of that value.[11] Hampton's position is that the crime (as a competitive victory) makes a statement about the relative value of offender and victim while the punishment makes a statement about the absolute value of the offender. Thus, Badman's crime says, "I am more valuable than Heiress," while the punishment says, "Badman's value is less than X," where X represents the overblown value that (the crime demonstrates) he places on himself. If Badman and Heiress are in fact of equal value V, then the punishment must say "Badman is of value V." The punishment seeks to diminish Badman, that is, to reduce his subjective sense of his own value as greater than V, *by according him the treatment that is appropriate for his true value.* But if Badman's treatment of Heiress is not appropriate for the value V, then neither is her similar treatment of him. Punishment demeans the offender, just as crime demeans the victim.

Can we say that depriving Badman of liberty is appropriate for his value (and thus not demeaning) because he deserves to be so treated, while Heiress does not? If the type of treatment that is appropriate depends only on the person's value, then to say that Badman deserves poor treatment is to say that his desert lowers his value—thus sacrificing the idea that all persons have equal value. We could say instead that the type of treatment that is appropriate for a person may depend on something independent of his value in this sense. But in that case, Badman's poor treatment of Heiress is not necessarily evidence that she is of low value, either—and it is precisely that aspect of his treatment of her that does count as such evidence that we must refute.

It may be objected that I have ignored the interplay of motives and actions that determines whether an action is demeaning. The motives of Badman and Heiress are not symmetrical. Badman (we may suppose) is motivated simply to satisfy his desires; thus he claims (acts on his belief that) his desires are more important than his victim's rights. But her motive—or the state's, when it acts on her behalf—is to assert moral truth; specifically, to show that Badman's claim of superiority is false. The act taken in response, to be effective in achieving this goal, must show that her right to liberty is more important than Badman's desire for her parents' money. But such a showing can be made by requiring compensation for the harm done, thus shifting the consequences of the wrongdoer's behavior back to him, as is regularly done in the context of civil suits. When the state requires Badman to return any money he has obtained from Heiress's parents to them, and to compensate her for the harm done by the kidnapping, it makes the desired showing that he cannot effectively place his desires above their rights—that he has no power over them. Punishment, rather than shifting the harmful consequences, adds new ones.

It may also be objected that it is unlikely that restitution and compensation can restore Heiress to her prior state; such measures cannot really "undo" the crime and thus cannot refute the evidence of Badman's superiority. As noted above, it is unfortunately true of many (though not all) crimes that the harm they do cannot be undone by compensation. But it is equally (if not more) true that the harm done by such crimes cannot be undone by punishment, either. Undoing the harm cannot be the criterion of refutation. The question is rather one of the *meaning* of requiring compensation or inflicting punishment, with respect to the rights of the victim and her status relative to that of the offender.

It is clear that requiring compensation can assert rights. If I breach my contract to sell you my house, in effect claiming that the contract is not binding (or indeed that my desire to keep the house is more important than your right to it), you may win a civil judgment against me to the effect that the contract is binding, and I will have to carry it through. The law's forcing me to do so is precisely a refutation of my claim that my desires are more important than your (contractual) rights.

The crime of kidnapping ranked Badman's desire for money above the rights of others, thus demeaning them and providing false evidence of his value relative to them. Requiring compensation correctly ranks Heiress's right to her liberty and her parents' right to their money above Badman's desire for that money, showing that all concerned are of equal value. Why, then, the need for punishment?

It may be suggested that we can make the appropriate statement here only by punishment because (or if) Badman lacks sufficient resources to pay adequate compensation (or because compensation would in any case be inadequate). Punishment so conceived is an alternative way for the state to make an authoritative declaration of the rights of the victim and the relative values of the parties, where compensation will not serve. Consider, however, what the content of that statement must be, given that the state, like Badman, acts to deprive someone of his liberty.

If the crime of kidnapping is understood to make a false statement about the victim's value by ranking the offender's desires above her right to liberty, then the punishment of imprisonment must be understood as a statement that some right or desire of hers is ranked higher than the offender's prima facie right to liberty. If it is a desire, it is necessarily true that the desire, whatever other content it may have, can also be correctly described as a desire to see Badman deprived of his liberty. It may, for example, be her desire to see him suffer, as Jeffrie Murphy suggests,[12] or her desire to deny his superiority, as Hampton suggests. But this entails, in context, that she desires to see him deprived of his liberty, as the specific form the suffering or denial of superiority is to take. Although Heiress may desire the deprivation under some descriptions but not under others (for example, she may not specifically desire that Badman be prevented from seeing the birth of his child, even if that is an effect of his imprisonment), if no one desires it under the description of a deprivation of liberty, going forward with such deprivation would be facially unjustified. If, for example, Heiress desires to see Badman suffer *as long as* such suffering violates none of his rights, the violation of his rights to make him suffer could in no way be justified by reference to Heiress's desires, regardless of her status. For Heiress's desire to have a chance of justifying Badman's suffering through violation of his rights, she must at least desire that he suffer *even if* the suffering violates his rights. Thus, Heiress's desire that Badman be deprived of his liberty is ranked above his prima facie right to that liberty. The necessary implication of this is, again, that she is more valuable than he.

The conclusion that punishment asserts that Heiress is more valuable than Badman can be avoided if it is her *right* to have him (for example, suffer through being) deprived of his liberty that is ranked above his prima facie right to his liberty. But of course she has no such right apart from her right (if she has one) to have him punished for wronging her.

Could we say that Badman has lost his right to liberty through his actions? The punishment would then coherently make the true statement that Badman has no right (against the state) to his liberty, while the crime would make the false statement that Heiress has no right (against Badman) to her liberty. But what is it that has overridden Badman's prima face right to liberty, and thus caused him to lose his all-things-considered right to it? Whatever it is, it must be something more important than his prima facie right to liberty (which would cause him to lose his all-things-considered right to it)—and, presumably, still, some right or desire of his victim.

If we say instead that the crime does indeed reduce the wrongdoer's value, the victim's desire to see the wrongdoer suffer (proportionally to the crime) may be correctly ranked above the wrongdoer's right not to suffer.[13] Her desire to see Badman suffer is correctly ranked above his (prima facie) right not to suffer, because (in virtue of his act) he is lower in value than she. We can then say that the punishment is justified, while the crime is not, because the crime provides false evidence that one person is lower in value than the other, and the punishment provides true evidence to the same effect. The punishment does not demean Badman, because it reflects his true low value.

The statements made by crime, restitution, and punishment would be as follows:

> *Crime*: Badman's desires are more important than Heiress's rights; thus, Badman is more valuable than Heiress. (False)
>
> *Compensation*: Heiress's rights are more important than Badman's desires; thus, Badman is not more valuable than Heiress. (True)
>
> *Punishment*: Heiress's rights are more important than Badman's desires (Badman is not more valuable than Heiress) *and* Heiress's desires are more important than Badman's rights (Heiress is more valuable than Badman). (True)[14]

But it seems odd to say that the crime can be annulled through an authoritative statement that the offender is of low value. If punishment is to "annul" the crime, all persons should return to the status they had before it was committed. The assertion of the lower value of the offender in virtue of his act appears instead to relegate him permanently to a new, lower status. The retributivist may say that, once the offender has been punished, he is no longer of lower value than others, in the sense that he is no longer deserving of punishment; after he has been punished, then, he returns to the status he had before the crime. The offender's return to equal status is asserted by releasing him from prison. Again, though, we must ask what the implications are for the meaning of the crime. If Badman released Heiress after payment of the ransom, would that similarly signify her return to equal status, and thus his relinquishment of the claim that he is more valuable than she? Presumably not, or there would be no need to punish him in order to refute that claim. But if his claim about her value survives her release, then the state's claim about his value must likewise survive his.

It is also difficult to see what would be meant, in this context, by saying that he deserves punishment before he serves his sentence, but not after. If it is in virtue of the lower status he has as a kidnapper—a status he will keep after the sentence is served—then there seems to be no reason not to continue punishing him indefinitely. But no retributivist subscribes to such indefinite punishment.

It may seem that these problems can be solved by separating the offender from her act. If punishment makes a statement, not about the value of the offender, but instead about the value or validity of her act (the truth of her statement), then it succeeds in restoring the status quo ante and asserting the moral truth without raising the problem of assigning a lower value to wrongdoers.

What kind of statement would satisfy these conditions? Recall that punishment necessarily makes a statement parallel to the statement made by the crime. In order to say that the punishment does not make a statement about the value of the offender (as a whole person), we must also say that the crime does not make a statement about the victim (as a whole person). If it does not do this, then the entire motivation for punishment as affirming the value of the victim disappears.

It seems, then, that regarding the state as the agent of the victim puts the state in the untenable position of making the same kind of false statement about the offender as that the crime makes about the victim—demeaning him in the way that he demeaned her. This result springs directly from the fact that both crime and punishment are intentional inflictions of harm.

We are thus led to the possibility that the state does not act as Heiress's agent in punishing Badman, but rather acts on its own behalf. For this line of argument to succeed, we can't just view the state as a disinterested third party, for then the penalties that it imposed would simply have the character of new crimes. Instead, we must view the state as standing above the individual members of society. Such a view would also allow us to preserve the equality of persons: if all persons are equal, but the state (or "society") is more valuable than any person, then we can coherently claim that the state's desires, though not those of other persons, may override the rights of individuals. Jeffrie Murphy has suggested that criminal acts are those in which a private person usurps the functions of the state—arrogating to himself the right to determine property rules, for example—so that it makes sense to regard the state as aggrieved in such instances, even where there is no individual victim.[15] This approach would enable us to account for retributive punishment for crimes lacking any obvious victim, such as possession of illicit drugs, trafficking in pornography, and driving while intoxicated.

It turns out, however, that the idea that the state is more valuable than any individual has unwelcome implications. If the state were more valuable than any individual, to the point that the "wishes" of the state were more important than the rights of individuals, it would follow that *any* deprivation of right by the state would be justified. Punishment, as an assertion, would be indistinguishable from the arbitrary deprivation of rights by the state. Moreover, as Hampton notes, it is the relative rankings that are important. If the crime ranks Badman above Heiress, and the punishment ranks the state above Badman, the statement made by the crime has not been corrected. In order for the punishment to affirm the value of the victim, the statement made by the punishment must in some way refer to the victim, and not just to the state.

It appears that punishment can assert that the offender is less valuable than the victim, in just the same sense that the crime can assert that the victim is less valuable than the offender. But to make the statement that both are of equal value, we must instead require compensation. What, then, of those situations in which compensation is obviously inadequate or where the offender is unable to pay? Suppose that Badman has not kidnapped Heiress but killed her instead, just because he felt like it. And suppose that there is no one to whom he could pay compensation, even if he had any money. How can we reassert that her rights are more important than his whims? I have argued that if we respond by punishing him we are only adding parallel false claims to those he has made. What we can do instead, as I shall discuss in chapter 8, is to make a much more literal assertion of the right through verbal or symbolic condemnation, and offer the offender an opportunity to make amends if he can, or to expiate his wrong through other positive actions. I do not suggest that such measures on our part will annul the crime, particularly if it is an especially serious one: the grave wrongs done by crime often cannot be annulled. The best we can do, in some situations, is not to make things worse than they already are by adding new wrongs.

III. Punishment as Expressing Justified Anger

What, then, of the anger of victims? Even if we cannot claim to be annulling the crime, must we not punish in order to assuage their justified anger at the uncompensable harms they have suffered? Even if the victims are not angry, ought we not ourselves to be angry and to demand satisfaction in the form of punishment? Some have argued that the satisfaction of vengeful or retributive anger is itself a route to preservation of the moral order.

Walter Berns, arguing in favor of capital punishment, suggests that if we are not angry when injustice is done, it means that we care for no one other than ourselves.[16] Berns thus lionizes justified anger as the foundation of a community that cares about its members and about justice. "A moral community," he says, "is not possible without anger and the moral indignation that accompanies it."[17] He sees the capacity for moral indignation as giving meaning to communal life; without it, he argues, there is nothing to separate humans from animals and no reason for us to live. Because he associates anger with the desire for, and even pleasure in the anticipation of, revenge, he suggests that if we are not willing to act on that desire we are morally bankrupt.

Imagine, for example, that Badman kidnaps Heiress and holds her, terrorized, for days or weeks, until her parents come up with the ransom. Suppose further that neither her parents nor any other member of the community reacts with anger toward Badman. Badman is pursued and caught, perhaps, but no one demands that he be punished. Surely, Berns would suggest, something is seriously wrong here. If Heiress and her parents had any self-respect, they would be deeply angry at Badman's treatment of them and demand punishment. Moreover, if other members of the community had any respect for them, they too would be angry and join in that demand.

I shall argue that this view is only partly correct, in that anger is a justified response to wrongdoing, and a failure to react with anger may sometimes reflect a failure to respect oneself or others. But, I shall argue, we can be angry without demanding harm to the offender; thus, that demand requires a separate justification. Although anger is often justified, it is never a morally required response to wrongdoing and is seldom the morally best response. Anger is the morally best response to wrongdoing only where it provides needed courage to take action that is morally preferable on other grounds.[18]

It may seem odd to speak of emotions as requiring justification or otherwise having moral status. Many view emotions as events that simply happen to us, and over which we have no control. But beliefs, and particularly evaluative judgments, play a key role in emotion. Consider, for example, the grief that one feels on learning that a close friend has died. This feeling, as it occurs, is certainly beyond our control. But then suppose we find out that the report of our friend's death was mistaken. Grief evaporates as soon as the information can be processed—because the emotion is founded on our belief in the fact of her death. To the extent that we can be held responsible for our beliefs, we can also be held responsible for the emotions that follow from them.

There is another component here, which some have characterized as the belief that the person reported dead was important to us. A person who expressed deep grief, but denied that the dead person had any importance to him, would seem to be contradicting himself.[19] This, I would argue, is not a belief, so much as an attachment to that person. We might believe, on the cognitive level, that the person in question has no importance to us at all—perhaps because we severed ties with her long ago under unfortunate circumstances. The upwelling of grief shows, however, that the attachment survives. It will do no good to try to persuade us that the person is not worthy of our regard, that we have not thought of her in years, and so forth; the attachment persists on the emotional level, largely inaccessible to cognitive input. We can, to a limited extent, be held responsible for our attachments as well as our beliefs, insofar as their formation is in our control. Thus, a parent who has managed to escape emotional attachment to her child is subject to criticism, as is a person who is not moved by the plight of a stranger in need of rescue.

Anger is similarly structured, in that it is founded on the judgment that we, or some other person to whom we are attached, have been the victim of undeserved harm. We are responsible for either making or not making this judgment; it reflects on our underlying attitudes about what constitutes harm and what is deserved. When people react unsympathetically to a victim of date rape, for example, they may be at fault for failing to make the appropriate judgments that she has suffered harm, and that the harm is undeserved. Or, equally, they may be subject to criticism for failing to show the appropriate degree of attachment to the victim, assuming that they have made the appropriate judgment. In our example, if Heiress's family and community agree that she has suffered an undeserved harm, but are unmoved by that harm because they have no attachment to her welfare, they are subject to criticism on that ground.

We may also become angry, not because we are attached to the person harmed, but because we are attached (on the noncognitive level) to the value flouted by the wrongdoer. One person may be consistently angered by unfairness, another by racism or sexism, a third by antipatriotism, and so on; this anger may be deep even if the value-flouting behavior is purely symbolic. Again, we have some responsibility for the values to which we become attached. We have some choice over the activities we engage in to foster specific values, although we may also develop such attachments through situations we are thrust into, rather than through chosen activities. These attachments are part of our moral character, and we are subject to criticism for them insofar as they are under our control. Failing to react with anger when some important value is flouted is a moral failure where its root is a lack of attachment to that value. Thus, even if we thought that community members could not be criticized for their lack of attachment to Heiress's welfare, we might criticize them for their lack of attachment to the value of liberty.

It is possible, however, that the members of the community are appropriately attached to the value of liberty, and to the welfare of Heiress, and that they correctly judge that she has been undeservedly harmed, and yet that they react to the kidnapping with sorrow rather than anger.[20] The difference between sorrow and anger is that sorrow accepts the harm, while anger rejects it. We may ask, then, whether sorrow's acceptance reflects moral failure.

Anger requires some idea that things might be (or might have been) otherwise; that one expected, or had a right to expect, that they would be otherwise. One may be angry at expected harms, but is more likely to be angry at unexpected ones. The person who loses her family in a wartime bombing is less likely to react with anger if the bombing has been widespread and long maintained. This, I think, is not a moral failing; rather, it is because anticipation often facilitates acceptance. Anger's refusal to accept harm is closely associated with a (conscious or unconscious) internal agitation, a demand for action in response to the harm. This demand may take the form of an impulse to harm the offender with blows, words, or a pointed withdrawal of interaction; to go on a rampage of destruction, indiscriminately smashing objects, or to embark on a course of action to effect change. Sorrow is passive, anger active. The internal demand for action is an often powerful motivating force that can lead the angered person to act in disregard of obstacles and constraints that would otherwise impede action. If action is called for, then anger may be a morally better response. I consider this point below.

Fear, with an associated impulse to avoid future harm rather than to fight back, is another possible reaction to a judgment of undeserved harm. Faced with a physically powerful assailant making outrageous demands, you are more likely to be afraid than angry; once removed from his immediate presence, and seeing yourself as again protected by the social group, you are more likely to be angry at his behavior. (This will also be true if the person threatened is a loved one, rather than oneself.) Fear requires an additional judgment that future harm is likely, but it is not this alone that separates it from anger. Given such a judgment, one might still be angry, both that the past harm has been done and that the future harm is threatened.

The central difference between fear and anger is that fear includes a re-action of avoidance, which in turn is based on the judgment that one lacks power to avert the threatened harm in a more active way. With re-spect to past harms, fear is not possible. One may move between anger, sadness, and fear with respect to the same undeserved maltreatment. Fear of being harmed in the future may be combined with sadness over past harms, and may harden into anger over time. Or the anger of a slum dweller over repeated thefts or physical attacks may give way to sadness and resignation as the possibility of changing the situation recedes into the realm of the improbable, and the attacks come to be expected. The central judgment of undeserved maltreatment is unchanged; it is the sub-sidiary judgments about the possibility of controlling the behavior that have changed.

The impulse of anger is not merely an especially fervent desire that the harm not have occurred; it incorporates as well a desire to control (in turn requiring that I can conceive of controlling) the course of events. Hurri-canes and blizzards, for example, are unlikely to anger me, because it is difficult to imagine controlling the weather. Oftentimes my desire to ex-ercise control is unrealistic, as when I am angered by the rude or careless behavior of another driver who passes me at a high rate of speed; but it is this desire that will make me angry rather than upset at his behavior. Similarly, members of oppressed social groups become angry with the in-dignities forced on them only when they see some prospect of change. Anger, then, requires a perception of power or potential power, including the possibility of obtaining a measure of control by making changes in ex-isting power relationships.

Anger may be said to be justified whenever I correctly judge that some person has been undeservedly harmed, or that some value of mine has been unjustifiably flouted. The anger itself is distinguished from the cor-responding judgment only by (a) my attachment to the person or value in question; and (b) the strong internal refusal to accept this harm. Assum-ing that my attachment to the person or value is unobjectionable (as will usually be the case), I am obviously justified in (internally) refusing to ac-cept any undeserved harm, and thus the anger based on this judgment is also justified.

One might also be mistaken in the judgment that one can, or might be able to, exercise control over the situation. But this judgment, while necessary for anger (rather than fear or sadness) to occur, does not seem to affect the question of whether anger is *justified*. Consider, for example, the anger of a slave by heredity in a deeply entrenched system of slavery that is widely accepted by both slaves and masters. Her anger may be impotent or unwise; but, because she receives treatment no human being deserves, her anger—her internal rejection of that undeserved harm—is justified.

Anger, then, may be said to be justified whenever I correctly judge that some person has been undeservedly harmed, or that some value of mine has been unjustifiably flouted. Because crimes typically involve undeserved harms and the flouting of important values, the anger of crime victims and of other citizens directed at criminal offenders will usually be justified.

It is natural to argue, however, that because anger impels action, while sorrow does not (and fear causes only avoiding behavior) anger is a morally superior response. The angry neighbor or community will not merely offer sympathy, but will take action to rectify the wrong. Berns takes the position that anger inevitably demands harm to the wrongdoer, and that acting on this demand is required where anger is justified. I shall argue that, while anger inevitably demands action, it does not inevitably demand harm to wrongdoers, and that the justifiability of taking action is separable from the justifiability of the anger itself.

The angry person demands action (either internally or externally). Does it follow from the fact that his anger is justified that his demand for action is also justified? Because justified anger implies a correct judgment that unjustified harm has occurred, it clearly follows that his demand that the harm be rectified (in the sense of "undone") is also justified. At the same time, it is evident that his demand for action may also take inappropriate forms. Angry people often make a bad situation worse through ill-considered or destructive actions; that their anger is itself justified does not invariably mean that their angry actions—or demands for others to act—are also justified.

Does anger necessarily include a demand that the offender be harmed? Most assume that anger requires an object in the form of a person whom we regard as responsible for the harm done.[21] In cases where we become angry without such an object, it is tempting to conclude that we are absurdly ascribing responsibility to impersonal or inanimate objects.

But consider the anger that is a recognized stage in the process of reacting to terminal illness. Though under such circumstances one is disposed to look for someone or something to blame, the depth of anger will be fed as much by the perceived unfairness of one's fate as by the perception that others could have acted to prevent it. This anger seeks an object, but it does not require an ascription of responsibility in order to exist. It seems to make perfect sense to say, "Even though I recognize that no one is at fault, I am angry *that* I am dying young; that I will never see my children grow up; that all the efforts I took to preserve my health were in vain."[22] Similarly, without ascribing blame, one may be angry that one has become pregnant despite taking precautions, that one was born severely handicapped, and so forth.

Even where wrongdoers can be identified, the demand for action may be focused more on other forms of redress. Consider the anger of those who fought against segregation. While in many instances they could identify the perpetrators, their demand was not for harm to those perpetrators, but rather for redress of their grievances—for change in the rules and practices that constituted segregation.

Undeniably, there is some relationship between anger and the desire to harm, at least for some people in some circumstances. I may harm someone *in anger*; anger can make it possible for me to harm people whom I otherwise would never harm. Anger's motivating force can cause me to disregard what otherwise would be obstacles to action, making it more likely that I will speak sharply, act coldly, strike out, and so forth. Anger as such, however, is separable from the desire to engage in these harming behaviors. Anger demands action, but not necessarily in the form of harm to others. At the very least, it is possible for me to be angry with X without desiring to harm him. Anger requires, not a demand for redress as such, but rather an internal refusal to accept harm, a demand for action.

Anger may thus be defined as a judgment that undeserved harm has been incurred, accompanied by an attachment to the person or value harmed, and an internal refusal to accept that harm, including a demand for action.

The specific form of anger that demands harm to its object is vindictive anger. Other attitudes toward the objects of anger are not only possible but common. One may contemplate present or prospective harm to others, including enemies and wrongdoers, with compassion, pity, or indifference. Anger does not preclude such benign or neutral attitudes toward harm to the offender, as the demand for action may be directed toward forms of redress that do not harm the offender, or that do so only incidentally. Angry strikers may demand higher wages or safety measures; angry tenants may demand repairs; angry governments may demand return of territory. Nor is this a function of the seriousness of the wrongdoing. While restitution and apology will not ease grief over the death of a loved one, they may assuage anger (and indeed may do so much more effectively than punishment of the offender).[23] The bereaved person who recognizes this may direct her anger toward obtaining such relief, rather than toward seeking harm to the offender.

Further, it is clear that justified anger may be accompanied by demands for (or the taking of) unjustified action. For anger in its vindictive form, as distinguished from simple anger, to be justified, there must be a separate justification for the action to which it impels the angry person. Justified anger rests on a correct perception of undeserved harm, and a demand that such harm be rectified is therefore justified. But a separate (retributive) argument will be needed to establish the relationship between harming the wrongdoer and rectifying the harm. The victim's preference for harm to the wrongdoer cannot fill this gap.

If the demand for harm to the wrongdoer does not spring from vengeful impulses but instead from the sober judgment that retribution is the appropriate response, it is a retributive rather than a vindictive anger.[24] As vindictive anger springs from the belief that one will enjoy seeing one's enemies suffer, so retributive anger springs from the belief that it is right that wrongdoers suffer. Given this belief, a perception of undeserved harm, and an attachment either to the person harmed or the value flouted, will automatically result in an angry demand for action in the form of (an appropriate degree of) harm to the wrongdoer. The justification of retributive anger, as distinguished from anger *simpliciter*, is, however, the same as that for vindictive anger: it is justified if and only if it is right that wrongdoers suffer. If this central tenet of retributivism is true, then retributive anger is justified in any instance where unjustified harm is inflicted by a culpable party; if it is false, then anger in its retributive (or vindictive) form is never justified. Both vindictive and retributive anger require separate justification for the harm that they seek. It is plain that the existence of justified anger, whether of victims or citizens, adds nothing to the retributive justification for harming wrongdoers, although it will, as Murphy points out,[25] serve as a motivation for seeking retribution that might otherwise be lacking.

Berns's argument for the importance to the moral community of acting to harm wrongdoers therefore depends on an independent showing that this is the best response to wrongdoing. Anger is one way, although not the only way, in which a community can demonstrate its concern about undeserved harm and the attachment of its members to one another. That anger, however, need not be directed toward harming wrongdoers in order to serve these functions, and is not justifiably so directed unless such harm can be justified on other grounds.

Anger is often conceived of as externally caused, so that the entire responsibility for my anger rests on those who have provoked me. But as we have seen, the subject contributes to anger in a number of ways. The judgments, attitudes, and attachments of the subject are necessary for anger; the object of anger contributes (at most) the ground for the judgment of unjustified harm; even this may be lacking in cases of baseless anger. Anger is, to a greater degree than is normally recognized, within the control of the subject; to a large extent, we can decide whether and when to react with anger.

It may seem empty to characterize anger as justified if we also say that acting to harm its object is not permissible. But to preclude harm to the wrongdoer is not to preclude action of any kind. To say that the anger is justified is to say that the harm in question should not have occurred, and to agree with that underlying judgment and the visceral refusal of the harm. Acting to seek constructive change or redress of our injuries would therefore be fully justified. Anger that seeks harm to the wrongdoer, much like the anger that seeks to vent itself in the destruction of property, can and should be redirected to constructive action.

Where constructive action is not possible—as for injuries that cannot be redressed—anger can be recognized in other ways. Here we can draw upon our typical response to anger that has no person as object, such as the anger of an earthquake victim who loses the use of his legs. Clearly, it is possible to provide meaningful recognition of such anger and the underlying judgment that the harm is undeserved. We can provide emotional support and practical help. We can seek to prevent similar losses by others. We can provide symbolic recognition and acknowledgment that the anger is justified. In short, we can recognize, understand, and attempt to alleviate anger.

In Western society, punishment of the offender serves as our mode of recognizing justified anger arising from wrongdoing. Against this background, failure to punish is inevitably seen as a failure to recognize the justified anger of the victim. But it is important for us to recognize that, insofar as punishment simply serves to provide such recognition, it could profitably be replaced with other symbols, including purely symbolic condemnation of offenders. This is not to suggest that such replacement would be easy. The tradition of punishment is ingrained in our culture; the culturally derived sense that it is the appropriate response to wrongdoing is likely to be resistant to change. But feelings equally deep, and equally rooted in history, have eventually yielded to social change, from broad social changes such as the replacement of aristocracy with democracy to narrower ones such as the trend toward acceptance of gay marriage.

Anger has, in other times and places, commonly been directed toward ends other than harm to the wrongdoer. As we saw in chapter 1, restitution, rather than harm to the wrongdoer, was a common response to wrongdoing in many ancient and medieval societies. In the South Pacific atoll of the Ifaluk, justified anger is acknowledged through a stylized speech that a designated person will give to the angry person, recognizing the angry person's desire to fight, but appealing to his compassion, his desire for the respect of the community, and the bad consequences of violence to urge him to exercise self-control.[26] A decision to exercise self-control is the expected, and almost universally attained, outcome.

U.S. culture tends to glorify anger and to regard it as an inevitable feature of social interaction. The claim to be angry is often made with some pride; the person who strikes, or even kills, another out of uncontrollable anger is one kind of folk hero. The stifling of anger is seen as unhealthy and dangerous, and the failure to become angry in an appropriate situation is easily interpreted as weakness. Reginald Denny, a man who was severely beaten during the Los Angeles riots following the Rodney King verdict, faced widespread ridicule for his open goodwill toward the two men accused of beating him. Anger fits in well with our rather egalitarian, yet competitive and atomistic view of social life: one has the right to be angry with almost anyone, and there is no particular reason to think they have considered your interests, or that you should consider theirs. This culture of anger plays itself out in an ongoing tragedy in which violence becomes the most self-affirming response to injury or insult; violence is then met with responsive anger and violent punishment. We can, and should, choose otherwise.

Do we have the ability to control our angry responses? Anger, contrary to what our culture tends to convey, is not the inevitable concomitant of self-respect, nor is violence its necessary outcome. A lack of self-respect is one reason why a person would not become angry, seeing any harm inflicted as deserved, or regarding herself as entirely powerless. But anger will also be averted by the mature recognition that there are things one cannot change, undeserved harms that will have to be accepted. Such a perception converts anger to grief, sorrow, or resignation. Anger is appropriate when there are steps that can be taken to rectify the harm, and may be necessary when taking those steps requires a degree of courage or disregard of obstacles. Anger toward criminal offenders is thus an emotion to be encouraged only insofar as it motivates us to do what is (on other grounds) morally best. If punishment is not the optimal response to crime either in terms of social welfare or in terms of moral appropriateness, there is every reason to seek to mute (or at least to redirect) our angry responses on both an individual and on a social level.

As we have seen, the subject has more control over his own anger than is usually supposed. As anger is not the only possible response to undeserved harm, we must ask when it is a desirable response, and how one goes about changing it. Consider how one responds to a spouse who has failed to perform an agreed-on task, resulting in inconvenience to the other. One can dwell on his inconsiderateness, magnify one's own contributions to the household, dredge up past examples of conflict, and become quite angry over a minor matter. Or one can do the opposite: minimize the importance of the transgression, criticize oneself, and decide to forgive him. To the extent that the sources of anger are evident, the degree of anger we choose to feel is often within our control. In the domestic context, it is quite likely that we will consciously decide what degree of anger, if any, will be useful in resolving the conflict, and what degree will be destructive.

Within our immediate circle, it is obvious that mutual communication of expectations and abilities and the establishment of fair arrangements will reduce the overall incidence of anger, and that this is a result toward which we should strive. We could instead take pride in our capacity for anger, claim the right to it in response to every undeserved harm, and demand the satisfaction of our anger through harm to those who had wronged us. It is plain, however, that a move in that direction would be destructive, and that we should seek to control and dissipate our anger except where anger is necessary to achieve important goals that are otherwise unobtainable—as when it supplies needed courage to demand a more equitable distribution of duties where gentler persuasion has failed. Rather than encouraging pride in anger regardless of consequences, the larger society would also do well to seek similar limitations.

4

Retribution and Social Choice

> If you suffer your people to be ill-educated, and their manners to be
> corrupted from their infancy, and then punish them for those
> crimes to which their first education disposed them, what else is to
> be concluded from this, but that you first make thieves and then
> punish them? —Thomas More, *Utopia*, 1516

I. Introduction

In contrast to utilitarians, Kant holds that each individual must be respected as an end in himself; no person is to be used as a mere instrument
for the furthering of another's purposes, but instead must be treated in
ways that respect his own choices.[1] We must respect the choices of others, according to Kant, because, from a rational point of view, all persons
have equal moral worth; thus (other things being equal), it is irrational to
subordinate any other person's desires to our own.

The paradigm cases of using persons as mere means to one's own ends
are deception and coercion. Such actions deprive the victim of (meaningful) choice, reducing her to the status of a tool of the other. Coercion simply overrides the victim's choices in favor of those of the coercer, as when
I enforce, at gunpoint, my choice that you fund my luxuries. Deception
deprives the victim of the information needed to make a meaningful
choice, as when you choose to give me money on the basis of my false
claim that I am collecting for a worthy cause. In either case, I disregard
your choices in favor of my own, treating you as a mere means to my ends
rather than as an equal. In this obvious sense, punishment, because it is
patently coercive, treats offenders as mere means to society's ends. Kantians (beginning with Kant himself) have sought to show that coercion is

in this instance permissible because it is founded on the prior consent of the offender.

Kantians argue as follows for the proposition that the offender, in committing a crime, consents to be punished.[2] Ideally, everyone would explicitly consent to given rules. Given a decision to break those rules later, consent to punishment would be complete. Punishment would not use the offender as a mere means to social ends: instead, the criminal law and its punishments could be viewed as serving the ends of the offender himself. Of course, it seldom, if ever, is actually true that an individual to be punished has explicitly consented to the law, but we can reasonably dispense with this requirement where there is a set of fair rules that are for the advantage of all. Typical criminal laws against killing, theft, and so on, obviously meet this requirement. Those who break the law take unfair advantage of their fellow members of society because they seek to obtain the benefits of social organization and of the self-restraint of others without accepting the accompanying burden of their own self-restraint. It is fair to punish lawbreakers in order to eliminate the unfair advantage thus gained and thus to restore the fair balance of benefits and burdens.[3]

Rather than claiming that the good done by punishment outweighs the harm, these theories seek to avoid the charge of treating offenders as mere means to the ends of others by resting the justification of punishment on the presumption that all must consent to a system of rules and penalties. I shall argue that the most plausible versions of retributive theory ultimately rely on an appeal to the social control function of punishment, as do utilitarian theories. But I shall argue that the consent of those most likely to be punished cannot be presumed on this basis, in part because punishment subjects them to increased risks of the same harms it is supposed to prevent, and in part because punishment is not the only available method of social control.

Kant says:

> No one suffers punishment because he has willed *it*, but because he has willed a *punishable action*; for it is no punishment if what is done to someone is what he wills, and it is impossible to will to be punished. Saying that I will to be punished if I murder someone is saying nothing more than that I subject myself together with everyone else to the laws, which will naturally [include] penal laws if there are any criminals among the people.[4]

The final phrase of the quoted passage reveals the rather quaint assumptions that the commission of crimes is confined to a specific type of person ("criminals") and that it is possible that some societies will have none of these people and thus be crime-free. Later versions of retributivism have dropped these assumptions in favor of the more modern idea that any of us may commit crimes. But the apparently generous assumption that we are all potential criminals obscures an important truth: that some individuals—not because they are a separate breed of "criminals," but because of their social circumstances—are much more likely to commit crimes than others.

Arguments appealing to rationality as a surrogate for consent, in the face of the evident unwillingness of the supposed consenter, always run the risk of imposing the values of the elite and the powerful on the rest. This concern is most acute where (as in punishment) the brunt of the "rational" policy is to be borne by the less privileged—again, even if their situation is not the result of injustice. Jeffrie Murphy has argued that, given the often abysmal level of social services and legitimate opportunities available to the disadvantaged, among whom most offenders are found, it seems absurd to claim that the typical offender has taken more than his share of social benefits and must accept additional burdens.[5] Moreover, he argues, contemporary Western society actively fosters motives of greed and selfishness that can lead those deprived of legitimate opportunity to commit economic crimes. He observes that "there is something perverse in applying principles that presuppose a sense of community in a society which is structured to destroy genuine community."[6] Building on this critique, I shall argue that, even where the rules are facially fair and evenly applied, where social arrangements are not unjust, and where individuals do not break the rules unless they choose to do so, the goods claimed for retributive punishment are not sufficiently compelling to justify the imputation of consent to all, and particularly not to those most likely to incur punishment.

Retributivist theory depends on a view of crime as the sole responsibility of a morally flawed criminal offender who freely chooses the wrong course of action over the right. The primary cause of crime, for the retributivist, is the bad moral decisions of offenders. But variations in the crime rate across time and place are linked to social factors not plausibly connected to natural variations in moral wickedness. As discussed in chapter 2, crime rates vary across societies and over time within the same society. The rate of homicide in the United States today is three times that of Canada and eleven times that of Japan, while the U.S. rate doubled in the 1970's and 1980's before declining to its former level in 2000.[7] The rate of "contact crimes" (rape and robbery, for example) in 1999 was 4.1 percent in Australia, 1.9 percent in the U.S., and only 0.4 percent in Japan.[8] Overall 1999 victimization rates ranged from 30 percent in Australia to 15 percent in Japan and Northern Ireland. Most importantly for present purposes, crime rates also vary most remarkably from one community to another within the same society: homicide rates in U.S. urban areas are five or six times those in rural areas, and rates in California are three times those in Maryland.[9] In all countries, the crime rates in urban areas are about 60 percent higher than those in rural areas. It simply is not plausible that all of these variations are attributable to random differences in the numbers of bad choices made by individuals.

As discussed in chapter 2, higher crime rates are associated with income inequality, cultural emphasis on material wealth to the detriment of other values, and a lack of structural support for institutions such as the family, education, and the polity. On the local level, strain theory suggests that, when life difficulties become overwhelming, people turn to crime to find solutions to their problems.[10] Structural factors such as the degree of urbanization, industrialization, and residential mobility affect crime rates, possibly because they lead to changes in patterns of learning and the availability of role models to imitate.[11] Crime rates are also affected by the level of supervision, the opportunities for crime,[12] and the attachment of individuals to social values. The attachment of individuals to social values is, in turn, affected by the level of social organization.[13]

Although most specific crimes may appropriately be said to reflect bad moral choices, the overall rate of crime depends on larger social conditions, and some individuals, at some places and times, are at far greater risk of making bad choices than others. This point does not depend upon the claim that the conditions in which those individuals find themselves are, in and of themselves, unjust. It depends only upon empirical connections between certain kinds of social conditions and crime. To the extent that these connections are known, the choice of a society to punish those who break its criminal laws must be evaluated in the context of its choice to foster other conditions conducive to crime. As More suggests, to "make thieves, and then punish them" is not a defensible course of action. Thus, the retributivist claim that we can assume the consent of all to the law and its punishments is valid only if we can assume consent to a larger package of social choices: those that determine the probability of becoming eligible for punishment, as well as those that allow for its imposition.

Most criminal offenders choose to commit crime *knowing* that there is a penalty, and even having a fair idea of what that penalty will be. By itself, however, this is not enough to justify imposing that penalty. The bank robber who announces that she will kill anyone who provides information to the police is not therefore justified in doing so—even though we might say that the informant chose to risk being killed. Now suppose that the informant is among the confederates of the robber, and that they have entered into a pact of silence, with death as the penalty. The robber, plainly, is still not justified in killing the informant, despite his explicit consent to the rule and later decision to break it. Nor is this simply because the agreement itself is in furtherance of criminal purposes: the same would apply if, for example, a woman gave her best friend permission to kill her if she ever got involved with a man again. In a more mundane example, the permission of a patient does not, by itself, justify the surgeon in amputating his limbs. And we do not ordinarily think that the state can legitimately command individuals to give up their liberty or risk their lives for no reason, even if we think that they have consented to a social contract. The explicit consent of the offender to be punished, then, even if it could be established, would not be an independently sufficient ground for punishment. The retributivist must also show that punishment serves some good purpose: we must have both consent and a reason to punish. Where we lack explicit consent, and seek instead to punish on the basis that we can assume everyone's consent, the good done by punishment must be significantly more compelling—just as the good done by medical treatment of an unconscious person must, to warrant the assumption of consent, be significantly more compelling than the good done by treatment of a person who has given explicit consent.

Although retributivists typically insist that their view is not teleological, they nevertheless have argued that retributive punishment serves important purposes. The purely retributivist strand of this argument suggests that punishment is good without reference to further consequences—because it is good that the guilty suffer, whether simply to give them what they deserve, to convey condemnation of their behavior, to remove the unfair advantage taken by the offender, to annul the wrong, or to vindicate the victim. An associated, less purely retributive strand takes note of the assurance of (almost) universal compliance provided by punishment: those disposed to comply with the rules are assured that they are not providing a benefit to others without receiving reciprocity. We saw in chapter 3 that it is difficult to make sense of the claim that punishment annuls crime or vindicates victims. In this chapter, I shall first argue that giving offenders what they deserve doesn't provide an adequate basis for imputing consent to all; neither does the removal of unfair advantage, when taken as an end in itself. The most plausible basis on which imputed consent to retributive punishment can rest, I argue, is the role that it plays in social control, that is, the assurance it provides to those who willingly comply with the law that others will do so as well. I shall then fill out the argument, suggested above, that consent to punishment cannot be imputed to all on such a basis.

II. Pure Retributivism

It seems on the face of it obvious that everyone—including those most likely to commit crimes—must agree to rules such as "no killing" and "no stealing" as necessary for minimal social harmony. One cannot reasonably argue that such behavior is tolerable. But making a rule does not by itself do anything about the incidence of violations, and the pure retributivist is not particularly concerned to reduce it—he is concerned only that wrongdoers should be punished. A rule that there is to be no killing seldom, if ever, translates into there actually being no killing. For the retributivist, the rule is best characterized, not as "no killing," but rather as "a person who kills another will herself be killed," or, conceivably, twice as many killings.[14] Any set of persons who would not agree to permit crime would, at least initially, have the same set of reasons for not agreeing to permit retributive punishment.[15] The reasonableness of the rules in question, then, is not by itself sufficient to ground consent to punishment.

Rule retributivists argue that the concept of a law or rule cannot be understood without the concept of punishment for violating the rule. To decide to have a law is to decide that violations will be punishable; correspondingly, to question the punishment of violations is to question the law itself.[16] The good done by punishment is thus coterminous with the good done by having the rule. There are two problems with the rule-retributivist view as a justification for punishment. First, the consequence attached to the rule does not have to be a retributive penalty, in the sense that its primary aim is the suffering of the offender. The rule can instead be enforced only by preventive means, or there may be a formal or compensatory penalty. The university may be said to have a rule that faculty must wear academic regalia to commencement ceremonies if those not so attired are barred from attending, even if this secretly delights those barred. In the legal arena, if I agree to your price for painting my house but fail to pay the bill when the job is done, the courts will enforce the law by compelling me to pay. The law does not aim at my suffering— indeed, it is inappropriate to say that I have been punished—but rather at the compensation of the other party to the bargain. To have a rule is to establish some consequence for breaking it, but that consequence need not be punishment. Second, if the rule does have a criminal penalty, it may be true that the rule itself is reasonable, while the rule with the particular penalty attached is not: "No littering" is a reasonable rule, but "No littering on pain of death" is not. In short, the retributivist must provide a justification for the criminal penalty, as well as for the rule itself, and that justification must go beyond a showing that it would be better if no one engaged in the prohibited conduct. Simply showing that the rules are for the advantage of all, then, is not a sufficient basis for imputing consent to punishment.

For Kant, the relevant good achieved by punishment is the suffering of the guilty. Given that we generally regard it as undesirable for people to suffer, why might we think that the suffering of the guilty is good? Kant's own response to this question is twofold. First, society is obligated to punish the offender in order to avoid being complicit in the crime. Second, the offender must be punished because he deserves to suffer. In a famous passage, Kant declaims:

> Even if a civil society were to be dissolved by the consent of all its members (e.g., if a people inhabiting an island decided to separate and disperse throughout the world, the last murderer remaining in prison would first have to be executed, so that each has done to him what his deeds deserve and blood guilt does not cling to the people for not having insisted upon this punishment; for otherwise the people can be regarded as collaborators in this public violation of justice.[17]

The backward-looking nature of retribution is nowhere more plain. Unless we are to take seriously the archaic idea of "blood guilt" that can be washed away only with blood, however, we must ask in what sense executing that last murderer will exonerate the community from complicity, rather than staining their hands with fresh blood. They have, presumably, not aided in the commission of the crime before the fact. Perhaps if they fail to act, they may be said to be condoning the murder, or failing to hold the murderer accountable for his deed. But execution—or other punishment—is not the only possible way in which they can act. As a way of disassociating oneself from the crime, execution is dramatic, but extreme. Why will a verbal or symbolic condemnation not serve as well? Why must they punish the offender, rather than, for example, seizing his property and giving it to the victim's family as restitution? The community's need to disavow this act does not, without more, show that they need to do harm, much less serious harm, to the offender. Recently, moral reform theories have specifically addressed why hard treatment might be necessary to the expression of condemnation. Those arguments will be considered in detail in chapter 6; for now, I turn to Kant's second reason for regarding the suffering of the guilty as good—that it gives each what his deeds deserve.

Some retributivists will say that the good of giving people what they deserve is self-evident and incapable of further analysis. But if a system that gives people the harms they deserve is self-evidently good, it would seem to follow that giving people the good they deserve, and indeed, meritocracy in general, is also self-evidently good.[18] In fact, as commitment to a principle of giving people the good things they deserve does not involve accepting any risk of hard treatment, the case for imputing consent to meritocracy appears stronger than the corresponding case for punishment. Yet it is plainly untrue that meritocratic distribution is a good so compelling that we can assume consent. The virtues of meritocracy in comparison to other principles of distribution may reasonably be disputed. Reasonable people may similarly disagree about whether punishment should be meted out on the basis of desert, particularly if they do not think any other good will come of it—and if they do think other goods will come of it, they may prefer to maximize those goods rather than adhere strictly to desert. It would, indeed, be less offensive to reduce a person's share of the social surplus, claiming to have his consent to meritocracy, than to imprison him, claiming to have his consent to a system of punishment.

Desert is a complex matter. Even if we were to decide in favor of a commitment to desert, we would then be left with the impracticable, if not impossible, task of determining, for each offender, just what he does deserve and how that differs from what he has already got. As W. D. Ross suggests:

What we perceive to be good is a condition of things in which the total pleasure enjoyed by each person in his life as a whole is proportional to his virtue similarly taken as a whole. Now it is by no means clear that we should help to bring about this end by punishment of particular offences in proportion to their moral badness. Any attempt to bring about such a state of affairs should take account of the whole character of the persons involved, as manifested in their life taken as a whole, and of the happiness enjoyed by them throughout their life taken as a whole, and it should similarly take account of the virtue taken as a whole, and of the happiness taken as a whole, of each of the other members of the community, and should seek to bring about the required adjustments.[19]

The view Ross discusses here, besides requiring investigations of truly daunting scope, entails that we should make efforts to give people the good things that they deserve, as well as the bad. It also implies that victims, having suffered wrongs that they do not deserve, should be made whole. If desert is not to have this central place in our thinking about social justice in general, some supplementary reason must be given as to why people must be given the punishments they deserve. The justification for retributive punishment cannot be found solely in the idea that wrongdoers deserve to suffer, in the absence of a general commitment to desert.

As Elizabeth Wolgast points out, there is a difference between the core retributivist belief that wrongdoers deserve to suffer (and that it is good if they do) and the judgment that it is permissible for any person to bring about that suffering.[20] Perhaps it is good, in some cosmic sense, if fate brings down on the head of the wrongdoer the same type or degree of suffering that he caused another; but if we as humans bring down that suffering, we may yet be doing what is morally wrong. Perhaps it will serve the gossip right if she finds her own reputation trifled with; this does not justify us in wagging our own tongues.[21]

There are thus several issues raised for any theory that justifies punishment on the basis that it is deserved: What is the basis of negative desert, and how does punishment provide that desert? Do those who are in fact most likely to be punished have negative desert, in light of their small share of social goods? What reason do we have to impose negative deserts, in the absence of a general commitment to desert? Finally, is the good supposed to be done by imposing punishment according to the specified basis of desert sufficiently compelling that it is fair to say, even of those most likely to be punished, that their consent can be assumed?

A series of efforts have been made to account for the importance of negative desert on the ground of the principle of fairness, or reciprocity. This principle holds that accepting the benefits of a fair scheme of cooperation creates a reciprocal obligation to do your part in maintaining it.[22] Herbert Morris argues that the criminal law benefits you by defining rights—such as rights to life and property—with which others may not interfere.[23] In order for everyone to realize this benefit, all must bear the burden of restraining themselves from interfering with others' rights. The person who does interfere with the protected rights of others renounces a burden that others have assumed and thus gains an unfair advantage. Thus far, the argument is an account of how the individual has failed to live up to his obligations, rather than of why we should therefore impose punishment. Morris suggests that, by punishing, we can remove the unfair advantage. This is an argument from desert: he has something he does not deserve, and we are in a position to remove it. As discussed above, the stance that we must remove undeserved benefits appears gratuitous in the absence of a like commitment to relieve undeserved burdens. But the reciprocity theory has something further to say. By establishing a system of punishment, we can also increase everyone's disposition to comply with the rules, thus assuring those who comply voluntarily that they are not assuming an unfair share of the burdens of cooperation. Thus, the theory aims at two goods: that of giving offenders what they deserve, and that of enhancing social control.

The reciprocity theory, I shall argue, is at its strongest when it relies on the ability of punishment to reduce crime: it is difficult to establish that punishment does indeed function to remove unfair advantage, especially when the social circumstances of the typical offender are considered. Social control is the strongest argument, even for retributivists: but, as I argue in section III, we cannot presume the consent of offenders on the basis of crime reduction effects.

There are two respects in which crime may be said to be "unfair." The offender gets an undeserved benefit which it is not fair for him to get, and the victim suffers an undeserved wrong. Punishment is easily seen as counterbalancing benefits to the offender, but does not in any obvious way reduce the victim's burden. An account of punishment that relies on the importance of rebalancing benefits and burdens must either explain how punishment benefits the victim, or explain why it is more important to reduce the benefits to the offender than to relieve the burdens of the victim. Proponents of this kind of view have generally focused on reducing the benefits of offenders, as indeed seems to be the primary function of retributive punishment. But why is it only the negative side of the equation that gets our attention? Egalitarians are routinely scorned for their insistence that it is better to have equality at a lower level of wealth than to allow inequalities from which not everyone can benefit. But to insist on punishing the guilty simply in order to make sure they have no unfair advantage goes further: it is as if, noticing inequalities of wealth, our principal concern were that the wealthy be brought down to the average, rather than that the poor should be made better off. Thus, the removal of unfair advantage is an unattractive idea from the outset.

The argument that punishment removes an unfair advantage also depends upon an initially fair distribution of the relevant advantages. This point is more than a formal caveat, given that the burden of punishment universally falls more heavily on socially marginalized groups who enjoy only a small share of social benefits. If we consider "unfair advantage" in the context of all social advantages, it will be difficult to show that the typical criminal offender has more than his share.

Jeffrie Murphy argues:

> A man has been convicted of armed robbery. On investigation, we learn that he is an impoverished black whose whole life has been one of frustrating alienation from the prevailing socio-economic structure—no job, no transportation if he could get a job, substandard education for his children, terrible housing and inadequate health care for his whole family, condescending-tardy-inadequate welfare payments, harassment by the police but no real protection by them against the dangers in his community, and near total exclusion from the political process. Learning all this, would we still want to talk—as many do—of his suffering punishment under the rubric of "paying a debt to society"? Surely not. Debt for what?[24]

With respect to better-situated offenders, we would have a better chance of making the case that, as a result of crime, they had more than their fair share of advantages. The embezzler who feathers her nest with the funds of others, the blackmailer who uses his ill-gotten gains to buy a Ferrari, or the stock swindler who adds a fifth million to her net worth by dealing on insider information certainly seem to have taken unfair advantage. To the extent that this is true, however, we can easily redress their unjust enrichment by repossessing their wrongful gains—

and give them back to the victims, thus reducing the victims' unfair burdens as well. We cannot as easily remove the "unfair advantage" taken by a middle-class murderer—but it is also not as easy to say just what his unfair advantage consists of, nor how it can appropriately be removed by punishment. He may have killed in a calculated move designed to reduce his economic burdens, as did one father of a handicapped child to avoid the continuing burden of his medical expenses. He may instead have sought to kill an estranged spouse in order to gain custody of their children (which is of course denied as soon as the offense is detected). Or he may have killed a beloved family member in a fit of rage that he immediately regretted, having gained only a momentary release of emotion—and having been left with a much greater emotional burden. There is thus no correlation between the seriousness of the crime and the unfair advantage it has brought the offender. In each case, it is not so much the offender's gain, as the victim's loss, that seems most unfair, and which, moreover, seems to govern the retributive intuition that the penalty should be matched to the seriousness of the crime. But the losses of victims, insofar as they can be redressed at all, are much more obviously redressed by restitution than by punishment.

Morris himself says that the unfair advantage consists of taking the benefits of a system of fair rules while refusing to assume the burden of self-restraint.[25] But, again, there is no correlation between the degree of self-restraint necessary to refrain from a particular crime and the seriousness of that crime. As Richard Burgh argues, if punishment sought to impose burdens equal to the renounced burden of self-restraint, tax evasion would be punished more severely than murder.[26] If the benefits and burdens argument is to succeed in vindicating retributive punishment, it must characterize the unfair advantage to be removed as varying with the seriousness of the crime.

It is also plain that the burden of self-restraint is typically much greater for some population groups than for others. Resisting the social factors conducive to crime will be quite difficult for some, quite easy for others. From this perspective, the free riders are not those who commit crimes, but rather those who are protected from the need to exercise self-restraint. As a number of critics have noted, it is not true of most of us that we have to exert effort to restrain ourselves from violent crime. Thus, the fair balance of benefits and burdens, understood in terms of a burden of self-restraint, is illusory to begin with.

Richard Dagger has argued that the fairness argument must be combined with some other measure of seriousness to arrive at the just measure of punishment—because the unfairness of crimes does not vary in proportion to their seriousness, it only provides the basis for one part of the punishment.[27] Each offender is to receive two punishments, one for unfairness, and the other corresponding to seriousness. But this means that the major part of the deserved punishment is unaccounted for by the reciprocity argument. If the crimes are equal in unfairness, but vary in seriousness, it follows that the punishment for unfairness, as such, must be a token one: otherwise, the "unfairness" component of punishment would be disproportionate for minor crimes.

George Sher suggests that the unfair advantage to be compensated for through punishment should instead be understood as the amount of extra freedom that the offender gains in violating a moral prohibition of a particular strength: as the prohibition on murder is more stringent than that on tax evasion, the amount of freedom one claims in murdering is greater than that one claims in evading taxes.[28] Punishment proportional to the degree of moral wrong then restores the proper balance by compensating for the amount of extra freedom seized by the offender. In particular, reducing the protection afforded the offender from acts that are ordinarily morally wrong compensates in exactly the right way for his failure to assume his share of the burden of providing such protections to all.

Sher suggests that social policies other than the criminal law, although they may create unfairness, are not relevant except insofar as they mitigate the wrongness of the offender's act, which might itself, in some very limited contexts, be understood as a justified "punishment" of its victims for other injustices he has suffered.[29] Although some (or most) offenders may have suffered other hardships, these do not subtract from the degree of deserved punishment because the satisfactions of which they have been deprived are not commensurable with protection from acts that are morally wrong. That is, to be protected from suffering what is (ordinarily) morally wrong, you must yourself refrain from moral wrongdoing.

But if what is important is simply to maintain a correct balance, and the balance is one between exposure to wrongs and inflicting them on others, it appears that the victim of crime must be permitted some free wrongdoing.[30] Sher responds to this concern as follows:

> Even if X has previously wronged Y, it hardly follows that a fair balance
> of benefits and burdens is restored when Y in turn wrongs Z. If Y does

this, then the original wrongdoer X is still left with the double benefit of moral restraint upon others plus his own freedom from such restraint; and the current victim Z is left with the double burden of moral restraint on his acts plus the absence of constraint on the acts of (some) others. Thus the original unfairness is not removed but displaced.

The end result here is certainly unfair to Z, and X remains doubly benefited. But Y—the offender we propose to punish—seems to be exactly even, having both suffered the unfair burden of injustice done by X and appropriated the unfair benefit of extra freedom from wronging Z. The situation described by Sher is unfair, but the situation after Y is punished is even more so: both he and Z will have more than their share of the burdens.

The best possible situation here is that in which X never wrongs Y, and Y never wrongs Z. Given that X has wronged Y, the best result follows if Y does not wrong Z—that is, the wrong done to Y does not justify his wronging others. Correspondingly, given that Y has wronged Z, the best possible result is that we do not in turn wrong (or at least harm) Y by punishing him. Wrongs done by crime cannot be undone, and doing additional wrongs (or harms corresponding to wrongs) only compounds the problem. Limiting the relevant advantages to those of wrongdoing thus raises as many problems as it solves.

It is difficult, then, to give a satisfactory account of the nature of the unfair advantage said to be gained through wrongdoing and how it can be removed by retributive punishment. Insofar as the notion of desert has intuitive appeal, and assuming that some future account will flesh out the sense in which punishment is deserved, it is also difficult to explain why priority should be given to giving people what they deserve in consequence of wrongdoing, rather than across the board—and, especially, why priority should be given to punishing wrongdoers rather than compensating victims.

That offenders may deserve to be harmed does not seem to provide a compelling reason to establish, or to consent to, a system of punishment. For such a reason, we must look beyond the pure retributive idea of desert, and consider the promise of the institution of punishment to protect us from deliberate harm by others.

III. Retributive Punishment as Promoting Social Control

Matt Matravers has recently proposed a justification of punishment that gives a new twist to reciprocity theory. Rather than begin from the assumption of moral equality, as Kantians do, or from the assumption that coercion is in general unjustified, Matravers begins from a Hobbesian perspective and seeks to provide an account of why self-interested agents—not in a hypothetical contract situation, but situated in society, and examining their existing commitments—have reason to accept moral constraints on their behavior in order to secure the benefits of social cooperation.[31] The commitment to accept moral constraints is simultaneously a commitment to accept sanctions, both to provide "sufficient security" that others will observe the rules, and to provide assurance to those who comply voluntarily that they are not being taken advantage of by others. He suggests that, for the self-interested agent, consent to moral constraints (including the constraints of the criminal law) *is* consent to coerced compliance, in that the agent sees that she will benefit from adopting a cooperative approach, but recognizes both that this will be to her advantage only if everyone else also adopts that approach, and that she may on some occasions be tempted to put narrow self-interest first. Punishment serves the dual purpose of providing a straightforwardly self-interested backup motive for compliance and assuring that others will not do better as free riders. The level of punishment necessary to these ends is a function of the seriousness of the violation and the overall stability of the cooperative scheme: the more serious the conduct, and the less stable the society, the more severe the punishment must be in order to preserve the motive to cooperate.[32]

Matravers's argument completes the rule-retributivist argument by providing a standard for the level of punishment, and provides a motivation for having a system of punishment in its perceived necessity to secure ongoing cooperation. The scope of this justification has some important limitations. It is a "constructivist" justification, in that it begins from no moral premise, but rather seeks to ground moral motivation in self-interest. We can each further our self-interest, Matravers argues, through cooperation with others; and in the effort to secure and retain their cooperation, it is beneficial to each of us to be, and to be seen as, cooperators ourselves.[33] Such arguments, he notes, apply only to those members of a reasonably just society who have reason to accept the cooperative scheme in that they are not systematically exploited or otherwise maltreated by others, and who in practice show their acceptance of that scheme by co-operating most of the time.[34] With respect to this group, it justifies only the imposition of whatever type of sanction is necessary to preserve co-operation. Punishment—understood as the deprivation of life, liberty, or property imposed for an offense—may or may not be necessary, depending on other social conditions. Those who do not see themselves as having reason to cooperate are literally outside the "moral community" of cooperators: self-interested agents have no reason to accept obligations to those with whom they have no expectation of being able to cooperate in the future.[35] Thus, Matravers suggests, such persons are "Locke's 'wild Savage Beasts'" whom we may coerce at will.[36] In this respect, his argument is orthogonal to mine (and to those of Kantian retributivists) in that he begins from the explicit assumption that coercion is in general justified (or not in need of justification), while I begin from the opposite assumption.

But insofar as Matravers seeks to provide a rationale for coercion among self-interested cooperators, his arguments are similar in structure to those of Kantian retributivists. His self-interested cooperators will have reason to accept a system of punishment only if it secures important goods, and he appeals to some of the same goods as retributivists: those of social control, moral censure, and prevention of free riding. For those who begin from the assumption that coercion is not justified, the question is whether they can provide an account of reciprocity that extends to all, importantly including those who do not wish to cooperate. Fundamentally, if we cannot provide an account of punishment that justifies the punishment of such persons, then we must choose between rejection of punishment and rejection of Kantian theory, the latter being Matravers's choice.

It initially seems that the idea of punishment as social control is anti-thetical to retributivism. As noted above, Herbert Morris suggests that both removing the unfair advantage gained by the offender and providing assurance that others will comply are factors in the good done by punishment. Many retributivists, including Kant, take the position that the prevention of crime, while important, is not part of the justification of retributive punishment, which stands justified regardless of further good consequences. Punishment is just insofar as it is deserved; consideration of consequences is entirely secondary. In this light, Morris's reference to punishment as increasing the disposition of others to comply seems out of place.

To the extent that retributivism depends on the importance of restoring an antecedently existing correct moral order, however, the retributivist is committed to the importance of that moral order. If it is important to restore it after the fact, then surely it is also important to preserve it from disturbance—to assure that moral duties are observed, rather than merely that wrongs are redressed. In other words, if it is important to give wrongdoers what they deserve, then it is also important to assure that victims do not suffer wrongs they don't deserve. Punishment, in addition to redressing wrongs, provides a motivation for people to observe their duties. The social control function of punishment can in this way be seen as part of retributive theory, not for pragmatic reasons but for moral reasons. Thus, despite its consequentialist appearance, social control could serve as one of the goods justifying retributive punishment.

Social control also plays a key role in the trust-based retributivism proposed by Susan Dimock. She argues that, if law is understood as a mechanism for creating and maintaining conditions of trust in a community, those who break the law are appropriately punished both to express condemnation and to provide an incentive for compliance.[37] The purpose of law, she suggests, is to establish and maintain conditions consistent with basic trust. Those who violate the prohibitions of the law undermine the foundations of that trust, which the law must then take steps to restore. The measure of punishment is the importance of the rule, because the importance of the rule determines the extent to which the fabric of trust is destroyed, and also because the importance of the rule determines the importance of deterring violations. That this is a version of reciprocity theory is implied by its derivation from "the purpose of law": it is not taken to be applicable in a state of nature or as between enemies. In addition, punishment would itself count as a violation of trust, comparable to that of crime, in the absence of implicit agreement.

Clearly, if we cannot trust others even to respect our physical safety, for example, something is seriously wrong. One way to seek to restore the foundations of trust would be to assure that, when things go wrong in that way, we seek to determine the roots of the problem and to rectify it. It does not seem, initially, that punishing the violator will do much to restore the conditions of trust. If the underlying problem is left unsolved, then we have no reason to expect that others will respect our physical safety in the future. It is also unlikely that offenders who have been incarcerated in the company of other offenders are for that reason more trustworthy. Dimock argues, though, that by punishing violators we can restore "the objective conditions of trust" by affecting the assessment of risk associated with violations. That is, if we threaten to harm offenders, and make clear that we will in fact do so, others can be assured that criminal behavior is risky and therefore less likely. The more severe the threatened punishment, the more confident we can be that the violation is risky and unlikely to be undertaken. It is clear, in her argument, that without this (perceived) effect on risk assessment, there would be little reason to punish.

What the arguments of Matravers, Dimock, and the fair play theorists have in common is an appeal to the deterrent function of punishment, transplanted from its native utilitarian soil. If Kantian arguments are not to fall to the objection of using persons as mere means to social ends, they must show that the deterrent scheme is for the benefit of all, including those most liable to be punished. As the scheme will impose on those punished the very kinds of harm that the scheme seeks to prevent, there is a problem: the more likely you are to be punished, the less likely you are to find the benefits of the scheme worthwhile. If the ex ante probabilities are equal for all—if everyone is equally likely, or able, to choose crime or not—then the fact that it is an advantageous scheme for the group is the only relevant fact. But if there is too much imbalance in the ex ante probabilities of being punished across social groups, those bearing the brunt of the punishment are just being used for the ends of the rest. (In Matravers's terms, those getting the short end of the stick have no reason to cooperate.) Great weight therefore rests on the equal ability of all to choose crime or not. But, as we have seen, some are more likely to make bad choices than others.

Their choices, bad as they are, are made against a background of conditions that, for a variety of reasons, make good choices less likely. Again, the point is not that these conditions are unjust: we can assume, for the sake of argument, that they are not. Rather, the point is that these conditions, themselves the result of choice at the social level, are conducive to the choices of individuals to commit crimes. It is true that this choice is in the hands of the individual, in the sense that if he does not decide to commit the crime he will not do so. But, knowing this, we would be foolhardy to assent to a system of retributive punishment under circumstances where the avoidance of such choices requires, if not superior virtue, then at least better than average self-control. To do so would be to invite, in the form of punishment, the very harms we are seeking to avoid in the form of crime.

We know we can avoid these consequences by making the right choices, but knowing this isn't always enough to induce us to rely on our ability to do so. Suppose that you want to lose weight and are considering whether to pay a substantial sum of money for a "guaranteed weight loss" program. The program staff promises that if you comply fully with the program, you will in fact lose weight; they further emphasize that compliance is a matter of choice on your part. But if, on questioning, you learn that only 20 percent of those who enroll actually manage to comply, you will probably hesitate to sign up—anticipating that it will just be too difficult for you to make the required choices. Because the same is true of the choice to avoid crime, it is not reasonable to impute consent to a system of punishment to everyone. In particular, we cannot presume the consent of the very persons most likely to incur punishment. To do so is as misguided as presuming consent to a dangerous medical treatment of the patients most likely to suffer its ill effects.

Retributivists tend to assume that the rate of crime at any given moment is a result of the choices of individuals who choose to commit crimes. I suggest that the crime rate can equally well be seen as a result of social policy choices. Consider the analogous case of automobile accidents. We may (and typically do) say of one of the parties to the accident that it is his fault for failing to observe traffic rules—perhaps he was driving too fast and failed to stop for a red light. But we don't explain differences in accident rates over time or from place to place by reference to the choices of drivers. Instead, we explain these differences on the basis of the choices of transportation engineers and local policymakers. If there are too many accidents at a particular intersection, we may install speed bumps or signs warning of the upcoming traffic signal if it is not visible from a distance. Rather than simply increase penalties for violations, we look for ways to make it easier for drivers to comply with the rules, knowing that human fallibility in certain areas is relatively predictable. Just as, in deciding on transportation policy, we may reduce or increase the rate of accidents, in making other types of policy choices we may reduce or increase the rate of crime. The difference is only that policy choices (apart from penal policy) affecting the crime rate are less often explicitly designed for that purpose. It is no more true that we must adopt a policy of punishment for purposes of social control than it is true that we must agree to make other policy choices that decrease the crime rate. Reasonable people may disagree about how best to exercise social control, as well as about what rate of crime is acceptable. The key point is that the reasonableness of a system of retributive punishment (and thus the reasonableness of imputing agreement to everyone) cannot be considered in isolation from other social policies that affect the crime rate and, concomitantly, the likelihood that one will decide to commit crimes and thus become subject to punishment. Crime is not simply the result of bad choices made by individuals, and the reasonableness of the social choice to impose punishment in order to reduce crime is impaired where other social choices have predictably resulted in its increase.

Morris suggests that if all our actions are viewed as simply a product of external forces, nothing we do is worthy of respect or admiration. The recognition that your actions result from choices is important (even if those actions are bad): "[W]hen what we do is met with resentment, we are indirectly paid something of a compliment."[38] The compliment that Morris has in mind is the underlying judgment necessary for resentment that we are the authors of our actions and could behave otherwise if we so chose. In fact, however, our actions are in part the product of personal choice and in part the product of social context. This, indeed, must be true if it is to be true that punishment provides an incentive to avoid wrongdoing, as punishment—like other incentives—is also part of the social context. While it is generally true that we will not do wrong unless we so choose, it is also true that the chances of our making that wrong choice are influenced by factors outside our individual control. Although it is disrespectful to assume that a person cannot control his behavior, it is equally disrespectful to assign him sole responsibility for doing so while cultivating the conditions that will make it more difficult for him to avoid wrongdoing. An extreme form of this kind of disrespect is the entrapment of suspects by law enforcement officials into crimes that they would not otherwise have committed. Society's respect for individuals is best demonstrated by an appropriate sharing of responsibility between those who commit crimes and those who set social policy. The burden of preventing crime should not be entirely placed on the shoulders of potential offenders.

I want to emphasize that this argument does not in any way suggest that the individual who, finding himself in a situation conducive to crime, chooses to commit that crime has any excuse based on the external circumstances that brought him to it. It remains true that he ought not to have committed the crime, that he could have refrained, and that he is wrong in choosing to commit it—just as it is true of everyone that even strong temptation to do wrong must be resisted. Instead, the focus of my argument is on the question of how we may respond to wrong-doing.

It is important, of course, to prevent wrongdoing. But this does not, ipso facto, show that it is necessary to punish. There would be more wrongdoing without punishment, but there would also be more wrong-doing without welfare, public education, or progressive taxation—all of which are policies on which reasonable people can disagree. In part, there is a trade-off between punishment and other methods of social control. To the extent that this is so, nonpenalty methods are preferable as long as they do not have other significant drawbacks. For example, relatively costly social measures to combat the effects of income inequality, family instability, unemployment, and local social disorganization to reduce mo-tivation and opportunity for crime are preferable to high penalty levels, where comparable crime reduction effects can be achieved. There is fur-ther reason to choose such policies insofar as they shift the burden of pre-venting crime from the disadvantaged (who incur the most punishments) to those who are financially well-off (who pay the most taxes).

It may seem that there are compelling reasons to choose that policy which most reduces the crime rate. But on examination, this is clearly not so. The policies that would minimize crime must be considered in light of the other effects they would have. For example, broad use of electronic surveillance would probably reduce crime but would also reduce privacy. Similarly, punishment probably reduces crime but also causes harms com-parable to crime to those punished. Among the various social control methods open to us, punishment has some of the most serious draw-backs—particularly when considered from the point of view of those most likely to be punished. Surely, there is a need for some measure of crime pre-vention. But there is no *necessary* answer to the question of how much crime, and of what type, is intolerable. The need for some measure of so-cial control, then, does not compel us to choose a system of punishment.

The retributivist may argue that punishment is preferable to other crime-preventive measures, such as those provided through environment, education, and social expectations. She may raise the specter of a popu-lation so disciplined in mind and body, through gentler mechanisms of so-cial control, that crime is an option only for those of exceptional imagi-nation and courage. Better, she might say, to allow liberty to violate the law and then punish than to constrain the will through social engineering.

But penal institutions are continuous with other disciplinary measures. In that sense, the justification of punishment must be continuous with the justification of other ways of preserving social order. The issue is not whether we punish or whether we exercise social control; rather, it is to what extent, and in what ways, we ought to use social power to limit human behavior. Given unlimited knowledge and ability to manipulate social circumstances, there would be a direct trade-off between crime prevention and freedom from social control. At one extreme, there would be little crime and little freedom. At the other, there would be a great deal of crime and little social control of any kind. It would be possible to maintain society at any point on this spectrum by determining the necessary level of social control. For any given level of crime prevention, it would be true that we could, by increasing other forms of social control, decrease the amount of punishment. Punishment is part of the social control package. There may be many reasons for choosing some point on the social-control spectrum short of complete eradication of crime. But the reasons for that choice are not reasons for imposing punishment instead of other forms of social control; they are reasons for refraining from any form of social control, including punishment, to increase crime prevention beyond that point.

IV. Restitution

At several places in this chapter and the previous one, I have suggested that restitution better fulfills the goals of retributivism than does punishment. Restitution can serve the purposes of vindicating rules, the removal of unfair advantage, affirming the rights of victims, and the (partial) annulling of crime. But because I have argued that none of these purposes provides a compelling enough good to assure consent, it follows that consent to a system of requiring restitution cannot be presumed in order to serve them. Moreover, because the payment of restitution will, like any penalty, fall more heavily on those social groups most disposed to crime, it will be especially problematic to impute consent to them. Thus, the justification of harm-shifting remedies cannot rest on an imputation of consent. In the next chapter, I shall argue that a justification of these remedies can nevertheless be found in the principle associated with self-defense.

V. Conclusion

Retributivist theory takes the crime as given and the offender as a morally free individual. Crime represents an aberration, a moral flaw in an otherwise civilized world. I have argued that it is naïve to consider the individual in isolation from his social context. Insofar as it is true that changes in social conditions can reduce motivation and opportunity for crime, we are obligated to make those changes, rather than to impose retributive punishment, at least up to the point where the costs of those changes to individuals begin to approximate the costs of punishment to individuals. Retributive punishment is a social policy, and its reasonableness must be considered in conjunction with that of other social policies that may reduce or increase the occasions for such punishment.

5

Punishment as Self-Defense

It is good to kill an admiral from time to time, to encourage the
others.   —Voltaire, *Candide*, 1759

I. Introduction

We saw in chapter 2 that the core of the objections to utilitarian theories
is that we have a moral duty to treat individuals with the respect due to
persons, rather than to use them as mere instruments to our own ends.
This is the same concern that prevents us from killing off the more needy
members of society to benefit the rest. Harming some to benefit others is,
at best, morally precarious. Social contract theories seek to show that
punishment results from the choice of the offender, rather than from the
choices of others, and so does not use her as a mere means. Such theories
must show both that the offender chooses to commit the crime and that
her consent to the associated punishment may be assumed. I have argued
that it is not reasonable to impute to all offenders consent to the system
of rules and penalties. If the right to punish can be made to rest on the
right to self-defense, however, we may impose punishment without consent to a system of punishment, relying only on the offender's choice to
commit the crime. Alternatively, the self-defense view could be taken to
cover those who cannot be expected to consent to punishment, thus serving as a supplement to the social contract view, which would be applicable to those who could be expected to consent.

Basing punishment on self-defense promises to integrate retributive
and crime-preventive purposes in a particularly neat fashion. The use of
defensive force is limited to aggressors, thus satisfying the desert requirement of the retributive view. But such force is used for the purpose of
averting harm, corresponding to crime-preventive purposes. If we can
base punishment on the right to self-defense, we can account for a policy

of aiming at deterrence while limiting punishment to those who deserve it: this theory would not be consistent with punishing the innocent to prevent crime.

Simply warning the offender that we will punish her if she chooses to commit a particular crime is not adequate to make the offender responsible for her own punishment, just as the robber's warning that if you resist she will shoot you does not justify her in doing so. We must also show that the punishment itself, or its attachment to the crime, results from the offender's choice. Otherwise, any consequence that we chose to attach to another's chosen course of action would be justified, and this cannot be so. The self-defense theory of punishment seeks to justify the attachment of the penalty to the crime through an analogy with the natural right of self-defense. When someone comes at you with a knife, you may use force to repel her without seeking her consent to be governed by a rule permitting such force. Your use of force against her may be said to flow from her choice in that her action forces you to choose between harm to yourself and harm to her; under those circumstances, you are justified in choosing harm to her. The aggressor's action represents a choice that someone will be harmed, in that she has chosen to take an action that makes such harm inevitable. The right to self-defense is thus appropriately exercised against enemies, with whom there is no question of sharing a social contract. Self-defense is exercised against those with whom reasoning has failed, or with whom there is neither time nor opportunity to reason. Clearly, we must be cautious before consigning any area of our relations with our fellow citizens to this category.

The principle of self-defense does not directly justify punishment, as in the case of punishment the wrongdoer has already inflicted her damage, and the question is one of doing additional harm to her. But proponents of the self-defense theory seek to collapse the distinction between self-defense and deterrent punishment, arguing that both flow from the same underlying principle. If successful, this argument would require us either to accept punishment or to reject the right to self-defense. I shall argue that the analogy fails: preventive violence is sometimes justified, but punishment does not fall under the relevant principle. The harms we do in enforcing self-defensive threats of punishment are neither necessary in the sense required by self-defense nor are they imposed on those who are responsible for the harms that will otherwise be done to innocents; thus, self-defense does not provide a justification for punishment independent of utilitarian and retributive rationales. What the analogy with self-defense surprisingly establishes instead is a right to compensation for past harms.

II. What Justifies Self-Defense?

I shall accept, for present purposes, the general account of self-defense that is given by proponents of its extension to punishment. On this view, the moral basis of self-defense is the shifting of inevitable harms from innocents to those who have made them inevitable.[1] On grounds of distributive justice, where the aggressor makes it inevitable that some must suffer harm, we are justified in choosing that the aggressor, rather than others, will be the one to suffer it (subject to constraints of necessity and proportionality). Harm is permissibly shifted away from those who have no causal responsibility for the current threat of harm and on to those who do have such responsibility.

Self-defense has two features that will be important for present purposes. First, the amount of force that I use must both be *proportional* to the harm threatened and *necessary* to prevent the harm the attacker threatens. For example, if you're running at me with a knife, and I have a Star Trek–style phaser gun set to "stun" that I can use to stop you, I would not be justified in setting it to "kill," even if I know you intend to kill me with the knife. Force meeting the proportionality requirement may not be used unless it also is necessary for self-defense. For the use of force to be necessary to prevent a particular harm, that harm must normally be imminent; otherwise, other ways of preventing it may usually be tried before it does become imminent. We are rightly skeptical of individuals (and nations) who claim that their use of apparently aggressive tactics was a "preemptive strike" against an anticipated future attack. It is not that such tactics are never justified, but that they are justified only when they really are necessary; as a corollary, it follows that those who resort to them must be in a position to know whether they are necessary or not. Simply knowing that the other party is ill-disposed toward us is not equivalent to knowing that the use of force is necessary.

Although the self-defensive use of force is subject to the necessity constraint discussed above, there is no requirement that it should be sufficient to prevent the attack. As with ordinary self-defense, one may use proportional force in an effort to repel an attack as long as there is at least some chance that it will be effective. The implications of this are worth following out. Suppose we threaten ten potential attackers with death if they kill their intended victims. And suppose we know that the threat has only a 10 percent chance of success; that is, it is likely to be effective against only one of the attackers. If in fact only one attacker is deterred, and the other nine kill their victims, we would then be justified in killing the nine successful attackers, because we were justified in threatening them in the first place. This is an important difference from utilitarian deterrence theory, which would indicate that we may not kill nine (or two) to save one. Broadly, then, there are only the most minimal constraints of effectiveness on punishment conceived as self-defense: any threat that might work will be justified and will be justifiably enforced.

We could not, of course, kill the nine attackers *seriatim*, after they killed their victims, in order to deter the tenth attacker, because that would clearly be using them as mere means to the end of saving the tenth victim. But the self-defense theorist will argue that we are not using the nine successful attackers as mere means to deter the tenth, because each chooses, in face of the threat, to attack anyway and so to incur the retaliatory harm. Note, however, that (as in the retributive argument) the attacker chooses the crime, not the punishment; it must be separately established that the threat and its enforcement are justified. The offender's choice to attack does not by itself show that we are not using her as a mere means.

Second, it is not the comparative moral badness of the aggressor, but rather his responsibility for the specific harm in question that justifies our shifting harm to him. If Charles Manson's cellmate threatens my life, I may not kill Manson to distract him; and if I, with my near-perfect moral character, threaten Manson at gunpoint, he is justified in defending himself, regardless of his past crimes. These two features of self-defense, I shall argue, vitiate the self-defense argument for punishment.

The shifting of harm to aggressors is most clearly permissible where the harm set in motion by the aggressor cannot be averted entirely, but can be diverted away from nonaggressors and on to him. The harm the aggressor has made inevitable still occurs, but it falls upon him rather than upon others. The wrongdoer who attacks me with a knife cannot complain when my defensive blow drives the knife into her own body. A harm different from that threatened may be done to the attacker where it is necessary to prevent the harm she intends to do to others: I may kick the knife out of the attacker's hand, even if I break several of her fingers in doing so. The proportionality limitation on such other harms may be seen as a substitute for the diversion to the aggressor of the specific harm she has set in motion.

Up to this point, the argument does not justify retrospective harms that simply add to a harm already done. Once we have failed to avert an attack, we are not justified, on grounds of self-defense, in inflicting additional harm on the aggressor. (If she has wounded me in a knife attack on Friday, my kicking her on the following Tuesday is not self-defense.) Such harm does not redistribute, but rather simply increases, the harm done. Past harms cannot literally be shifted to those who caused them.

What the redistribution principle does support, with respect to past harms, is after-the-fact compensation. Losses can permissibly be redistributed from victims to the wrongdoers responsible for them where this is feasible—for example, the assailant can be made to pay the victim's medical expenses and to pay monetary compensation for his pain—because, although such payments cannot "undo" the harm done by the attack, they do in a meaningful sense shift harm from the victim on to the person responsible for it. Even though, as discussed in chapter 4, a right to compensation cannot be based on imputed consent, such a right does follow from the principle underlying self-defense. A right to compensation can be enforced without punishment, through the means normally used by creditors, as will be discussed further in chapter 8.

Deterrent punishment is similar to the case of retaliatory, rather than redistributive, harm, in that it imposes new harms on past wrongdoers without shifting harm away from their (past) victims. The core of self-defense arguments for punishment is that the threat of punishment occurs before the crime, and thus is justified on defensive grounds. Thus the challenge is to show that the threat of retrospective harm is justified, and that carrying out the threatened harm, after the fact, can also count as defensive.

If we are justified in actually harming aggressors in order to prevent their harming us, it appears a fortiori true that we are justified in threatening them with that harm if by doing so we can prevent them from harming us. If I may actually kick the knife out of the attacker's hand, I may certainly threaten to do so. In fact, if (I know that) threatening harm will be sufficient to stop the attack, I am obligated under the necessity constraint to make the threat rather than to use actual force; and, in many instances, I won't know whether actual harm is necessary unless I try the threat first. What concerns us, however, is not the uncontroversial threat to inflict sufficient harm on the aggressor to avert her attack, but rather the threat to inflict retaliatory harm if she succeeds in harming us.

It is tempting to think that, as threats of force are less harmful than the actual use of force, it is justified to threaten an amount or type of force that we would not be justified in actually deploying, as a way of avoiding the imposition of actual harm. Suppose that A is about to shoot B, and we can stop him by spraying Mace in his face. We also know that while the threat of pepper spray won't stop him, the threat of being shot himself will. Wouldn't it be better to threaten to shoot him in order to avoid having to harm him with Mace? And if this is permissible, wouldn't it also be permissible to threaten him with retaliatory rather than preventive harm if that will be more effective in stopping him?

Issuing threats that we would not be justified in enforcing raises both moral and pragmatic problems. Such threats are manifestly manipulative: they seek to change the behavior of other moral agents by creating false beliefs about our intentions, enabling us to substitute our judgment for that of the other person. As we aim to persuade the other that we will act in ways in which we would not be justified in acting, we seek to mold her choices by considerations that are not only false but unjust. Considered as a way of changing the behavior of others, this is no different, morally, from the actual use of unjustified force. It is also unwise policy, in that if the aggressor ignores our threat of unjustified force, we will either have to act unjustly or reveal our threats to be empty, thus devaluing any future threats we might make. To show that threats of retaliatory harm are justified, then, the self defense theory must show that the actual imposition of the harm is justified in case our threats are ignored. There are two approaches to this problem: one seeks to show that the retaliatory harm is itself necessary for defensive purposes, and the other seeks to show that threat and enforcement stand or fall together, so that, in effect, the threat justifies the actual imposition of the harm.

Daniel Farrell argues that the retaliatory harm we impose for deterrent purposes can be considered defensive. With respect to specific deterrence, he argues that the necessity requirement can be extended to cover harm that, while not necessary to avert the current attack, is within the limits of proportionality, and is necessary to avert a future attack by the same aggressor. With respect to general deterrence, he argues that those who ignore our threats endanger us, so that we may shift harms to them to defend ourselves from that danger. I shall argue, first, that the principle of self-defense does not justify retrospective harm for purposes of specific deterrence: either the harm is not legitimate self-defense, or it is not retrospective and must be justified in terms of future dangers. Second, I shall argue that those who ignore our justified threats do not have sufficient responsibility for future dangers from others for our enforcement of our threats to count as self-defense.

Farrell postulates a single aggressor who engages in repeated attacks. I can repel the current attack through the infliction of x amount of pain; but then (I know) she will attack again, at a time when I am more vulnerable. But I also know that the infliction of some additional amount of pain $(x + y)$ in defending myself from the current attack will be sufficient to prevent her from attacking next time. Here, Farrell argues, it may be necessary (a) to threaten more harm than is necessary for immediate self-defense (to threaten $x + y$), and (b) to carry out that threat, if the threat alone does not suffice to deter the offender. If this additional prospective harm is permissible, he suggests, retaliatory harm for the same purpose would also be permissible.

Suppose that I warn the knife-attacker that if she attacks me I will spray her with Mace (x) and also break her hand afterwards (y). She ignores my threat, attacks me, and I inflict both harms. But because we know that simply spraying her with Mace (x) is all that is necessary to repel the current attack, breaking her hand as well (y) can only be justified on the basis that it is necessary to repel future attacks; *ex hypothesi*, it is not necessary to repel the current attack. The doing (and the threatening) of this additional amount of harm must stand or fall on the basis of its being necessary to prevent the next attack; the current attack is only marginally relevant, in that it might provide some (not conclusive) evidence that there will be another one. And if there were no present attack, and I had arrived independently at my beliefs about the likelihood of the next one and the measures necessary to prevent it, I would be equally justified in taking those measures. The aggressor's current attack, in the face of my threat, is not, by itself, enough to show that she forces me to choose between harm to her and harm to myself with respect to the next anticipated attack. If we find it difficult to accept that I would be justified in breaking the offender's hand when she is not attacking me in order to prevent her doing so in the future, we should also find it difficult to accept that I can inflict this additional harm when she is attacking me, but lesser force (Mace) would suffice for immediate self-defense.

One factor that makes the use of the additional force plausible, I think, is that typically one does not have time to reflect or sufficient information to choose the exact amount of force necessary to repel the attack; thus, some leeway is allowed in real-life cases of self-defense. One might have believed (or be able to convince others that one believed) that it was in fact necessary to break the attacker's hand to avert the current attack, perhaps because she might quickly recover from the Mace spraying. But, given knowledge of the exact amount of force necessary, using more than that is clearly unjustified. Any additional force to be used requires a separate justification. The fact that the next attack is not imminent counts strongly against the justification of using (additional) force now to prevent it, just as it would if there were no present attack.

In criminal law, self-defense or defense of a third party justifies the use of force only when one is in imminent danger. Efforts to extend the defense to situations in which one is the subject of repeated attacks (as in the battered spouse defense) have been criticized on the basis that it is implausible that one cannot find other means to avoid the harm before the next attack. Supporters of such an extension of self-defense argue that, because of the special psychological effects of being battered by a loved one, the battered spouse may effectively be unable to seek outside help or to leave her abuser, who is in any case likely to pursue her if she does leave. It is not my purpose here to debate the merits of the battered-spouse defense, but rather to point out the uphill nature of the battle to extend the boundaries of self-defense to include nonimminent attacks. Caution in extending the boundaries of self-defense is warranted in that the expected attack may never materialize; the victim who expects to be incapacitated may seek help from others; or the victim may be able to escape or to develop passive defenses to ward off the attack. It will be seldom indeed that a future attack will be sufficiently certain, and sufficiently unavoidable, that nonimmediate self-defense can be justified.

It is thus far from clear that Farrell's victim of repeated attacks may take any measures beyond those necessary to repel the immediate attack, unless the usual alternatives are for some reason unavailable. And if she may take such measures, they are justified only because necessary to the prevention of her next attack, not because of the present attack. If we may not do additional (or retaliatory) harm in such an instance, it follows that we may not threaten to do such harm either, even if a threat of otherwise unjustified harm would be more effective than a threat of justified harm. Either the threat, or the doing, of harm for the purposes of specific deterrence is justified only insofar as the harm is necessary, or reasonably perceived to be so.

We need not worry that clever aggressors, who could be stopped by the infliction of proportional harm, will escape by making sure that the amount of force necessary to stop their lethal attacks is minimal, nor yet that we must expose ourselves to dangers that we know we could prevent by a just use of force. If we can stop lethal attacks with a minimum of force, we are still spared from harm. And if we do know that the application of force is necessary to prevent a future attack, we may use that force, within the limits of proportionality. What we may not do is knowingly use more force than necessary with respect to either attack, or use force that is purely retaliatory.

Farrell goes on to argue that punishment for general deterrence purposes can be justified on self-defensive grounds, because one aggressor's disregard of our threat will leave us more vulnerable to attacks by others if we don't follow through on the threat. It is his choice to disregard our threat, Farrell suggests, that puts us in the position of having to choose between harm to him and harm to innocents (by other aggressors), and we may therefore choose that he, as a culpable aggressor, will be the one to suffer harm. I shall argue that the present aggressor's ignoring of our threat does not render him responsible, in the sense required for justified self-defense, for our consequent increased vulnerability to attacks by others.

Note that, by itself, enhancing the effectiveness of future threats against others is not a sufficient reason for harming the offender. It may well be that we could deter future offenders by showing ourselves to be ruthless in any number of ways, but we are restricted to demonstrating our ruthlessness in contexts where it is justified, and in particular, where it is not a mere use of our victim as a means to our end of deterring others. We may not choose to inflict a sound thrashing on the local hoodlum with the most formidable reputation, even if doing so will effectively protect us against attacks by others. It is important, then, to show that the aggressor is morally responsible for forcing me to choose between retaliatory harm to her and acceptance of future harm to myself, rather than simply being in a position where harm to her will serve my ends.

The aggressor's causal contribution to the future harms we seek to avert is that her ignoring of our threat has affected the motivations of other potential aggressors, so that they are now more likely to attack us if we fail to carry through on the threat. But does this make her morally responsible for our danger?

It is evident that a causal contribution alone, particularly if it is a minor one, will not be enough to justify harming the aggressor (or harming him more than otherwise justified) to avert the attacks of others. For example, if Supervisor fired Employee for unsatisfactory performance, Supervisor may be said to have played a causal role in Employee's later showing up at the workplace armed with a machine gun. Suppose that the only way we can stop Employee from massacring her former coworkers is by turning Supervisor over to her. There is some truth in the statement that Supervisor's action in firing Employee caused us to have to choose between harm to him and harm to others, just as there is some truth in the statement that the aggressor's ignoring of our threats causes us to have to choose between (greater than otherwise justified) harm to her and harm to others from prospective crimes. But this causal contribution would not justify us in turning Supervisor over to Employee in order to secure the release of the hostages, even if Supervisor knew in advance that Employee was likely to react violently if fired. He simply is not morally responsible for the wrongful acts of Employee, despite his causal role, and so we may not shift harm from the innocent hostages on to him.

So far, we have assumed that the actions of the causal contributor are morally permissible. Does moral responsibility for the acts of others to which one has made a causal contribution (and thus the permissibility of harm-shifting) depend on the wrongfulness of the causal act? I think not. Suppose, for example, that Supervisor fired Employee because she was about to discover Supervisor's embezzling activities. Even though this is a wrongful act that plays a causal role in Employee's rampage, Supervisor still is not morally responsible for Employee's violence, and we still may not shift harm from the innocent hostages on to him. Nor does this depend on the degree of wrongfulness of Supervisor's behavior. If Supervisor had killed Big Boss, who would have reinstated Employee the previous day, thus averting the crisis, we still could not justify turning Supervisor over to Employee to protect the hostages.

It is evident, I think, that even though Supervisor has made it inevitable (or perhaps just more probable), through his wrongful act, that someone will be harmed, his contribution to that future harm is just too indirect to justify shifting harm on to him. In the case of punishment, too, the main moral responsibility for our increased vulnerability must be assigned, not to the current punishable wrongdoer, but rather to the anticipated wrongdoers to whom we are vulnerable. We are more vulnerable as a result of the current offender's action only through the mediation of future offenders' increased willingness to harm us. It thus seems that the future vulnerability created by the offender's ignoring of our threat cannot justify our enforcing it after it has failed to deter the offender.

One reason why we may not harm Supervisor to defend the hostages is that harm to them requires the intervention of another moral agent (Employee). It is tempting to say that the reason we may not use self-defensive force against Supervisor is that Employee's intervention absolves him from responsibility for the prospective harm to the hostages, taking as our principle that we may shift harms from innocents only to the wrongdoers who directly cause them. There are, however, some situations in which we may use self-defensive force against a person who is not the last decision maker in the causal chain leading up to the harm we are trying to avert.[2]

Suppose that Ruffian, aware of Employee's wish for revenge, offers to supply her with a machine gun suitable for the purpose. While we would want to stop short of killing Ruffian to divert Employee from her course, it would certainly count as self-defense to intercept Ruffian before he can deliver the machine gun and to forcibly restrain him from doing so, even though Employee is another moral agent who must make the decision to attack. The same would be true even if Ruffian only seeks to affect Employee's motivation—perhaps by telling her that Supervisor fired her because of racial animus, knowing that she can be counted on to react violently to such news. Here, Ruffian acts *in order to* cause danger to the hostages, rather than simply in disregard of the danger to them. The wrongfulness of Ruffian's behavior, unlike that of Supervisor, consists precisely in its malicious causal contribution to the hostages' danger. Without this kind of intentional contribution to the current danger, other causal contributors—even if they have acted wrongly—may not be harmed to avert it.

The principle, then, is that harms may be shifted from innocents only to wrongdoers who act with the intention of causing the specific harm we seek to avert. This principle would not permit the punishment of offenders for general deterrent purposes. There may be some few offenders who commit their crimes for the purpose of encouraging others to do likewise (tax protesters, perhaps), but most are simply indifferent to such effects.

The causal contribution of the offender who ignores our threat of punishment will seldom, if ever, be a more significant factor in the decisions of others to commit crimes than the manifold social and psychological factors that lead them to criminal activity. I have argued above (chapter 2) that we cannot even be sure that deterrent effects occur. But even if punishment has significant general deterrent effects, those effects are not in themselves determinative of the crime rate. As discussed in chapter 4, the rate of crime stems from a complex combination of structural, social, and psychological factors. Correspondingly, the degree of our vulnerability to future crimes varies to some extent with each of these factors. To say that the individual offender within this picture is causally and morally responsible for any significant part of our vulnerability to the crimes of others can only seem hopelessly naive. It is not that the individual offender even in the most dismal of circumstances is not responsible for her own acts—but to hold her thereby responsible for our vulnerability to the multifariously caused acts of others in her situation is arbitrary indeed.

Some have sought to show that the imposition of retaliatory harm counts as self-defense just because it has been threatened in advance.[3] The threat, of course, is prospective; and it can make no relevant difference to the potential aggressor whether the harm threatened will occur before or after his wrongdoing. Suppose that I can construct a device that will detect wrongdoing and inflict harm on the offender (as spikes on parking lot entrances inflict tire damage on those who seek to avoid paying at the exit). The harm done by the device is not defensive, but the device itself is. It seems that, given necessity and proportionality restraints on the harm to be done, we would be justified in activating such a device for purposes of self-protection. The device represents the initiation of a real threat of punishment (rather than a bluff) because once activated, it cannot be deactivated after the aggressor has acted. The suggestion of these writers is that making a threat of retrospective punishment is like activating such an automatic retaliation device (ARD); when we are justified in making such a threat (conditional on wrongdoing), we are justified in simultaneously establishing a real risk that the threat will be carried out (if the condition is met).

The human application of threatened punishment differs from the automatic retaliation device in that there is a separate decision to carry out the punishment, and this decision must also be morally justified. Warren Quinn argues, however, that punishment is analogous to the automatic retaliation device because the moral status of the threat/punishment does not change over time.[4] If the offender has a valid objection to being punished after the crime, she should have been able to raise this same objection beforehand, when the threat to punish was made (and the risk of being punished was established). If she had no valid objection to the threat, then she can have no valid objection to its implementation. Quinn thus assimilates threat and enforcement to one event, so that any amount of force justified in self-defense is justified in retaliation, as long as it is threatened beforehand. I shall argue, however, that when our threats are ignored we learn that they were not justified with respect to those who ignore them, and so we may not carry them out against those persons.

Quinn, like Farrell, argues here that the threat is justified on grounds of self-defense (which does not require the consent of the attacker). Quinn argues here that if we are justified in threatening some amount of harm, we are justified in creating a conditional risk that the harm will actually be done. And, if the condition is met, he argues, we are thereby justified in carrying out the threat, because (a) the permissibility of risk creation is the same as that of the imposition of the same harm, and (b) the permissibility of either does not change over time. Thus, if before the attack we are justified in threatening harm H (and creating a conditional risk that it will happen), we are by the same token justified in imposing harm H (creating a 100 percent risk of that harm) when the condition is met. Quinn's theory thus seems to avoid the problem raised by Farrell's that the harm prevented by punishing a particular offender is not a harm for which she may reasonably be held responsible. Instead, Quinn casts the punishment of the offender as "an unavoidable empirical consequence" of the protection created by justified self-defensive threats and concomitant conditional risks of punishment.[5]

One constraint on self-defensive threats, as we have seen, is that they must be necessary to protect against the threatened harm. If we know in advance that a particular measure is not necessary for our protection, we may neither threaten it nor impose it. Moreover, if (I know) I can avert your attack without harming you at all—perhaps simply by letting you know I am armed—then that is the course I am obligated to take. Similarly, although I need not know that my defensive measures will be effective for them to be justified, if I know (for certain) that a particular measure will be absolutely ineffective in preventing your attack, I am not justified in threatening or imposing it. What is known to be ineffective for a particular purpose cannot be regarded as necessary to that purpose. For example, while I might be justified in sneaking into your house and stealing your weapons in order to defend myself, I would not be justified in sneaking in and stealing your favorite book (assuming that doesn't reduce your willingness to attack).

It also follows that if, in the process of imposing some harm that I believe is necessary to defend myself, I discover that it is either unnecessary or completely ineffective, I am obligated to abandon it. Suppose, for example, that (perhaps as a spouse threatened with battering) I believe initially that I can avert the attack that you threaten only by putting a nausea-inducing substance in your food each day. If I subsequently learn that it is not necessary to do this in order to avert your attack (you can be stopped by a reminder of ethical duties), then I am obligated to stop putting the substance in your food. Equally, if I learn that the nausea-inducing substance, while making you uncomfortable, has absolutely no effect on your willingness to beat me, I have no self-defense justification for continuing to use it and am obligated to stop doing so.

Now suppose that I threaten you with some retaliatory harm that I believe has some chance of stopping your attack. I am justified in making the threat, let us assume, because I reasonably believe that it may be effective. If I learn, at any time, that it will not be effective at all, then I ought to withdraw the threat. But if in fact you attack and harm me anyway, in face of the threat, I have learned, precisely, that this threat is ineffective against you. To impose the harm now, after the fact, is to impose a harm that (I now know) has no defensive value against you. If I had had this information in advance, I would not have been justified in issuing the threat in the first place. It therefore seems that the justification for issuing the threat cannot carry over to become a justification for imposing the harm. The threat is justified against those against whom it will be ineffective only because we do not know this in advance. If the subsequent enforcement of the threat is justified, it can only be on retaliatory or utilitarian grounds—grounds that are themselves suspect, as I have argued in earlier chapters.

It may be objected that, while we have learned that the threat was not an effective deterrent, we have not learned that the actual imposition of the threatened harm will be ineffective. For the aggressor may well have underestimated what it would be like actually to suffer the harm we threatened, and, once having suffered it, may be deterred by the same threat that failed to deter him the first time. But suppose that we had all this information before issuing the first threat. We would then have known that the threat (as opposed to simply imposing the harm without threat) would be ineffective, with respect to the first attack, as long as the attacker continued not to appreciate what the harm threatened would really be like. And if our threats are known to be ineffective, we are not justified in making them. With respect to the second and subsequent attacks, the same would be true. At any point, our imposition of the threatened harm would change the attacker's attitude, but, if we are not justified in imposing it simply to change his attitude, the fact that we have previously threatened it does not create a justification for doing so. On Quinn's view, the enforcement of the threat is justified because the threat is justified, and the threat is justified where the threat itself (not the imposition of the harm) can protect us. Thus, he says, the imposition of the harm is justified "by the period of protection that *precedes* it."[6] Because Quinn's argument derives the justifiability of imposing the harm from the justifiability of the threat (unlike Farrell's, which appeals to the deterrent value of the harm itself) we are justified only in making threats that have some chance of effectively protecting us, and consequently never justified in carrying them out when they turn out to be ineffective.

Would we be justified in simply imposing the harm, rather than making the threat, in order to assure that the first (or any subsequent) attack did not occur? There may be some rare circumstances where we would be, but these will be circumstances in which the imposition of that harm, at that time, is necessary to the prevention of the attack—rather than necessary to the effectiveness of future threats. Similarly, we may not impose the harm here simply to show the aggressor what it is really like.

It is true that in the situation described, with respect to attacks by this specific aggressor, we can protect ourselves against future attacks by carrying out the original threat. Note, however, the parallel between this argument and Farrell's argument for the use of additional force not necessary to prevent the current attack. The force we use in carrying out our threat, like our action in breaking the knife attacker's hand after averting her attack, protects against the next attack, and as such can be justified only with reference to it, including necessity to that purpose. If we can justify it with respect to the next attack, we don't need to rely on the previously issued threat to justify it. If we can't justify it solely by reference to the forthcoming attack, it is not defensive: it cannot be defensive with respect to the past attack.

We are not, however, in the position of determining whom we may threaten, and with what, on a case-by-case basis. Rather, we are in the position of having to determine whether or not to establish (or continue) an ongoing practice of punishment. The establishment of an ongoing practice of making and carrying out threats differs from a threat made on one occasion in several ways. It is justified, if at all, not by the prospect of some specific attack but rather by a general prospect that attacks will occur. Its necessity is therefore not relative to the imminence of any particular attack, but rather to the inevitability of attacks in general. It will thus be easier to show that a system of deterrent punishment is necessary to the prevention of future harm than to show that the punishment of a given individual is necessary to that end.

If our choice is conceived as one of whether to have a system of punishment or not, it appears that the choice is between increased harm to nonaggressors through not having such a system and increased harm to aggressors through having such a system. After all, it is wrongdoers who are punished and innocents who are protected; so it appears that the institution of punishment properly shifts harms from innocents to the wrongdoers who are responsible for them.

This can be so, however, only if we aggregate all of the wrongdoers into an undifferentiated mass, such that "all of the wrongdoers" are responsible for "all of the crime." Such a move is made by Philip Montague:

> Imagine a society S that contains a subclass S' of individuals who are both strongly inclined and quite able wrongfully to kill or injure innocent members of S and who will do so if not directly prevented from acting. Innocent members of S are therefore at risk of being injured or killed because of the inclinations and abilities of those in S'. . . . Assume . . . that risks of harm to innocent people that those in S' create cannot be reduced without somehow harming the latter. Under these conditions harm is . . . unavoidable from the standpoint of S as a whole, though S does have some control over how this harm is distributed. A distribution

involving threats of punishment will favor innocent members of S over those in S', while a distribution not involving such threats will have the opposite result. [The fact that] those in S' are to blame for the fact that there is unavoidable harm to be distributed . . . presumptively requires S to establish a system of legal punishment.[7]

In practice, there is of course no such neat division between those who are prone to commit crimes and those who are likely to be victimized. None of us can claim not to be a potential wrongdoer, any more than we can claim not to be a potential victim. In general, the two correspond: the risk of victimization is highest in the same demographic groups that are the most crime prone. Most often, people victimize others who move in the same circles as they do: muggers seek victims in their own neighborhoods, drug dealers kill other drug dealers, and white-collar offenders victimize white-collar stockholders. This does not mean that every member of a given demographic group is equally likely to commit crimes, but it does mean that those who are likely to commit crimes are also at risk of victimization—and those risks are probably higher for the offending population as a whole than for the nonoffending population. "Those in S'" are all of us.

According to Montague:

the forced choice faced by S is not whether to punish individuals; rather, it is a choice whether to establish a system of punishment in the face of risks to innocent members of S created by those in S'. Hence, the problem noted earlier as associated with applying [the principle of distribution of harm] to *individual* punishment (i.e., that punishment is after the fact of harm being done to innocent persons) does not arise.[8]

As noted earlier, we would not be justified in shifting harms from the innocent members of S to the members of S' simply on the ground of the moral superiority of the innocents. Supposing that there is a famine in which some must starve, we are not justified in taking food from the morally worse and giving it to the morally better: the morally worse (we may suppose) are not responsible for the food shortage, although they are responsible for other harms. Nor may we set up a system of food distribution, in advance of any shortage, under which food will be redistributed from the morally worse to the morally better, even though this might provide a salutary incentive to moral behavior. Only if the food shortage has been caused by wrongdoing, and some must starve, may we choose that those wrongdoers will be first to go—it is their fault that we have to make such a choice. A fortiori, we may announce in advance that he who (culpably) causes a shortage of food will be the first to suffer its consequences; we may shift harms from their intended (or random) targets to those who have set them in motion. It is important that the members of S' be responsible for the existence of risks to the other members of S. Moreover, if the members of S' have varying degrees of responsibility for risks to other members of S, we cannot make a wholesale shift of harms from non-S' to S' (as Agamemnon held all Trojans, even those yet unborn, responsible for harms some Trojans had done). For example, we cannot hold those responsible for the risk of shoplifting liable for a risk of murder created by other members of S'. The harms to be borne by individual members of S' (or the risk of harm to be imposed on them) must prevent or reduce risks of harm to others for which they are individually responsible.

Is it true that those we decide to harm in establishing a system of punishment are responsible for the fact that we have to make a choice about whether harm will fall on them or on others? It is true in the weak sense that if no one was going to harm anyone else, there would be no need for any intervention in the distribution of harms. Montague thus suggests that those who are going to harm others, if they are not prevented from doing so, are responsible for the need to redistribute harm. And we can apparently identify with precision those who are going to (or rather had been going to) harm others, by their in fact harming others after the system is in place. But of course, the point of establishing a system of deterrent punishment is to prevent some people from doing the harms they otherwise would have done, and these are not the ones who do harm despite the existence of such a system. S' can be subdivided into "deterrables" and "undeterrables." A decision to establish a system of punishment is a decision to punish the undeterrables (or at least the undeterred) in order to deter the deterrables.

To make the point clearer, suppose that we know that if we establish a system of punishment we will be able to catch drug dealers, but not murderers, and that we can deter murder, but not drug dealing. Suppose further that we can deter the murderers by punishing the drug dealers. We are, in a sense, forced to choose between harm to drug dealers and harm to innocents (i.e., potential murder victims). But the drug dealers we apprehend are clearly not to blame for our having to make this choice, and if we choose to harm them, we will have to find some justification other than self-defense. We would not be justified in lumping them together with the murderers as "wrongdoers" and claiming that they are collectively responsible for threatened harm.

The case is not otherwise if our deterrable offenders, as well as our undeterrable ones, are drug dealers. We can deter some future drug dealers by punishing those not deterred so far, and we are, in a sense, forced to choose between harm to undeterrable drug dealers and harm to innocents. But the undeterrable drug dealers are not to blame for our having to make this choice. In short, we are simply in a position to use undeterred drug dealers for the social end of preventing future drug dealing.

It may be argued that it is the propensities of those in S' that cause the risk to other members of S, and that they are therefore to blame for that risk. If they were to blame for the risk, we would be justified in shifting the risk on to them. But, unless they have deliberately cultivated their propensities for crime, they are no more to blame for the risk thus created than AIDS victims are to blame for the risk posed to public health by their condition. In both cases, members of the group in question are responsible for actions they take to harm others, and in neither are they to blame for the abstract likelihood that they may take such actions. For Montague's argument to succeed, the case of punishment for deterrent purposes must be distinguishable from that in which we simply decide that, as some will inevitably be harmed, we will choose that harm falls on the morally worse rather than on the morally better.

Montague points out that it is only the risks of harm that are shifted by the system of punishment: no one is actually punished unless they in fact commit a crime. Instead, we lower the risk that innocents will be harmed by raising the risk that wrongdoers will be harmed. But again, if we are *not* imposing harms on those who are deterred by our threats of punishment, then we have shifted the harm that *they* would otherwise do on to those we do harm, that is, those who are not deterred by our threats. And if we are imposing harms on those who are deterred (by subjecting them to a greater risk of overt harm), we are doing so on the basis of their propensities, and not on the basis that they have, through their actions, made it inevitable that some will suffer harm. This point is parallel to that made above in connection with Quinn's argument: once we learn that our threats are ineffective, we are not justified (on grounds of self-defense) in carrying out the harm threatened; similarly, we may not (on grounds of self-defense) establish a system in which harm will be imposed on those who are not deterred by our threats.

A system of punishment established for deterrent purposes essentially represents a decision that one group (actual offenders) will be used as a mere means of deterring a second group (deterrable potential offenders) from harming a third (innocents). The fact that a person's decision to join the first group is voluntary and culpable does not confer on us the right to use them in this way. Our right to self-defense is limited to a right to harm others in efforts necessary to prevent the specific harms they threaten; we may therefore seek to prevent people from joining the first group, and we may harm them in the process. Our right to shift harms after the fact from innocents to wrongdoers is limited to the harms that those wrongdoers have done—not those that others might do in the future; we may therefore require offenders to compensate their victims for the harm they have done, but we may not require them to bear burdens associated with preventing the future offenses of others, nor may we threaten to do so.

So far, I have argued that we do not have a right, corresponding to the right to self-defense, to punish offenders. It might be argued, however, that we have a *reason* to establish a system of punishment, in order to convert risks of being victimized into risks of being punished if we victimize others. If all can agree on this reason, retributive punishment could be founded on this agreement, in combination with the offender's choice to commit the crime. This may seem to be a stronger reason than either desert or social control taken separately, and thus to provide a firmer basis for the social contract argument. This appearance is deceptive, however. The social-control version of the Kantian argument already incorporates both considerations, as it is an argument for retributive (desert-based) punishment in order to achieve the good of social control. Once the imputation of consent is required to make the argument go through, the self-defense argument loses its advantage over the Kantian retributive argument—that it supports a right to punish irrespective of the offender's consent. An argument to this effect would thus encounter all of the objections raised in chapter 4.

Quinn explicitly argues that such a system would be consented to. If we each had access to a personal ARD (and the right to use it), some would implement the devices at once, preferring the protection offered over the unprotected state. Those who initially feared punishment more than desiring protection would not immediately implement their ARDs, but would still be subject to the risk of punishment by those who had implemented them. If asked for permission to be included among those protected, they would then have no reason to refuse, as doing so would increase their protection without increasing their risk of punishment. Analogously, a system of punishment based on the right to make and enforce self-defensive threats would gain universal consent in the same fashion: one may as well agree to have one's own rights protected by defensive threats, given that one will be subjected to them in any case. This argument, however, explicitly presupposes the individual right to establish and carry out defensive threats, and only shows that the individual right can logically be extended to the social level. If we remove this assumption, the argument still shows that everyone would consent, but the consent loses its justificatory force. Suppose we assume instead that some people prefer to make and enforce the threat of death against anyone who infringes their rights. They then offer to include others, who are already subjected to the risk of being killed by their defensive measures, under the protection of their scheme. The others, assuming they cannot organize effective resistance, can be expected to consent for self-interested reasons; but their consent provides no justification for the implementation of the scheme.

III. Conclusion

The natural right of self-defense may be invoked as a justification for harming others only where the harm that we do is necessary to prevent an imminent attack and is directed against those who act culpably with the intention of causing the specific harm that we seek to prevent. Punishment, as retrospective harm, does not meet these criteria. It is directed against those who have harmed us in the past, with the aim of preventing others from harming us in the future. The actions of those we harm through punishment do not have sufficient effect on our vulnerability to future harm to make the assignment to them of responsibility for future harm legitimate. When we shift harms from potential victims to past wrongdoers, we shift harms for which the past wrongdoers are not morally responsible; in so doing, we use the past wrongdoers as mere means to our own ends. We may require wrongdoers to compensate their victims for the harms that they have done, but we may not harm them in order to prevent future harms by others.

6

Punishment as Communication

I. Introduction

Moral reform theories seek to show that punishment is justified (in whole or in part) because it conveys a moral message—a message that may benefit the offender by improving his moral character. These theories take as central that the source of wrongful behavior is the failure of the offender to appreciate the wrongfulness of his conduct, that this failure is a defect of moral character, and that hard treatment (punishment) is necessary to the communication that the conduct was wrongful.

Moral reform theory shares with retributivism a focus on individual moral responsibility. As we have seen, it is problematic to assume that the commission of criminal acts results from a moral weakness not shared by others; moral character plays into circumstances to determine which individuals will offend.

Character defects may, however, be a necessary condition for the performance of at least some kinds of criminal acts, perhaps, for example, those that display gross indifference to the suffering of others; punishment of such acts might legitimately address moral character. I shall argue, however, that aiming at the moral good of the offender, either alone or in combination with other purposes, is not sufficient to justify punishment. Moreover, state punishment cannot address the offender on a moral level—whether to make a forceful communication of the wrongness of the act, or to change his moral character for the better—so that the effort to do so, and to justify criminal punishment in these terms, is misplaced. This remains true even where the laws are just and evenly applied.

II. Moral Reform Theories

Rehabilitation of offenders seemed for a while an attractive and humanitarian alternative to harsh deterrent and retributive views. Criminal offenders often have troubled family backgrounds plausibly thought to result in poor social adjustment that might be addressed through appropriate therapy, thus benefiting both the offender and society. Punishment that benefits the offender as well as society is apparently easier to justify than punishment that harms the offender for the social good. Apart from the problematic record of rehabilitation in practice,[1] however, its apparently kindly face conceals an essentially manipulative approach to offenders. To see this, one need only consider the possibility of subjecting unruly protesters to aversion therapy or psychosurgery to make them more law abiding.[2]

Herbert Morris provides the definitive critique of the rehabilitative ideal in "Persons and Punishment," arguing that the theory's view of the offender as a mere product of social forces, and its treatment of punishment as a benefit to the offender, are inconsistent with treating him as a person in the Kantian sense.[3] Moral reform theory, in contrast, begins from the Kantian position that individual autonomy must be respected; its purpose is not to change the offender as such, but rather to persuade him to choose to change his own behavior as a result of the perception, induced by punishment, that his previous behavior was morally wrong.

The principal proponents of this view are Morris himself (in a later article), R. A. Duff, and Jean Hampton.[4] Beginning from the premise that the state must take measures to announce the wrongness of certain acts and to prevent them from occurring, they argue that, because the state may not use offenders as mere means to the goals of others, these measures must respect the autonomy of offenders and be taken out of a concern for the offender's good. Duff, for example, criticizes deterrent theories for providing the offender with morally irrelevant prudential reasons for complying with the law; avoidance of penalties is a self-interested, not a moral, reason for refraining from criminal acts.[5] Duff suggests that, to treat the offender as our moral equal, we must instead supply relevant, moral reasons for compliance—that is, the reason we give the offender must be our reason for having the rule in the first place. Punishment can supply such reasons, and thus induce genuine repentance, under the right conditions—where it can serve as a penance appropriately imposed by a community of which one is a voluntary member and whose shared values one has flouted. Those imposing the punishment must do so with the intent of inducing voluntary repentance and thus bringing the offender back into the moral community. Given these aims, the punishment must not coerce or manipulate the offender's will. Instead, because it seeks to address him as a moral agent, to persuade him of the wrongness of his act and gain his free agreement, it must also leave him free to disagree and to experience the punishment as pure coercion. Although in punishing we aim at the offender's moral good, the offender's autonomy is part and parcel of that moral good. Thus, it would be internally contradictory to seek his moral good through means that did not respect his autonomy.

The good aimed at is a change in the offender's moral character; the underlying premise is that criminal acts are freely chosen as a result of defects of character. Punishment proportional to the gravity of the offense is the only way the state can communicate to the offender that his act was wrong, and how serious the wrong was. Ideally, punishment is to convey the moral wrongness of the conduct, communicating that the victim has been harmed, and to what degree, by inflicting a corresponding amount of pain on the wrongdoer. Where Morris stresses the potential for restoring the offender's attachment to the good, Hampton emphasizes that, for offenders who do not value the interests of others, injuring their own interests may be the only way to communicate how they have harmed others, and to impart the message that the conduct is prohibited, which is a necessary part of conveying that it is seriously wrong.

Hampton emphasizes that the punishment will also show the offender and others that there is a limit on permitted conduct, while Duff emphasizes instead that it will restore his relationship with the community by expiating the wrong. Morris subscribes to both these secondary purposes. The action is thus taken out of concern for the good of the offender as well as out of concern for the good of others. Unlike rehabilitation, which seeks to change the offender's character against (or regardless of) his will, punishment directed at moral reform, according to its proponents, does not unacceptably invade the autonomy of the offender as long as he is left free to reject the moral message sought to be conveyed by punishment. Punishment is therefore justified as long as it attempts to promote the offender's moral good.

Both Duff and Morris limit the application of their theories to circumstances in which the rules are fair and the offender shares the values on which they are based. What we should seek to do through punishment, they argue, is to bring the offender back to what may reasonably be said to be his own values and to restore him to the good graces of a community of which he is a full member.

I shall argue that the aims of moral reform, insofar as they differ from the aims of other purposes of punishment, are insufficient to justify punishment, and that they do not cure the problems of other justifications. In part this is because the connection of character defects to crime is questionable, and in part it is because the aim of moral reform implies a strong paternalism. Even if these aims were sufficient to justify punishment, the state is not in a position to promote, or even to aim at, the moral good of the offender, and so cannot draw on this justification. This would be true even in a more ideal society in which the laws were just, fairly applied, and showed equal concern and respect for all.

As we saw in chapter 4, the moral defects of offenders are not the primary cause of crime: if they were, crimes would be more evenly distributed across time and place. To the extent that offenders may be seen as persons of average moral character who find themselves in circumstances more conducive to crime than do others, it is inappropriate for the state to seek to improve their characters rather than to change their circumstances, and presumptuous of those whose circumstances are more fortunate to suggest that their characters need improvement. Having a character defect—even of a specific type—is not a sufficient condition for crime. But is it not at least a necessary condition? We may assume that the laws are just, as the scope of just punishment is necessarily limited to the enforcement of just laws. Insofar as the laws are uniquely just (that is, required by justice), it will also be true that the offender ought to share the values underlying the laws. Insofar as they instead represent one of many possible approaches to justice, it will not necessarily be true that the offender who does not share those values has a defective character. For example, it would be false to say that the offender ought to share the value of protecting private property, as society might equally well be based on communal property instead. Less globally, the offender may legitimately disagree with society's judgment regarding the sale or use of drugs, the appropriateness of violence in dispute settlement, or specific marriage and tax laws. In this disputed area, we must rely for the justification of punishment on the idea that the offender ought to share the value of accepting society's judgment as to such matters, or, more directly, that it is wrong for him to disobey the law, simply because that is the law. I shall separate, for purposes of discussion, punishment (for moral reform purposes) of offenders who have contravened basic precepts of justice from punishment of offenders who have disobeyed legitimately enacted laws, the justice of which can be disputed.

Let us begin with the offender who breaks laws not in themselves required by justice simply because he is insufficiently attached to the value of obeying the specific edicts of the government. Let's assume that he personally disagrees with the law, even though it has been duly enacted. It might be a law concerning sale of particular drugs or permitted levels of air pollution, enacted to secure particular policy aims. Our offender may disagree with the importance of the results aimed at, or may think that the means chosen are not necessary to those ends. According to the moral reform view, we would then punish him with the aim of communicating the wrongness of disobeying government edicts, in order to remedy the moral defect reflected by his disagreement. But it is not so clear that the lack of an attachment to the state and its edicts, whatever they happen to be (as opposed to an attachment to the welfare of others), is in fact a moral failing. Do we really want to induce such an offender to say, as Duff suggests offenders should, that "I recognize and am distressed by the harm which I have done to others. I see that I have harmed myself, by injuring my relationships with others—by separating myself from God or the Good; from those whom I have directly wronged; from other members of the community whose values I have betrayed; and from myself as someone who truly desires good rather than evil"?[6] The history of civil disobedience and conscientious objection remind us of the value of questioning the law's commands. There may be arguments for enforcing the law, whatever it happens to be (after all, policy must take some direction or other); that does not necessarily imply that those who disobey such laws are morally defective. Possibly such an offender has disobeyed simply to further his own interests at the expense of others; but where the law in question is not required by justice, this will not be true in every case. Some will disobey out of a genuine disagreement with the policy. We will not be able to tell which are which, nor will we be able to justify punishing all on the ground that they have demonstrated moral defectiveness.

Duff argues that many *mala prohibita* should be seen as wrongs, in that they inconvenience others or take unfair advantage of others' willingness to obey the law.[7] Thus, the breaker of such laws is properly seen as in need of moral improvement. This certainly applies to the driver who chooses to drive on the right rather than on the left, where the law specifies the left. But what of the householder who chooses to own a gun, in defiance of laws prohibiting it, because he does not believe that the proliferation of guns raises the level of social violence? Or the youth who chooses to sell a controlled substance, because he does not believe it is dangerous? Their respective beliefs may well be reasonable, even if ultimately proven false. Their sole moral defect, in that case, would be that of paying insufficient deference to governmental determinations. We would do well to hesitate to punish people in order to get them to recognize and remedy such a defect.

From the outset, then, the argument for morally reforming punishment is best restricted to punishment for acts that are morally wrong in themselves, and that therefore do demonstrate defective character (though not necessarily a character more defective than average). This is, of course, not a trivial category, as most common-law crimes are intrinsically wrong in virtue of the harm that they do to others.

The state has an interest both in the moral good of the offender and in the practical good of other members of the community, as reflected in criminal law. Although an argument might be made, following Plato,[8] that punishment is justified because it benefits the offender, there are serious difficulties with such a position, as I shall show in the next section. Thus, moral-reform theorists seek to find the basic justification of punishment elsewhere, and to argue that such purposes must be constrained by a concern for the good of the offender. Hampton argues for a new approach to crime prevention, while writers such as Duff and Morris seek to show a consonance of aims between retributivism and moral reform, such that we simultaneously aim at the moral good of the offender and at more traditional retributive goals. I shall argue that, because the idea that state punishment can aim at the offender's moral good is hollow, to require that it do so is effectively to argue that punishment is never justified.

I shall begin by showing that one can claim punishment is justified on the sole basis that it benefits the offender by promoting his moral good only by embracing one of two implausible claims: either that restraint of liberty for almost any reason is justified (extreme paternalism) or that it would be unreasonable for the offender to prefer physical liberty to moral improvement. Thus, moral reform theory is more plausibly construed as a constraint on other justifications, based on harm to others, rather than as a separate justification. As a constraint on deterrent and retributive theories, it has the potential of rescuing them from the respective charges of using the offender as mere means to social ends or of inflicting pointless suffering. But if other justifications of punishment are to be constrained by the requirement that they aim at the good of the offender, rather than simply at deterrence or retribution, it is essential that punishment can in fact promote the good of the offender. I shall argue that state punishment cannot, except in special cases, achieve the postulated good of moral reform, and hence that it is disingenuous to claim that it can aim at this good. Hence, my argument will be that the aim of moral reform rescues other theories at the expense of vitiating them: if we may punish for deterrent or retributive purposes only if we also seek to promote the moral good of the offender in punishing her, we may not punish for those purposes, because punishment cannot promote her moral good.

Moral reform theories generally justify state intervention both on the ground that the state has a legitimate interest in the moral good of its citizens (at least in the limited sphere of criminally prohibited acts) and on the ground that the rights of others are invaded by such acts. Punishment is seen as seeking to promote the offender's moral good by seeking his recognition of his wrongdoing and his free repentance, restoring his attachment to the good and his relationship to the community. At the same time, it is presented as serving either crime-preventive or retributive ends. These two lines of justification for state intervention are often not clearly separated. Thus I wish to begin by making clear that state punishment for purposes of moral reform cannot be justified on solely paternalist grounds—that is, on the sole ground that it is for the good of the offender.[9]

Parents punish children for their own good, seeking to improve their moral characters as well as their behavior. It is tempting to suppose that society might similarly punish criminal offenders for their own good, justifying the use of hard treatment by appeal to the good that ultimately will result for the offender. It will be useful to set out plainly the difficulties that lie in the path of such an effort.

III. Paternalism

Offenders who are subjected to punishment are deprived of liberty against their will. Compelling a person to do something against his expressed (or known) wishes for his own good is prima facie wrong because it is an interference with his autonomy, in the sense of self-determination: he is denied the right to make his own choices. Such interference must be justified, if at all, on the ground that the good at stake is more important than his self-determination. For example, we might say that restraining a panicky person from running back into a burning building to rescue a dog is justified because saving his life is more important than allowing him to choose to rescue his pet. The extreme paternalist holds that self-determination has no weight, so that any intervention that in fact promotes the good of the individual is for that reason justified. Intervention would be unjustified, on this view, only if it did not promote the good of the individual. For example, you would be justified in forcibly (or secretly) substituting some tastier, more nutritious foods for the hot dogs, Twinkies, and potato chips I have chosen to place in my shopping cart. The substitution would be wrong only if you were mistaken about the quality of the respective foods (if your judgment were not in fact better than mine). This position lacks plausibility because my self-determination is itself clearly a part of my good; the idea that we can thus casually substitute our judgment for that of another person is insulting because it is fundamentally inconsistent with the equality of persons.

A more plausible paternalist position holds that, although we must in general respect the self-determination of others, there are some instances in which the good at stake is sufficiently important to outweigh the good of self-determination. In such instances, the moderate paternalist argues that the individual's choice to forgo the good is unreasonable and therefore may be overridden. It is on this ground that most battles about paternalism are fought. Alternatively, we sometimes seek to intervene on the ground that the choice the person wishes to implement is not genuinely his choice (not voluntary): it is ill-considered, he is not in his right mind, or he is mistaken about key facts. As this latter category clearly does not apply to the offender who does not wish to be punished, let us consider the argument that his preference for physical liberty over the opportunity for moral reform is unreasonable and so need not be respected.[10]

Morris comes close to this position, arguing that punishment is needed to restore the offender's status as a "morally autonomous person attached to the good"—a good that she is not permitted to relinquish voluntarily.[11] In general, a person's preference not to incur great harm is considered reasonable, almost regardless of the compelling nature of the benefit that she can get by embracing the harm. The sacrifice of one's physical liberty required by punishment is, obviously, a great harm. The term "unreasonable" is properly applied to choices such as preferring the wind in one's hair to the safety afforded by a motorcycle helmet, or preferring to risk death by making an uninformed choice of medications rather than endure the inconvenience of getting a prescription. Such choices, while arguably defensible, are obviously problematic. On the other hand, the patient with the gangrenous leg who refuses amputation;

the daredevil who insists on leaping a canyon on a motorcycle; the novice who dedicates herself to poverty, chastity, and obedience, are seen as possibly eccentric but not as subject to forced intervention. These individuals risk death, maiming, the constriction of life—they make choices that most of us would reject out-of-hand—but we have no right to substitute our choice for theirs. Comparably, the preference for one's physical liberty over the moral improvement promised by punishment appears manifestly reasonable, even on the assumption that moral improvement is a greater good than physical liberty. At most, it seems, we can argue that the choice of physical liberty over moral improvement is not ultimately the best choice for the person; many of us will even have difficulty asserting that we would, in the same circumstances, choose moral improvement.

Alternatively, it may be argued that the choice of physical liberty over the prospect of moral reform does not represent the authentic preferences of the individual, but is instead comparable to the recovering alcoholic's fleeting desire for a drink or the patient's visceral fear of necessary surgery. There may be something to this assertion where the offender has strayed from his own moral values and has thus separated himself from a community that is important to him. His deeper and more lasting preference may then be for restoration to the community and to pursuit of his more important values, while his temporary preference is to avoid the deprivation associated with punishment. But to impute such preferences in every case is entirely to vitiate the value of self-determination. To argue that the offender's authentic preference is necessarily for moral improvement over physical liberty is tantamount to substituting our judgment for his. Even if we are right about his authentic preferences (as we would also be in the shopping basket example), to contravene his actual choice is to deprive him of self-determination in a very real sense.[12] There would be nothing left of self-determination if the "self" to be respected were assumed to be the same for every individual.

Even if (as seems improbable) it can successfully be maintained that moral reform (or one's status as a morally autonomous person attached to the good) is such a great good that even intervention as extreme as deprivation of physical liberty is justified on paternalistic grounds, we must also consider the probability that our intervention will achieve the good sought. Even the extreme paternalist will not require a reluctant patient to undergo painful treatments that are unlikely to succeed in saving his life. We therefore cannot justify punishment on paternalist grounds unless punishment is in fact reasonably likely to produce moral improvement, and we are willing to make one of the following claims:

1. We are always justified in intervening to promote the good of another (extreme paternalism).
2. Moral improvement is by far a greater good than physical liberty, such that the offender's preference for physical liberty is unreasonable.

In section V, I shall argue that we cannot expect state punishment under most conditions to result in moral reform. But even under the limited conditions where it is likely to do so (discussed in section VII), the paternalist must still show that the offender's preference not to be punished may be overridden for the reasons expressed in (1) or (2). Thus, the prospects for justifying punishment for purposes of moral reform on paternalist grounds are dim.

It may be objected here that the moral reform theory does not justify punishment strictly on grounds of the moral improvement that it aims at, but rather on the ground that it is a communicative effort, showing concern and respect for the offender by seeking to communicate to him the nature of his wrong. But because this is a coercive communication that injures the offender, the argument for coercion must still be made. If the offender does not wish to be shown concern and respect through deprivation of liberty, we must justify showing our concern in this way either by reference to his good or by reference to the good of others. If we seek to justify this deprivation by appeal to the idea that concern and respect are goods for the offender, then we will still need to show, at a minimum, that the offender's preference not to be shown concern and respect in this way is unreasonable.

IV. Nonpaternalistic Goals

It is, of course, difficult to imagine a situation in which the moral improvement of the offender could be separated from the good that it does for others—because it is the essence of being a morally good person that one treat others well. The state's interest in promoting the offender's moral good is therefore not limited to what it does for him. The state has a legitimate interest in protecting the rights of others. Punishing offenders, after the fact of the crime, simply in order to promote the good of others is problematic, as we have seen (chapter 2). State punishment must respect the autonomy of the offender and must not use him as a mere means to the ends of others; as the proponents of moral reform emphasize, he is not a dog to be trained, but an autonomous human being to be communicated with on a moral level.

No one would object to simple cognitive communication of the wrong done: the difficulty is to show that the use of hard treatment is essential to the communicative effort. Without such a showing, the theory is open to the charge of imposing gratuitous harm or treating the offender as an animal to be trained. At the same time, hard treatment must also be shown to serve a social purpose, as we have seen that the good of the offender alone is unlikely to justify state intervention.

Moral reform theorists appeal variously to deterrent or to retributive social purposes as the motivation for state intervention. The aim of improving the offender's moral character by communicating the wrongness of his conduct is then seen as a constraint on these other purposes. Conceivably, punishment for these purposes will be more acceptable if so constrained. Constraining deterrence by a concern for the moral good of the offender has the potential of rescuing deterrent theory from the objection that it uses offenders as mere means to the social end of crime prevention. Alternatively, if retributive punishment could be shown to serve the moral good of the offender, then we would need to consider whether that good was sufficient to motivate consent to such punishment, perhaps in combination with the other goods it is said to serve.

A. Constrained Deterrence

Hampton focuses on deterrence as the ground for state intervention, while arguing that any punishment imposed by the state must also be directed at the moral good of the offender. Punishment creates a barrier to unacceptable behavior, but does so for the good of the offender as well as for the good of others: "Punishment is justified as a way to prevent wrongdoing insofar as it can teach both wrongdoers and the public at large the moral reasons for choosing not to perform an offense."[13] We must accept, she suggests, that the justification of punishment is tied to crime prevention; but the goal of crime prevention is best achieved through moral education. On Hampton's view, then, there are two necessary and sufficient conditions for state punishment: it must be punishment for an act that has harmed others, and it must be aimed at the moral good of the offender. It is up to the offender, she argues, whether he experiences the punishment as a purely coercive deterrent or as a moral message. Thus, as long as we seek in punishing to communicate our moral evaluation of the offender's conduct and so to improve his moral character, we are justified in a practice that may (at his option) instead only serve the ends of society at his expense. If the offender is used as a mere means to social good, it is because he has, by rejecting the moral message aimed at his own good, chosen to be so used.

For this argument to work, however, there must be a justification for punishment independent of the good it might do the offender, if only he chooses correctly. Otherwise, in allowing him to choose which of two unjustifiable courses of action we will take, we afford him no real choice at all. If his real choice is not to be punished at all, then we are not respecting that choice. It is as though we tried to justify forcing an unwilling neighbor to clear our driveway of snow by pointing out that he can benefit from the exercise if he uses a hand shovel, and has only himself to blame if he chooses instead to use a snowblower so that he gains no benefit at all.

I have argued above that the paternalist justification does not work; a concern purely for the good of the offender would dictate that we do not punish him against his will. Thus, even if punishment benefits him, we are doing to him something we would not otherwise be justified in doing in order to benefit others—that is, we are using him as a mere means to the ends of others. Simply adding a constraint that we also aim at the offender's moral good will, therefore, not be sufficient to justify punishment for crime-preventive purposes.

B. Constrained Retribution

We saw in chapter 4 that the purposes commonly associated with retributivism are not sufficiently compelling to provide a basis for presumed consent to punishment. Morris argues that, for hypothetical persons seeking to reach agreement on a social contract, the prospect of moral reform would provide a powerful reason to choose punishment:

> Thinking of ourselves as potential, and thinking of ourselves as actual wrongdoers, and appreciating the connection of punishment with one's attachment to the good, to one's status as a moral person, would we not

select such a system, if for no other reason, than that it would promote our own good?[14]

Again, though, this argument depends on the success of the straight paternalist argument. To say that we would choose such a system is to say that we would choose paternalist coercion in cases in which our moral good conflicted with our physical liberty. There is no more reason to think we would make this choice than to think that we would choose, for example, forced consumption of healthful foods. Even if our moral good is preferable to our physical liberty (or our physical health is more important than our enjoyment of calorie-filled treats), we can presume consent to punishment for that purpose only if self-determination is always outweighed by the promotion of our good. Thus, adding the aim of moral reform to traditional retributive aims, or constraining those aims by the requirement that we also aim at the offender's good, will not justify punishment unless it is also shown that the strong paternalist argument succeeds.

Let us assume, however, for purposes of argument, that at least one of these three arguments (paternalist, constrained deterrent, or constrained retributive) succeeds, in the sense that aiming at the offender's good is a sufficient justification for punishment, either alone or in combination with deterrent or retributive aims. I shall argue that punishment (in the sense of hard treatment) cannot promote, and thus cannot be said to aim at, the offender's good, and that these arguments therefore fail.

V. Aiming at the Good of the Offender

In order for any one of the three arguments to go through, it must be shown, not merely that aiming at the offender's good is a sufficient justification for punishment, but also that it is possible for punishment, which on the face of it harms the offender, to be said to aim at the offender's good in some meaningful sense. Moral-reform theorists argue that punishment aims at the offender's good in that it uniquely serves the purpose of communicating the nature of the wrong, thus opening the door to repentance and moral improvement. Moral reform advocates do not rest their arguments on the efficacy of moral reform; in fact, it might be said that they advocate punishment aiming at moral reform regardless of its efficacy. A repentance guaranteed to result from punishment would not be a free repentance; in order for punishment to respect the autonomy of the offender, it must allow for at least the possibility that she will choose not to repent. Similarly, a forced restoration of one's identity as a morally autonomous person attached to the good, in Morris's formulation, would be a contradiction in terms. Moreover, to convey the desired message of the degree of wrongness of the offense, the punishment must be limited by proportionality to the offense, rather than continued to the point of actual repentance. Instead, moral reform theorists require that, in punishing (for other purposes) we must also aim at (rather than secure) the moral good of the offender. In so aiming, we show our respect for the offender as a person and our concern for her good. This moral good is ideally to be achieved through the free repentance of the offender, resulting from his recognition of the wrongness of her act.[15]

What does it mean, though, to aim at the moral good of the offender if, as the moral reform theorists insist, it does not mean that we necessarily achieve that good? These theorists don't mean simply that we subjectively hope that the punishment will morally benefit the offender; instead, they seek to show that punishment (hard treatment) is necessary to the communication of the moral message and, ultimately, to the offender's repentance and moral development. Recall that the reason why punishment must aim at the good of the offender is so that we will not be treating her as a mere means to social ends, but instead as a person who is valuable in her own right.

I shall argue that we don't have this aim or intention in the required sense—in the sense required to treat the offender as an end in herself—unless there is a reasonable chance of success, that is, unless the offender can be expected to receive the communication as sent and to change her moral character accordingly. Subsequently, I shall argue that state punishment typically cannot succeed in these efforts.

The end of moral reform is in itself unobjectionable. What is problematic is the use of hard treatment to achieve it. When we seek to justify the use of hard treatment on the ground that we are aiming at moral reform (or to rescue other justifications from objection on this same ground), we must at a minimum show that there is some reason to think that it will have the intended effect, even if we are for other reasons precluded from promising its efficacy. If I believe, for example, that sexual intercourse is proper only for purposes of procreation, I can't justify engaging in it when I know that the conditions for successful procreation are absent. Nor can I in good faith claim that I intended to keep a promise when I knew at the time of making it that I would in all probability be overwhelmed by other obligations that would prevent me from doing so.

Similarly, we cannot be said to "intend" to communicate *p* unless we believe that our target will receive the message as *p*. Suppose that a man wishes to communicate his social availability to women (*p* = I am socially available). He chooses what might, in logical and abstract terms, be considered an "appropriate" method: he (truthfully) tells every woman he meets he would like to have sex with her. Because of the likely effects of that particular form of communication on (most of) its recipients, and because the message received is not likely to be the one sent (that is, most women will interpret it as an insult), the purpose of communicating social availability cannot justify the attempted communication, even if the subjectively intended message is otherwise desirable and appropriate.[16] To give a more extreme example, suppose that I see you savagely kicking a defenseless person, but know only a few words of your language. If I know that, in your language, "stop" means "kill," I cannot justify yelling "Stop! Stop!" on the ground that I intended to discourage you from what you were doing (even if I have no other way of sending the message).

Similar reasoning applies if we know that the message is likely to be understood but rejected by most of its recipients. If I know that you think John is a liar, I can't justify choosing him to deliver a warning of imminent danger, even if he is otherwise best suited for the task. In the case of punishment, perhaps the message can be delivered only by the state (or by "society" in some form). We may know that offenders will reject any message coming from the state, yet have no alternative means of delivering the message. If I know you think I am a liar, and I can't turn the job of warning you over to anyone else, shouldn't I still warn you? Perhaps so— as long as no other harm is done by the warning. But now suppose that not only do you actively distrust me, but the only means I have of delivering the message is by causing you physical harm. (Perhaps my message is "don't go down that path" and I can only deliver it by tripping you every time you try to go that way—which you will of course interpret as simple malice on my part.) Our putative concern for the offender's moral character is hollow if it is predictable that we will not only fail to improve it but also do palpable harm.

Despite the nonteleological nature of moral reform theory, it will nevertheless be important to consider the mechanism through which punishment might be thought to promote moral reform in order to evaluate its claim that punishment must aim at the moral good of the offender. If, as

I shall argue, the mechanism through which moral improvement might occur is lacking, it will be shown that punishment cannot legitimately be said to aim at the moral good of the offender. To the extent that other justifications (such as deterrence and retributivism) are constrained by the requirement of also aiming at the offender's moral good, those justifications will fail, because the requirement cannot be met. Justification on straight paternalist grounds will also be shown to be precluded because of the improbability that punishment will result in the desired good of moral improvement.

I shall argue that the state, unlike the family, is not in a position to effect the kinds of emotional changes that are necessary to the improvement of moral character. I argue that good moral character has both a cognitive and an emotional component, only the latter of which can be affected by punishment. But in order for punishment to change emotional attachments, the offender must also be emotionally attached to the punisher in a way that most offenders are not attached to the state.

A person having a good moral character has a defensible view of what is morally right, is disposed to act in accordance with that view, and is morally autonomous, that is, she has the ability to make her own independent evaluation of what is morally right.[17] Moral development thus has both a cognitive and an emotional component. The cognitive component consists of the development of appropriate moral beliefs and the ability to apply them to new situations. The emotional component consists of the development of a disposition to act in accordance with those beliefs—that is, the development of a set of emotional attachments to values. Change or development of moral character involves either cognitive moral learning, the development of new attachments, or a conflict of attachments resulting in a change in the structure of attachments to values.

In a well-known essay, W. V. O. Quine postulates that our (cognitive) beliefs are (more or less) coherently structured, with some beliefs being more central to the entire system than others.[18] Faced with a choice, we will give up less central beliefs rather than more central ones; but even the most central ones (mathematical truths, for example) are subject to correction given a sufficient threat to other parts of the belief structure. The structure of our attachments to values is similar. We are deeply attached to some of our values, just as we are deeply attached to some of our beliefs, while we have only a mild degree of attachment to others. When multiple attachments can no longer be simultaneously sustained, we will typically choose to sacrifice the one to which we are less firmly attached.[19]

If my favorite food turns out to be cancer causing, I am likely either to discount its delights or to minimize my fear of cancer. If I discover that my religion conflicts with my sexual preferences, one or the other will have to be changed. Just as beliefs about logic and coherence have the function of adjudicating among conflicting beliefs, our most central values have the function of adjudicating among conflicting values. For example, I value my own material well-being; I also value the well-being of others. Sometimes (if not constantly) the two conflict. Sometimes it is possible for me to sacrifice my material well-being for that of others with little or no sense of loss; this is when my attachment to some third value, such as fairness, tells me that it is my own well-being that must give way. When we say that fairness demands that I pay my debts, we speak of a psychological as well as an ethical demand. The degree of my attachment to ethical values such as fairness can be measured by the extent to which I will in practice sacrifice other values (which need not be limited to my own well-being) to adhere to them.

Although values and beliefs are strongly interactive, they are not identical. At the extreme, I may hold ethical beliefs in the same way that I hold beliefs about theorems of geometry; it would take a lot to convince me that they are not true, but I do not really care about them very much. (I have no attachment to the good.) I may believe strongly (that is, fairly centrally) that discrimination against some group is wrong (giving up this belief would seriously disrupt my belief system), yet fail to be disturbed by instances of such discrimination: I simply judge them wrong, but they don't bother me. A person of good moral character has a structure of moral beliefs that is defensible on a cognitive level and a structure of attachments to values that is appropriate to their place in that belief structure. Such a person not only believes strongly that slavery is wrong, but also has a high degree of emotional aversion to slavery. In fact, a person who fails to have a defensible set of moral beliefs, but who is attached to a defensible set of values, will in one sense have a better moral character than the person who does have a defensible set of moral beliefs, but who is excessively attached to his own well-being on an emotional level. We can imagine, for example, a professor of moral philosophy who has developed a sophisticated moral theory of which he is justifiably proud, and to which he of course subscribes, but who miserably fails to put this theory into practice. Similarly, we can imagine a person who believes, on a cognitive level, in the relevance of many indefensible distinctions among persons, but who is yet, on an emotional level, given to an indiscriminate compassion which in practice leads him to ignore those distinctions.[20] Each fails to give effect to his cognitive moral beliefs—itself a moral failing—but the second is a morally better person than the first, in the sense that more of his actions will be morally defensible.

A person's moral character, then, consists in part of the complex of values to which he is attached and the strength of these attachments. Attachments to the welfare of particular persons and to religious and cultural values are necessarily, if messily, mixed in with attachments to ethical values. I say "necessarily," because these attachments can conflict across category boundaries, and the ways in which such conflicts are resolved reflect directly on moral character. The conflict is often both a conflict of beliefs, on the cognitive level, and a conflict of attachments on the emotional level, but may involve emotional attachments without corresponding beliefs. The degree of a person's attachment to the value of fairness, for example, is best measured in relation to the lengths to which he will go to discount his attachments to particular persons. (Note that this is not a conflict between fairness and loyalty; loyalty is, to some degree at least, independent of the felt degree of attachment.) Similarly, cultural values, such as the preservation of a deeply patriarchal social structure, may directly conflict with ethical values, as may at least a subset of religious values, such as obedience to the rulings of church authorities. I make here no substantive claim, either that ethical values must always be primary, or the contrary; I simply point out that all of these values occupy to some extent the same domain, in that the areas in which they influence behavior overlap to a significant degree.

For punishment to change moral character, then, it must either change our cognitive judgments or our value attachments. Punishment has been used, historically, in an effort to promote cognitive learning, although the practice is no longer fashionable. Recounting the story of his childhood in Ireland, Frank McCourt describes the methods of his schoolmasters:

> They hit you if you don't know why God made the world, if you don't know the patron saint of Limerick, if you can't recite the Apostles' Creed, if you can't add nineteen to forty-seven, if you can't subtract nineteen from forty-seven, if you don't know the chief towns and products of the thirty-two counties of Ireland, if you can't find Bulgaria on the wall map of the world that's blotted with the spit, snot, and blobs of ink thrown by angry pupils expelled forever.

They hit you if you can't say your name in Irish, if you can't say the
Hail Mary in Irish, if you can't ask for the lavatory pass in Irish.[21]

It need hardly be said that such methods are singularly ill-designed for
the imparting of cognitive knowledge. At most, the blow conveys that a
specific answer is wrong in the eyes of the teacher; it conveys nothing
about why the answer is wrong or how to arrive at a correct one. The
most charitable interpretation of the teachers' behavior is that they
sought to motivate their pupils to attend to their lessons, wherein cognitive information would be imparted through other means. Similarly, if the
offender believes (falsely) that his act of violence was justified because the
victim was a member of a particular despised group, the prison term can
teach that the authorities disagree with his assessment, but not that his
beliefs are wrong. Such cognitive deficits will have to be remedied
through methods apart from the punishment itself.

Hampton suggests that the punishment can convey information about
what it is like to be the victim of wrongdoing:

By giving a wrongdoer something like what she gave to others, you are
trying to drive home to her just how painful and damaging her action
was for her victims, and this experience will, one hopes, help the wrongdoer to understand the immorality of her action.[22]

There may indeed be some few cases in which the offender literally fails
to understand or appreciate what it is like to be harmed in the way he has
harmed others. For example, a slumlord who inflicts uncomfortable and
unsanitary conditions on his tenants may never have experienced such deprivations himself, and might well learn a valuable lesson about the nature of his wrongdoing by being required to live in one of his own build-
ings. But much more often, knowing from experience what it is like to be
a victim, rather than being the missing piece in the offender's moral understanding, is one of the factors contributing to his seeking to victimize
others. If the reverse were more typical, we would find more offenders in
the ranks of those who have suffered little harm or deprivation in their
lives. Hard treatment can convey useful cognitive information only in the
exceptional case where the offender lacks this kind of experience.

In what sense, then, can it be said that hard treatment is necessary to
convey to the offender that his act was wrong? It is evident that the hard
treatment is not directed at instruction in morals, but is rather designed

to assure the offender's appreciation of the message on some more visceral level. We don't want him merely to understand the idea that, for example, rape is wrong, or to agree with it on a cognitive level; we want him also to have a visceral attachment to the values inherent in that belief. Duff says:

> If someone has wronged me or another, I might try to make him hear—though I cannot and should not force him to accept—my criticism: I shout at him; I chase after him as he walks away; I stand in his way as he tries to leave. I force my criticism on his attention, knowing that he will initially perceive it only as an unwelcome and unfriendly intrusion, but hoping and intending that he will come to understand and accept it for what it is.[23]

Given the above account of good moral character, in order for punishment to reach the offender on the visceral level, thus changing her moral attitudes, it would have to result in a change of value attachments. But can punishment serve this function? It is natural to think that it can, because most of us have known it to do so in the context with which we are most familiar—that of parental punishment. Indeed, both Hampton and Morris explicitly invoke this analogy to suggest that this is a central and proper purpose of punishment. I shall argue, however, that the analogy between parental and state punishment fails because it is the child's emotional attachment to the parent—an attachment not existing between offender and state—that makes possible a change in value attachments as a result of punishment.

Let us first examine how parental punishment can change value attachments. One way that we can come to be concerned about those to whom we were previously indifferent is through the concern for them of others we care about. For example, we may be concerned about the welfare of a friend's lover, whom we have never met, because we know his welfare affects our friend. Still, we do not become as concerned about his welfare as our friend is, or as concerned as we are about the welfare of our friend. It is a secondary kind of concern; and if that person's welfare ceased to affect our friend, it would cease to concern us. A fuller transferring of values occurs, however, when we come to share the reasons our friend has for being concerned about someone. For example, we may adopt as our own the friends of our friends, not just because the original friendship provides the occasion for spending time with them, but also because we are disposed to look for and to appreciate the qualities our friend values in them. The same holds for the lower level of interest and concern those close to us display in the affairs of broader groups of people. We are more open to the persuasion of the friend than of a stranger. The stranger can rely only on rational arguments; the friend appeals to our predisposition to believe that the things he values will also have value for us, as well as to our desire to retain and to deserve his respect for the qualities that form the basis of the friendship. The parent who has an appropriate concern for the interests of all others is similarly in a strong position to transfer that concern to the child, who shares the parent's reasons for that concern, and who is predisposed to believe that the things the parent values will also have value for her.

When beliefs are shown to be inconsistent, I must either give up one of the beliefs or give up my belief in consistency. Similarly, when there is a continuing conflict in my attachments, I must give up one of the attachments or find some way to accommodate both. The disciplining of children is necessary to bridge the gap between the natural attachments of children and the attachments their parents wish them to develop. Children learn that (some of) their natural attachments conflict with their attachment to the parents, not merely when there is a direct conflict of interest but also when they act contrary to the parents' values. For example, the child naturally attached to her own self-interest realizes that she cannot continue to be selfish, even in private, and retain the genuine love and approval of the parent. Thus, it is crucial that her attachment to the parent be sufficiently strong to overcome the competing tug of self-interest. A weaker attachment may well result in the child's devaluing the relationship rather than compromise her natural attachment to herself (just as adults may accept a cooling of relations with friends rather than reconsider their most central values).[24]

For the child who is strongly attached to the parents, it will not be enough to gain their outward approval. Such a child who acts against the parents' values behind their backs will feel false and undeserving when praised for her good behavior. In Haim Ginott's telling example, a child praised by his parents for his good behavior on a car trip responded by deliberately upsetting the car's ashtray, filling the car with choking dust. It later turned out that he had been quietly wishing for (and constructing in detail) an accident in which his baby brother would be killed, but he and his parents would survive. The parents' praise at this moment created such a sense of guilt and falsity that he felt the need to reveal what he saw as his "real self."[25]

The significance of the child's attachment to the parents in promoting moral development can be seen by comparing our reactions as adults to situations in which we simply desire someone's approval instrumentally to our reactions in situations where there is a genuine relationship. It is common for us to desire to gain the approval (or to avoid the disapproval) of most of those we have dealings with; such approval in general makes life more pleasant and smooths the path to our goals. But in many of these situations, the approval serves to a greater or lesser extent a purely instrumental purpose. To take an extreme example, a prisoner of war will benefit from avoiding the disapproval of his guards, who have a great deal of power over him. Thus, he may make an outward show of compliance and even respect. Nevertheless, he will not hesitate, as soon as the guard's back is turned, to drop all semblance of compliance. His desire for the guard's approval is purely instrumental, and the guard's possession and exercise of power fails utterly to reach his inner character. At the other end of the spectrum is the effect on us of those people we deeply love and respect. We ordinarily do not find it satisfactory simply to gain the outward approval of our friends; instead, we wish to be loved for our real qualities. We also want our friends' approval to be an expression of their genuine feelings for the qualities we really possess; what we seek is a connection between true selves. Such relationships are deeply satisfying. In contrast, should I obtain requital of my love of another through lies, deceit, and a false display of the qualities I know she values, my initial satisfaction will prove hollow: it is not me, but only my false representation, that she loves.

The child, then, seeks the genuine approval of the parents. Punishment can play a role in expressing strong parental disapproval both by serving as a simple expression of anger and as evidence of what the parent is willing to do to prevent the behavior. There is thus a direct tie between the parent's initial deterrent intentions and the effect on character. Here, the contrast between the parent's usual behavior and the punishment is significant, because the child knows that the parent finds it difficult to impose deprivation on her, and so knows that the parent's desire to stop the behavior is strong.

The child moves from an appreciation of the parent's willingness to impose deprivation despite his love for the child to an appreciation of the parent's attachment to the value at stake. This creates an inner conflict between the child's attachment to the parent and her attachment to values different from those of the parent, ultimately leading to the child's adopting the parent's values out of her wish genuinely to deserve the parent's approval. When the state punishes, the offender may possibly be impressed with society's attachment to the value he has violated, and with its disapproval of his conduct. But this impression, like the prisoner of war's impression that the guards are determined to prevent him from escaping, cannot by itself change the offender's moral character. For such change to occur, the offender must take the disapproval that the punishment expresses to heart; he must experience a conflict of value attachments.

State punishment can thus reach only those unusual offenders who are sufficiently attached to the state (or society) to wish not merely to gain, but also to deserve, its approval. Those lacking this relationship and attached to values conflicting with those sought to be imparted will reject the message of punishment for the simple reason that it conflicts with their own values.

The offender, though not attached in the appropriate way to the state, may be attached in this way to some subgroup such as his family or church. If these groups indicate agreement with the punishment, though they are not the ones inflicting it, there will be a basis for moral improvement through the conflict of attachments thus created. Suppose, for example, that the offender is deeply attached to his parents, who tell him that he deserves the punishment he has been given. He will then have to choose between his attachment to his parents and his attachment to the values that caused him to offend. A mechanism similar to this can be seen to operate in "reintegrative shaming" projects, in which the shame of the offender's family members on hearing victims recount his behavior operates, at least sometimes, to awaken remorse.[26] It may be argued that, because moral reform is thus a possible, if indirect, result of state punishment, we can reasonably claim that it aims at moral reform in all cases, based on the hope that the offender will have sufficiently strong attachments to some person or group that will indicate approval of his punishment.

There are significant difficulties with such a justification for hard treatment, however. We could claim to have this hope in all cases only by cultivating ignorance of whether appropriate groups, with appropriate attitudes, actually exist for a given offender. Duff suggests that we have no right to assume of any offender that he is incapable of repentance, but such an assumption is not involved in the judgment that a particular offender is not deeply attached to any group that approves of his punishment. We would thus be left with a peculiar situation: our justification for punishing, based on aiming at moral reform, would depend upon the approval of some group to which the offender is attached. This peculiarity is the direct result of the state's own inability to claim such an attachment, and thus to aim directly at moral reform. Family members can be present at a trial or hearing and can express their views to the offender, but punishment (at least in the form of imprisonment) will typically separate the offender from them and from the experience of their condemnation, as they are not the ones carrying out the punishment. If the offender is not brought to repentance before punishment, the views of persons to whom he is attached will likely have diminishing significance as the punishment proceeds. Better, it would seem, to leave it to the group to which the offender does have an appropriate attachment to determine how it will chastise him, than to rely on that attachment to make the state's punishment effective in its aims.

State punishment, in itself, will typically not touch the moral character of the offender. For some offenders, approval of that punishment by groups to which they are attached might lead indirectly to moral reform. But the state may not assume that every offender has attachments that will result in such change, and making punishment contingent on their existence would effectively put the punishment decision in private hands, as well as leaving no justification for punishment in cases where no such attachments were found.

VI. Restoring Relationships

Morris and Duff argue that punishment, in addition to constituting an attempt to change the offender's moral character, is a way of restoring ruptured relationships. Morris argues that hard treatment is also necessary for expiation of the wrong and the restoration of relationships. As an illustration, he cites the incident in *Sophie's Choice* in which a young boy is grateful to his father for imposing deprivation on him when he forgets to tend the fire that keeps his invalid mother warm.[27] A mere reprimand, Morris suggests, could not serve to expiate the boy's feeling of guilt. But requiring him to suffer a deprivation similar to that which he has caused for his mother wipes the slate clean and allows the relationships to be restored. There is a sense that he has paid for his wrong through his own suffering.

Although the story as told by Styron is persuasive—we believe that the young boy is grateful for his punishment—it nevertheless does not seem typical of our thinking about punishment. Why is it that we think, at least in this instance, that suffering expiates guilt? Why might one ever embrace suffering? It is clear that imposing suffering on oneself is not always the best way to restore relationships ruptured by one's own wrongdoing. Consider the following superficially similar scenario. While a woman is out of town for a business meeting, her husband notices that there is a loose plank in their front steps. Intending to repair the step, he removes the plank. On the way to the hardware store, however, he meets a friend and they go to a bar and get drunk. He forgets all about the step, and when the wife comes home in the dark, she falls through the missing step and breaks her leg. Overcome with remorse, her husband takes a baseball bat and breaks his own leg as well.

This reaction, while it shows genuine repentance, also indicates a lack of common sense. A more appropriate reaction on the part of the husband would be to recognize that he has injured the relationship, and to do something constructive to restore it. Doing something for his wife that will affirmatively show that he does care about her welfare will go a lot further toward restoring the relationship than doing injury to himself. Yet if, as both Morris and Duff suggest, guilt can only be expiated through the acceptance of suffering, the husband's action ought to appear reasonable and restorative.

There are, I think, two kinds of reasons why acceptance or imposition of suffering can serve to expiate guilt. Both, I shall argue, are expendable. First, there is the idea that the suffering of the wrongdoer serves to restore an abstract cosmic balance. Nozick appeals directly to this idea, contending that the wrong must be given effect as a wrong in the life of the wrongdoer.[28] The metaphysics behind this idea are questionable at best. Where is this cosmic balance, and what does it matter if it is restored? Why, in terms of actual human lives, ought we to be concerned about it? We might, in any number of other ways, seek to maintain some abstract balance. We could, for example, plant a new tree for every one that we cut down; start a fire for every fire we put out; restore to its place every pebble we kick on our path; or assure a birth for every death. Some of these balancing moves are good social policy, and others are a waste of time or worse. Imposing suffering on the offender does not, in any obvious way, restore the status quo ante. Given the sobering history of reasons people have found to impose suffering on others or to accept it themselves—from the quest for physical attractiveness to serving the will of God—we would do well to be skeptical of the claim that suffering can serve some abstract goal.

Alternatively, suffering may seem to expiate guilt and serve, at least sometimes, to restore relationships, because the imposition of punishment is the way that we conventionally recognize wrongdoing. To the extent that it is conventional in our society to recognize the doing of wrong by imposing or offering penance, we can recognize that we have done wrong through penance, or indicate that others have done so by punishment. The cultural nature of this phenomenon is evident when we compare contemporary attitudes toward penance to those of the Middle Ages. Today, a person who wore a hair shirt or flagellated himself with an iron-tipped flail to demonstrate his repentance for his sins (however vile) would probably be considered mentally ill and would certainly be considered ill-advised. Even a milder penance such as shaving one's head would likely induce the same reactions of incomprehension and mild revulsion. We no longer attach the same value to suffering as a path to redemption as we once did. The voluntary acceptance of unusual burdens certainly demonstrates sincerity in a convincing way.[29] But this is not the only way to demonstrate sincerity, nor is there any reason why such burdens must be the unproductive ones of pure penance. Today, the wrongdoer who voluntarily seeks to do good to make up for his bad deeds is a more impressive penitent than the one who imposes suffering on himself for its own sake.

We are not so far along when it comes to imposing suffering on others and often tend to feel that wrongdoers cannot be accepted into society again until they have "paid their debt." But here too, it is evident that the mere completion of a prison term seldom serves to restore an offender to the community's bosom. Ex-convicts continue to be stigmatized as dangerous and untrustworthy; we seldom feel that an offender who has served his sentence is on the same footing as a person who has committed no offense. We look instead for positive indications—education gained, religious conversion, and, most of all, good works to determine whether the crime will be forgiven or forgotten.

Plainly, the prison term alone does not permit restoration of relationships. Today, we would probably not be willing to accept the positive indicators of change as enough to restore the offender to his previous status unless he had also served his prison sentence. But again, this is at least in part a matter of convention and existing law. In the case of a known offender who had escaped conviction on a legal technicality, we would be much more likely to accept positive indicators alone as grounds for reacceptance (rather than expecting the offender to impose gratuitous suffering on himself). We expect convicted offenders to have served their sentences, because that is the normal course of events and society's expected response to wrongdoing. These conventions are not entirely out of our control, as will be discussed in chapter 8.[30]

VII. Moral Reform in an Ideal Society

I have argued that the state cannot change, or even aim at changing, the moral character of the offender through hard treatment because the offender lacks the necessary attitude toward the state. Both Duff and Morris argue that, given that punishment must aim at the moral good of the offender in order to be justified, punishment is justified only in communities united by shared values and by mutual concern and respect[31] or where "there is a general commitment among persons to whom the norms apply to the values underlying them."[32] It may seem that, even if we cannot legitimately claim that punishment in today's society aims at the moral good of the offender, such a claim might have legitimacy in a more ideally ordered society. In fact, Duff and Morris are both critical of punishment under current conditions, and argue that the move toward more ideal conditions is required in order for punishment to be justified.

Morris would limit punishment to offenders who are attached to the values of the criminal law, appreciate their significance and have an equal opportunity to comply with them, yet freely decide to violate them. Duff would require that the law serve the common good of the community, which must be a "genuine community, united by shared values and mutual concern and respect."[33] In such circumstances, might the offender have the necessary emotional attachment to the state to facilitate moral reform?

As we have seen, punishment cannot convey cognitive knowledge, so if punishment is to be directed at moral reform, some change in value attachments must be contemplated. It might easily be true that the offender, while attached to the values of the criminal law, is not strongly enough attached, so that he has allowed (for example) his self-interest to override that attachment. (He values property institutions, say, but not enough to turn down a tempting opportunity to make off with someone else's cash.) But the changing of his value attachments through punishment will be possible only if he experiences a conflict of attachments such that he is constrained to reduce his attachment to his own selfish interests and to increase his attachment to the values represented by the law. The simple experience of interference with his own interest through punishment can only reinforce his attachment to himself; and any appeal to this attachment (of the form "this is what happens to you when you do wrong") would vitiate the claim that we are teaching a moral, rather than a prudential, lesson.

To be reached on the level of moral character by punishment, he must be sufficiently attached to the punisher to wish not merely to gain, but also to deserve, its approval. This attachment must be strong enough to compete with the offender's attachment to his own interest, so that he will choose to reduce that latter attachment in order to deserve approval. The fairness of the laws and their equal application to all (even if perceived by the offender) will not assure the offender's deep desire for the approval of the lawgiver, just as my participation in a tennis tournament with fair rules does not assure my wish to deserve the approval of the referee. I may wish instead to cheat at every opportunity in order to gain the prize, which I already know I do not deserve. If caught cheating, and punished for it, I may merely regret that I did not cheat more effectively. I will change my attitude toward rule compliance only if it conflicts with a deeper attachment. The ability of punishment to reach the offender (and thus the plausibility of saying we are aiming at his good) depends on his emotional attachment to the punisher, and not on the fairness of the laws or his attitude toward them. He must find the disapproval of the punisher, expressed in punishment, painful in precisely the sense that it represents separation from the punisher.

It is conceivable that in some society other than our own one might stand in such a relation to the state (or to society as a whole). Such relations might obtain in a tightly knit community of which the offender regards himself as a true member, so that his separation from it (and its values) is genuinely experienced as painful. In such a society, punishment might plausibly be said to aim at the offender's moral good, just as parental punishment aims at the moral good of the child. But, even if the other objections to paternalist, constrained-retributive, or constrained-deterrent punishment could be met, it would be far from clear that we ought to aspire to such a social structure in order to be able to justify the imposition of punishment. The desirability of the sense of belonging likely to be achieved in a closely knit community has to be weighed against the desirability of independence and individuality more likely to be found in a more loosely knit social structure. This conflict has been the subject of extensive debate between communitarians and liberals; I do not seek to enter that discussion here. Instead, I simply note that, if such a social structure is in fact established, the objection that the state cannot properly be said to aim at the moral good of the offender will not apply.

VIII. Conclusion

The argument that punishment is necessary to communicate the nature and degree of wrongness of the offense, or to expiate the wrong and restore relationships, has been shown to fail for several reasons. The straight paternalist argument (punishment to promote the offender's moral good) depends upon the acceptance of one of two implausible claims: either that we are always justified in intervening to promote someone else's good, or that the preference for physical liberty over moral reform is unreasonable. As well, it depends on the claim that punishment can in fact induce moral reform. But punishment cannot impart cognitive truth, and the state is not in a position to affect the value attachments of most offenders.

The failure of the straight paternalist justification also means that we cannot use our aim of promoting the offender's good as a way of avoiding the objection that, in punishing for crime-preventive purposes, we are using him as a mere means to social ends. Adding another unjustified alternative end, unchosen by the offender, simply gives him a choice of unjustified impositions.

Because the mechanism through which punishment can promote moral development is lacking in state punishment, constraining retributive theory by requiring that punishment also aim at the moral good of the offender would mean that state punishment could not be justified on retributive grounds. Perfectly just laws, evenly applied, would not suffice to assure the degree of emotional attachment to the punisher needed to establish the required mechanism for change in moral character.

Given a tightly knit community from which separation is psychologically painful to the offender, the mechanism for moral change through punishment could be present. In such a case, the paternalist and constrained-deterrent arguments would still fail to go through for the other reasons noted above. The constrained-retributive argument for punishment would apply in such conditions, but this does not by itself provide a conclusive reason for preferring this type of community to one that is more loosely structured and, unlike the society in which laws are fair and evenly applied, it is not self-evidently desirable.

7

Is Punishment Justified?

In the preceding chapters, I have considered the main lines along which current justifications of punishment have been proposed: that it does more good than harm, primarily through deterrence and incapacitation; that it is good to harm offenders, because doing so annuls the crime; vindicates the victim, assuages justified anger, preserves the moral order, or counts as justified self-defense; and that it aims at the benefit, rather than the harm, of offenders through moral reform. I have sought to establish that each of the proposed justifications fails, some on their own terms, and others when examined in light of the realities of criminal punishment.

I. Crime Prevention: Doing Good by Doing Harm

The purpose of crime prevention (or social control) runs through utilitarian, Kantian retributive, and self-defense justifications. Crime prevention is a worthwhile goal, but I have argued (chapter 2) that it is unlikely that punishment as presently practiced in the United States can meet the minimum utilitarian standard of doing more good than harm. Empirical studies using cost-benefit analysis have suggested that punishment is socially beneficial, but most of these studies fail to take into account negative effects on offenders. Those effects must be considered in a utilitarian reckoning and are likely sufficient to outweigh even the highest credible estimates of crime-preventive effects. Even if the good done by punishment did outweigh the harm, that would not be sufficient to establish that it is justified in utilitarian terms: it must also be compared to alternative (especially nonharmful) ways of reducing the crime rate. Given a small surplus of good over harm done by punishment, it would easily be overmatched by nonharmful social measures that made only modest reductions in crime.

Efforts to make punishment more productive of utility by restricting imprisonment to the most dangerous have failed so far, and can be expected to continue to fail, because crime is not a natural category, and the propensity to commit crimes is therefore not likely to be an isolable factor in individuals. We will therefore always have to incapacitate many who are not dangerous in order to incapacitate any who are, both reducing the net gain in utilitarian terms and raising serious questions of fairness.

Finally, punishment is unlikely to satisfy utilitarian criteria because the small amount of good it might claim to do must be weighed against other uses of social resources to prevent crime, as well as against other goods that might be done with those resources. Punishment begins at a great disadvantage in such calculations because it expends resources on doing harm. Alternative uses of funds, labor, and materials, even those that are not aimed at crime prevention, are thus likely to fare better in utilitarian terms as long as they are directed to nonharmful ends.

It could nonetheless turn out that, from a utilitarian point of view, some amount of more humane and more selective punishment would be justified. But even if punishment can be reshaped to meet utilitarian criteria, we may not harm some simply in order to prevent harm to others; to do so is to use persons as mere means to social ends—to fail to respect them as choosing beings and instead to treat them as raw material for the furtherance of social ends. In so doing, we are little better than the original offender, whom we seek to punish for violating the personhood of her victims.

Nor can we avoid this criticism by appealing to the natural right of self-defense. The future offenders against whom we would defend ourselves are distinct from the present offenders we harm through punishment. It is not self-defense to harm the offender who has defied our threats, even if his defiance leaves us somewhat more vulnerable to harm by others. When we shift harms from potential victims of future crimes to past wrongdoers, we are still using the past wrongdoers as mere means to our own ends. Similarly, because we must desist from harming others under the rubric of self-defense when we learn that the measures we are taking cannot deter them, we may not enforce our self-defensive threats against those who have shown themselves undeterred.

Constraining punishment for deterrent purposes by the requirement that it also aim at the offender's good, as urged by moral reform theories, similarly fails to treat offenders as ends in themselves, at least in the typical case in which such punishment contravenes the wishes of the offender. Giving the offender a choice as to whether the punishment will benefit him, or only benefit others (through crime prevention), fails to respect his choice not to be punished at all. Punishment for deterrent or incapacitative purposes remains unacceptable even when the prospect of moral reform is added.

Crime prevention also turns out to be important for the Kantian version of retributivism, as it appears to be the strongest of the goods proposed as a basis for imputing consent to a system of punishment. But such consent cannot be imputed to the very individuals most likely to be punished, where other social choices have made it more likely that they will commit crimes. This argument leaves some room for the imposition of punishment under an imputed social contract where these conditions have been met, but not under present social conditions.

I must acknowledge that it is possible that abolishing the institution of punishment—even gradually over a long period of time—would result in rates of crime that many would find intolerable. Such an eventuality would bring several factors into play. First, it would provide an incentive for more aggressive attempts to address the broad social causes of crime. A high rate of crime carries the message that there is widespread dysfunction: either those committing the crimes do not believe that their behavior is wrong, or they are desperate enough to do things that they know are wrong. But suppose that the limits of knowledge, and the social resources available, have been exhausted, and the rate of crime remains unacceptable by any standard. At this point it would be permissible to use punishment for social control to the extent that it had been shown *the only effective measure* to bring about a reduction in crime to tolerable levels, *and* that the risk of incurring punishment was, as a result of the social measures already deployed, both approximately equal for all and acceptably low in view of the probability of becoming a victim of crime if punishment was not used. Under these circumstances it would be reasonable—as it is not at present—to impute consent to punishment to those on whom it is inflicted. Supposing that we could not meet these criteria, we would first have to direct our efforts toward meeting them. In the meantime, we would be in the unfortunate position of a person waiting for a kidney transplant who considers the option of using inside connections to jump to the head of the list. Where the only quick way out of an intolerable situation is to trample the rights of others, the fact that the situation is intolerable does not lift our obligation to refrain.

Can we keep crime within tolerable limits without resort to punishment? In the next chapter, I shall argue that we can. Addressing the broad social causes of crime promises far greater reductions in serious crime than suggested by the most optimistic advocates of punishment. Such measures must be considered even under a utilitarian analysis, and are likely to prevail over punishment in utilitarian terms. And we cannot appeal to an imputed consent to punishment under Kantian theory unless those measures have already been implemented. In addition, the right to self-defense, while it cannot justify punishment, does justify both direct intervention to prevent crime and remedies, such as restitution, that shift the harm the offender has set in motion from the victim on to him.

II. Harming Offenders as Good in Itself

Hegelian retributivist theory claims that it is good to harm offenders—to humble their wills—because that is the only way that their crimes can be annulled. I have argued that punishment repeats the crime rather than annulling it in any meaningful sense. Punishment does not, of course, annul the crime in the sense of causing it not to have happened; in this it is crucially different from the preventive use of force, which can cause the crime not to happen. The use of coercion to defend rights may coherently be limited to such preventive uses. Punishment may be said to "annul the will" of the offender in the sense that it frustrates some of his wishes, but it does not, and cannot, annul his will to commit the crime once he has committed it.

The difficulty of making literal sense of the concept of annulling the completed crime through punishment suggests that it may be better understood metaphorically, as an assertion by the state of the victim's rights. But I have argued that Hampton's effort to explicate this concept by characterizing hard treatment of the offender as making a statement about the value of the victim is problematic. The correct statement that victim and offender are of equal value seems better made by restitution: the shifting of costs back to the offender demonstrates that the offender is not more valuable than the victim, thus affirming the value of the victim. Punishment, on the other hand, appears to assert that the offender is of lower value than the victim (just as crime asserts that the victim is of lower value than the offender). Such a statement is inconsistent both with the equality of persons and with the retributive goal of restoring the status quo ante. There appears to be no basis for justifying punishment as an annulment of the crime.

The anger of victims and society, while it may sometimes be assuaged by punishment, does not itself provide a basis for the infliction of punishment. Although anger is a justifiable response to the correct perception of undeserved harm, it is not an inevitable result of such a perception, nor is it invariably the morally best response. It is a morally preferable response—and thus a response deserving of encouragement—only where it serves as a needed impetus to morally preferable action. The demand for change that characterizes anger may move us to act in destructive as well as constructive ways. Anger as a response to crime will take its specific goal from underlying attitudes about harm to enemies—attitudes that must find their own separate justification. Thus I have argued that vindictive anger—which specifically seeks harm to the wrongdoer—will justify punishment only to the extent that such harm can already be justified on other grounds.

III. Harming Offenders for Their Own Moral Good

The attempt to promote the moral good of the offender cannot be the sole justification for punishment, primarily because such a justification is predicated upon unacceptable assumptions about when paternalism is justified. To justify punishment on the sole ground that it is for the offender's good requires that we either adopt the extreme paternalist position that we may override the self-determination of others as long as we do so for their own good, or show that it is unreasonable for offenders to prefer physical liberty to moral improvement, so that substituting our judgment for theirs requires only a moderately paternalistic stance. Neither of these positions is promising. The preference for physical liberty over one's own moral good is reasonable, as is the reverse preference.

Advocates of punishment as moral reform have instead sought to show that a concern for the promotion of the offender's moral good should be coupled with either a deterrent or a retributivist rationale. But constraining deterrent or retributive purposes by a requirement that they also aim at the good of the offender vitiates those rationales, because punishment cannot impart cognitive understanding, and the state typically lacks the kind of relationship with the offender that is necessary for punishment to affect his value attachments. These considerations would not be mitigated by perfectly just laws evenly applied. Such a justification for punishment might be applicable in a particular type of tightly knit community, where there is a significant emotional attachment of the offender to the community at large; but it is likely that such a community would be able to restore value attachments without resort to punishment.

IV. Conclusion

The grave harms done by punishment are not justified by any of these lines of argument. Insofar as punishment prevents crime, it does so by using offenders as mere means to the ends of others. Punishment repeats the crime, rather than annulling it, and creates new victims rather than vindicating the original ones. It does not serve the moral good of offenders or make any communication that cannot be made through language or symbolic means. It is time to consider how we might live in a world without this institution.

8

What If Punishment
Is Not Justified?

I. Introduction

We have seen that punishment as a social institution, and particularly as currently practiced in our society, is deeply problematic. The question naturally arises whether it is an institution that we can, in practical terms, do without. Is the price of a morally defensible approach to crime complete social disintegration? I think we need not become moral martyrs; that the criminal justice system is not in fact serving the functions we intend it to serve; and that measures short of punishment can serve many of these functions as well as or better than current punishment practices. Rather than seeking to prevent crime by deterring or incapacitating offenders, we can address the structural, cultural, and psychological causes of crime at the level of social policy while using defensive measures to discourage crime and force to prevent imminent harm. For crimes we cannot prevent, we can continue to try and convict offenders, communicating censure through symbolic condemnation and requiring offenders to compensate victims, as well as offering victims appropriate emotional support. Keeping a public record of convictions will expose offenders to a range of social sanctions that may lead them to seek reconciliation. For those offenders who are open to change or seek expiation, we can offer the opportunity for voluntary redress through reconciliation hearings, apology, and a level of social contribution commensurate with the seriousness of the crime.

The kinds of measures that might be used to replace punishment are implicit in the arguments I have given against the various justifications of punishment. With respect to prevention, I argued in chapter 2 that using punishment to prevent crime probably causes more harm than good; there are other ways to prevent crime without doing harm; and punishment uses offenders as mere means to social ends. Thus, we must seek out non-harmful methods of preventing crime to avoid these criticisms. In chapter 4 I argued that punishment is not properly characterized as fair reciprocity where, as a result of other social choices, some are much more likely than others to incur punishment, and social policies could be changed to reduce crime without imposing risks comparable to the risk of being punished. The obvious step here, as well, is to change the structural and cultural conditions known to increase crime before considering punishment.

We may not use punishment in self-defense because the past offenders we punish are not the cause of the future harms we seek to shift on to them, and punishment does not meet the necessity constraint on self-defense (chapter 5). What we *may* do is to shift harms from victims to the offenders who caused them, and to take self-defensive measures meeting necessity (and proportionality) constraints in situations where such measures can prevent imminent harm.

Because punishment is closely parallel to crime, it cannot annul crime or vindicate victims, and the anger of victims or others does not provide a separate justification for punishment (chapter 3). Crime can never be literally annulled, but, by requiring compensation, we can mitigate the harms that it does; and by offering emotional support to victims we can assuage their anger without using measures analogous to crime.

We may not punish offenders in order to promote their moral good because moral development as a sole purpose of punishment is unacceptably paternalistic, and state punishment cannot communicate the wrongness of the offense to offenders or promote their moral good (chapter 6). But we can communicate censure through symbolic condemnation, and we can seek to promote voluntary moral reform through the personal attachments of the offender.

I begin with changing conditions conducive to crime as an alternative to deterrent and incapacitative punishment. These conditions range from the broad social level, through the community and the family, to the individual psychological level. I suggest that change in these conditions holds out much greater promise of constructive change than punishment. Such changes are to be supplemented with more direct interventions to prevent imminent crime. Both sets of preventive measures are discussed in part II. Responses to unprevented crime are considered in part III.

II. Crime Prevention

At present, our main strategy for crime prevention is to try to reduce the motivation of potential offenders through the general threat of apprehension and punishment, and to isolate those who have already committed crimes. This strategy, I have argued, is not morally defensible. But it has other weaknesses as well. It does not address the sources of deep social alienation. Instead, by taking an aggressive stance, it encourages marginalized individuals to see themselves as locked in battle with the forces of order, so that getting away with behavior that harms others becomes the goal and refraining from such behavior becomes capitulation. This is a battle we should not fight. We should instead turn our attention to the underlying causes of crime and to the constructive measures that can be taken to respond to it.

We can assume that punishment exerts some downward pressure on the crime rate, although I have argued that this effect is likely insufficient to outweigh its negative effects. But punishment is not the only way to reduce crime, and I have argued that the possibility of achieving crime reduction in other ways undercuts both utilitarian and reciprocity arguments for punishment. Crime is not solely a function of the bad moral decisions of individuals. There is broad (though not universal) agreement among criminologists that social factors such as income inequality, poverty, unemployment, and local social disorganization contribute to crime. In addition, some individuals are at higher risk of committing crimes because of physical or sexual abuse, drug dependence, lack of job skills, and mental illness. The mechanisms by which these various factors affect the crime rate, and the extent to which they do so, are disputed,[1] and I do not pretend to resolve that dispute here. Instead, I shall discuss how, in an effort to prevent crime without punishment, we might address the causes of crime most commonly cited by criminologists today.

A. Reduce Income Inequality

Income inequality in the United States rose almost 25 percent on the Gini scale in the 1980's and is significantly greater than in other stable industrial democracies.[2] The connection between income inequality at the national level and violent crime is well documented worldwide.[3] Yet such inequality can easily be reduced by redistributive taxation, which requires much less in the way of resources than a prison system. Messner and

Rosenfeld suggest that income inequality is not an aberration, but rather represents a necessary backdrop to the culture of economic competition, providing significant stakes for players of the game.[4] If they are right, change in the income structure may have to be preceded by cultural change. Moving money away from the wealthy is also made more difficult by the political power that money can buy, while spending tax money on more prison space is politically easy. Thus, the social choice to date has been for income inequality, and for the costs that it imposes in the form of a higher rate of violent crime. It is open to us to continue to make that choice, recognizing that when we do so we are choosing a higher risk of victimization. Alternatively, we can wage a fight on both political and cultural fronts for greater equality and lower rates of crime.

B. Reduce Poverty and Provide Job Training

Since the Kerner Commission concluded in 1967 that "crime flourishes where the conditions of life are the worst," it has been a commonplace that poverty breeds crime. Poverty (absolute deprivation) is a separate issue from income inequality (relative deprivation). Poor countries do not always have higher rates of crime than wealthier ones, and the poor of the United States are better off in absolute terms than the poor of most nations. It is nevertheless true that higher rates of crime are found in severely impoverished communities and among the unemployed. Recent work suggests that it is not the temporarily unemployed, but the chronically unemployed young man who is likely to turn to crime.[5] Such individuals often face multiple obstacles to decent employment: poor literacy, lack of skills, learning disabilities, lack of role models or sources of effective counseling, drug dependency, and so on. If these problems could be effectively addressed, the burden of unemployment caused by economic fluctuations could be spread more widely across the population and would cease to be a crushing chronic burden on particular individuals and communities. These are not easy problems, but it would be relatively easy to put within reach of all families the resources that middle-class families now call upon when their children face school and other life difficulties. Not every middle-class family is able to rescue a troubled child from lifelong problems, but they have a much better chance of doing so than poor families. Services such as individual counseling, drug treatment, and help with finding a job are now sometimes offered to youths who have run afoul of the law; there is no reason, except lack of funds, not to offer those and other services to all. Doing so would, again, reduce the dramatic differences between rich and poor, lowering the stakes in the economic competition and probably decreasing economic efficiency. Again, we can choose: maximum efficiency, or lower crime rates?

C. Foster Social Organization in Crime-Prone Communities

Some communities, as Robert Sampson and William Julius Wilson have shown, have particularly high rates of crime even when compared to demographically similar communities. What these particularly crime-prone communities seem to have in common is a high level of local social disorganization, caused, in their view, by the interaction of larger social forces (such as housing discrimination and the transformation of the economy from an industrial to a service economy) with community-level factors (such as residential turnover and concentrated poverty). For example, the flight of more stable middle-class black families to the suburbs results in a higher local concentration of poverty, while high residential turnover contributes to the loss of community networks that aid supervision and accountability. At the same time, concentrated unemployment resulting from loss of nearby industrial jobs both reduces opportunities and decreases the availability of marriageable partners, so that single motherhood becomes the norm. In this environment, youths increasingly lack positive role models, and groups of unsupervised teens become more prevalent.[6]

These problems, many of which are attributable to poor public policy in the first place, can also be addressed by policy changes. More broadly distributed public housing can reduce concentrations of poverty. Since Wilson's 1987 work first highlighted this issue,[7] some efforts have been made in this direction. In recent years, however, the focus has been on denying priority to the poorest eligible families to achieve a more mixed population in public housing, and demolishing large public housing complexes.[8] The residents of demolished units have been offered vouchers, but the reduction in total housing stock has in turn increased the likelihood that more people will become homeless. Such policies may in fact decrease residential concentrations of poverty, but doing so at the expense of increasing the desperation of the poor simply trades one factor in high crime rates for another. These policies—and more globally, the sheer unwillingness of governments and taxpayers to spend money on housing for the poor—must change if residential concentrations of poverty are to be addressed in a meaningful way.

Key to the social disintegration of the communities Sampson and Wilson studied was the exodus of middle-class blacks to the suburbs. These residents had been the backbone of local organizations such as churches and community centers, as well as providing a local network of longtime residents who knew each other, knew each other's children, and were therefore a source of continuing support and supervision.[9] This kind of network, once disrupted, is not easily put back into place. But measures can be taken to encourage stability of residence, by preventing the development of the conditions that make neighborhoods unlivable. For example, when there is a sudden loss of jobs because a large employer closes down, assistance should be provided to jobless workers before their lack of income further reduces their available choices. They may need help in the form of retraining, resume preparation, or transportation to job sites, for example. What is likely to make the biggest difference, over all, would be acting on the understanding that job loss is not simply an individual misfortune, for the individual to deal with as best he can, but rather a community-level problem to which resources must be devoted. The current approach, at its best (a best it has not seen in recent decades) is to provide a fixed level of assistance to those individuals who have the initiative to seek it out; when that assistance is exhausted, the community in effect shrugs its shoulders and gives up on the problem. Many are thus left with nowhere to turn, or do not know where to turn in the first place. Again, these are frustrations unknown to the middle-class person, for whom there is always another (if a less desirable) option: unable to get a job at his former level, he accepts one at a lower level; unable to find work in his field, he retrains in a new one; unable to find work at all, he calls upon family and friends for aid until things improve; they, in turn, make sure that he is directed to appropriate medical or counseling resources. The gap left when these alternatives are lacking for an individual, and especially for a large number of individuals in a particular community, has to be filled if the blight of local social disorganization is to be halted.

D. Support Families to Reduce Stress and Increase Supervision

Both social disorganization and institutional-anomie theories of crime identify the tremendous strains on working families as significant contributors to crime. Lack of broad cultural support for the family as an important institution and for the nurturing of children as important work combines with economic strain to produce troubled, often dismembered, families unable to provide effective nurturing or supervision for their children.[10] Such children are easily recruited by rudderless peer groups that are fertile breeding grounds for criminal activity. Culture cannot be changed by fiat, but governmental agencies do not have to participate in spreading the message that the economic sphere is the only one that counts. Schools can support the idea that family life is as important as work life; community centers can offer classes on parenting as well as counseling and support for overburdened parents. Instead of viewing children as consumer luxuries for their parents, we must learn to see them as everyone's responsibility. Parents must be provided with the resources to give their children the attention they need for healthy development. From a broader point of view, this makes sense because without children, society will die. From the narrow point of view of crime prevention, it makes sense because if we refuse to help struggling parents, some predictable number of their children will turn to crime.

I am no expert on social policy, and no doubt my policy suggestions are unsophisticated, if not entirely wrongheaded. But the point is that there is a body of knowledge about the social factors associated with crime, and there is also a body of knowledge about how to address those issues most effectively. It is obvious that in many respects we have simply chosen not to address them, or to do so in suboptimal ways. My point at bottom is that we can and should draw on these bodies of knowledge to derive policies that will reduce crime without raising the serious moral issues associated with punishment, and that indeed have a much greater potential for long-term crime reduction than any penal policy.

It is worth noting that most of the social factors associated with reduced crime are also independently desirable as ways to foster individual development and flourishing. Some, however, will find many of them objectionable as interferences with economic efficiency, as contrary to the spirit of rugged individualism, or even (in some instances) as unconstitutional. Such critics must yet accept that the enforcement of a social preference for these values comes—insofar as we can tell from current research—at the price of a higher rate of crime. Punishment, I have argued, is ruled out as an approach to crime prevention. The question, then, becomes one of choosing between the alternatives of preventing crime through social measures such as those I have suggested above, on the one hand, and accepting the higher rates of crime caused by their opposites, on the other. What is not acceptable, I have argued, is choosing the set of policies that tend to increase crime, and relying on punishment to reduce the rate of crime thus produced.

E. Intervene to Prevent Imminent Harm

The approach I have suggested so far would not bring immediate dividends in the form of lower crime rates, even if it was wildly successful in the long term. But measures aimed more immediately at crime prevention need not be dispensed with entirely. As we have seen, the objections to using punishment as a method of crime prevention do not apply to direct intervention to prevent crime. When the police intervene to prevent burglaries or assaults in progress, for example, we don't need to strain the analogy of self-defense to justify such direct defensive action, taken before the harm is done.

We do not, of course, wish to restrict our crime-preventive efforts to the last ditch, nor do we need to do so. My objections to punishment and preventive detention do not apply to surveillance of those reasonably suspected of criminal activity or to disruption of criminal conspiracies or operations. The use of passive defenses—or what criminologists call "target-hardening"—raises none of the issues posed by punishment. We may use locks, bars, fences, alarms, and even barbed wire or tire-damaging spikes to prevent people from entering places from which they are legitimately excluded without exceeding our right to self-defense, assuming that any harm done by such measures is both proportional to the harm threatened by trespassers and necessary to prevent that harm. (We may not, for example, defend our right to collect entrance fees to parking lots through the use of land mines, or defend our homes from burglars with spring guns, because the force used is disproportionate to the property rights defended.) Those who ignore or circumvent these measures may be arrested and removed before they do further damage. The detention of an individual until the opportunity or motive for commission of a specific crime that he clearly intends has passed may well pass muster as defensible direct intervention (again depending on proportionality and necessity constraints). For example, participants in a barroom brawl might be detained until sober; members of feuding gangs might have their activities curtailed until they are able to resolve their differences. Such specific interventions raise far fewer problems than detention for inchoate "dangerousness."

III. Responding to Unprevented Crimes

Even full implementation of the measures I have suggested so far would not prevent all crimes, and might not prevent as many as punishment. Clearly, it will not do simply to ignore those that are committed. The harms—and the wrongs—done by crime cannot be undone, and for many victims of serious crime life will never be the same. It is important for victims, and for the community, that these wrongs be acknowledged and condemned in a meaningful way. For those harms that can be redressed, some means of redress must be provided. How can we do these things without punishment? I shall argue that they can be done through formal condemnation, requiring compensation, and providing an opportunity for voluntary reconciliation and the making of amends.

A. Communicate Wrongness through Trial and Symbolic Condemnation

The formal processes that we now use as a prelude to criminal punishment themselves serve many of the purposes ascribed to punishment, without raising the same serious moral issues. Even the preliminary public events of arrest and formal charging have been shown to have some deterrent effect for those most likely to care about their reputations as solid citizens. The trial provides an occasion for the victim to be heard and assures that blame is not improperly placed. Conviction by judge or jury in itself carries a measure of condemnation of the defendant's conduct and corresponding vindication of the victim. The cognitive communication that the defendant's conduct was wrong and is condemned by his community is well begun by the verdict and can be elaborated upon by the judge as she sees fit; it might be appropriate for the judge to announce some formal measure of just how wrong the defendant's conduct was, perhaps by comparing it to well-known earlier cases. Finally, the entry of the judgment against the defendant's name in public records will provide an appropriate caution to anyone who cares to inquire.

We may well fear that the offender will be untouched by the judge's words of condemnation, that he and others will be undeterred from similar behavior in the future, and that the court proceedings will not change his character for the better. We should remember, though, that the same objections apply with similar force to punishment. Those who don't care for the opinions of their fellows can rather seldom be made to do so through harshness; those who do care may well find the solemn public condemnation reason enough to repent.

B. Vindicate Victims and Reverse Some Effects of Crime by Requiring Compensation

Current victim-offender reconciliation programs are premised on the idea that the needs of victims are given insufficient attention by the criminal justice system, which may relegate them to the role of witness or exclude them entirely from the process. The victim-offender reconciliation proceeding or victim-offender mediation, in which the offender hears the victim's account of the crime and the harm that it did, can benefit victims in several ways. It provides an outlet for the victim's emotions, often leading to a reduction in fear and anger. The offender may offer an apology, backed up by willingness to make appropriate reparations. Victims may be skeptical of the sincerity of the apology,[11] but often find partial or symbolic restitution on the part of the offender more meaningful than compensation that comes from the state.[12] Although most studies show that the majority of victims feel they had an opportunity to be heard and are satisfied with the outcome, a significant minority report feeling worse after the hearing than before.[13] A great deal depends upon the sensitivity with which the hearing is conducted, and the skill of the leader in bringing it to a successful conclusion. Making such programs routine, rather than exceptional, would likely raise significant challenges in maintaining and improving the quality of the hearing and the outcome for victims. At minimum, victim participation must be voluntary and victims should be informed in advance of the possibility of an undesired outcome.

That said, the reconciliation proceeding, or something similar, has potential for addressing the anger of victims in a way that is much more appropriate than providing vindictive satisfaction through harsh penalties. I argued in chapter 4 that justified anger does not provide an independent basis for punishment. Anger in response to undeserved harm is justified anger, but the resulting demand for action in the form of punishment of the wrongdoer depends on the separate judgment that it is good to make wrongdoers suffer—a judgment that I have argued is unsupported. What we can offer to victims is, first, a clear recognition that they have been wronged; second, an opportunity to express their anger and to have it validated; third, the meeting of the demand for action by requiring compensation; and finally, the possibility that the offender will offer a face-to-face apology.

Currently, recognition that the victim has been wronged is bound up with punishment of the offender. Reconciliation hearings that are offered as an alternative to court adjudication bypass judgment and sentencing, thus potentially leaving victims feeling that the wrong done has not been recognized, to the extent that the reconciliation proceeding does not result in the offender's accepting responsibility. The nature of such proceedings may inhibit the facilitator from expressing any opinion at all. In addition, many offenders are not caught, and the victims of those crimes typically receive no recognition beyond the taking of their report by the police. Dispensing with punishment entirely, as I have argued we should, would remove one of the ways in which victims can obtain recognition that they have been subjected to undeserved harm.

It is important to remember, however, that the use of punishment as recognition of wrong done is largely conventional, and conventions can be changed—not overnight, but eventually. The process of trial and formal judgment can itself offer official recognition of the wrong. Appropriate compensation for all victims—including victims of crimes whose perpetrator is never apprehended—would provide further evidence that the victim's rights are valued.

In shifting the costs of the harm done to the wrongdoer, insofar as that is possible, we act on a principle similar to that underlying self-defense: where the offender's culpable actions have resulted in costs that would not otherwise have to be paid, we are justified in choosing that the person to bear those costs will be the offender. He incurs these costs in much the same way as he incurs other debts, for example, ordering food in a restaurant or destroying his own property. In shifting the harm from the victim to the offender, we do not impermissibly use the offender as a means to social ends; instead, we make him bear the consequences of his own choices. Importantly, in shifting harms in this way, we do not increase the total harm done, but only reallocate it to the person responsible for its existence.

Compensation is not subject to the same objections as retributive punishment. It is a question of the shifting of harm from the victim to the offender who brought it about, rather than a question of imposing an additional, gratuitous harm over and above that caused by the offense. The metaphors often used in defense of retribution ("paying one's debt to society," "restoring the balance," "removing unfair advantage," "annulling the crime") apply much more obviously and literally to compensation. The principle underlying self-defense—that harms may be shifted from the innocent to those responsible for them—does not support punishment, but does support making offenders pay the costs of their crimes. For the state to require offenders to undo, insofar as possible, the harm they have done is also unequivocally to affirm and vindicate the rights of victims—a function I have argued retributive punishment does not serve.

It will not have escaped the reader's notice that the shifting of harm from wrongdoer to innocent is exactly the principle that underlies civil liability. Many criminal defendants, of course, are unable to pay damages; some have thought that this is the primary reason we have the criminal law as well as the civil law. Nietzsche presents a darker version of this view: where the offender cannot pay with money, he must pay with suffering; punishment is compensatory because we revel in the suffering of others.[14] Rather than indulge such notions, we might do better to ask how else compensation can be assured.

Under the current civil law, tortfeasors who have no significant assets or income are considered "judgment-proof" and are rarely sued. Moreover, smaller judgments entered against individuals are seldom collected because collection, and the payment of its costs, are left in the hands of the successful plaintiff. In turn, plaintiffs who are aware of this state of affairs seldom pursue civil suits in which the stakes are low or the prospective defendant is not wealthy. As a result, a large proportion of the civil damages to which crime victims are even now theoretically entitled remains uncollected. Putting collection of civil judgments (and collection costs) in the hands of the government could significantly improve this situation. Assets and wages could be attached, or the amount of compensation could be added to the offender's tax bill and be subject to withholding. It may go further: the wealthy offender may move her assets out of the jurisdiction or find ways to hide them; the wage worker may quit his job and change his name rather than continue to see compensation subtracted from his wages. It seems that at this juncture we either have to shrug our shoulders and give up on obtaining compensation for the victim or resort to the threat of punishment to force the offender to pay. Note, however, that similar moves on the part of prospective criminal defendants are not unknown, and that it is open to the state to pursue the evasive offender and to charge him for the additional costs so incurred.

Compensation rates could be increased significantly over current civil collections through the use of measures short of the threat of punishment—even though there will be some instances in which we have to give up on the possibility of collection. Credit card companies, for example, continue to thrive even though their only legal recourse against nonpayment is the civil law (imprisonment for debt was abolished in the mid-nineteenth century). There are plenty of nonpayers who have been able to get away with it, but there are many more individuals sufficiently concerned with their reputations among lenders to keep the business of extending credit going. Failure to pay compensation for crimes might become part of one's credit history as well as part of one's criminal record; both would be of interest to potential employers, and it would be difficult for nonpaying offenders to escape a range of collateral consequences.

The victims of particularly stubborn nonpayers (or of the truly destitute) need not be left out in the cold. Victims could be compensated from a common fund to which convicted offenders would be required to contribute, rather than being compensated directly by the offender; the costs of administering the fund would be considered part of the costs of the offense, to be borne by offenders. The shortfall caused by nonpaying offenders could then either be distributed over all victims through less than full compensation, or made up by tax revenues (thus distributed over all taxpayers).

C. Provide Opportunities for Reconciliation with Victim and Community

Proposals to replace punishment with restitution often meet with the objection that to do so would be to trivialize the intentional harm done to victims through crime, and to allow the wealthy to purchase the right to commit crimes whenever they choose. But it is unlikely that a person once convicted of a crime would leave the courtroom to resume her life as before, whether or not he is required to make compensation. As Roger Wertheimer points out:

> Wrongdoing can justify denying the wrongdoer claims and entitlements—to protection against injury during the wrongdoing, to the profits of wrongdoing, to goods needed to compensate victims of the wrongdoing. Further, we may properly deny loyalty to the disloyal, deny equal opportunity to the treacherous, and deny to the disaffecting any

claim on our affections. We may justly deny a wrongdoer any claim to our generosity, benevolence, esteem, trust, and virtually any of our goods. We may desert those who desert us, abandon them to a desert of their own making, a lifeless, desolate wasteland bereft of the benefits of our community and society.[15]

Although Wertheimer makes these observations in support of retributive punishment, most of the consequences of wrongdoing he notes here have little to do with criminal punishment: they are either social consequences imposed by private individuals repelled by the offender's behavior or civil sanctions imposed by the state for the purpose of compensating the victim. The social consequences, by themselves, can contribute not only to retributive ends but also to crime prevention. The person convicted of theft could expect to find it more difficult to find employment, for example. Rapists and murderers could expect virtual ostracism and constant surveillance. The social stigma created by conviction would have a much greater impact without the intervening prison sentence; offenders who did have a stake in community acceptance might find themselves seeking ways to restore themselves to the good graces of the community.

In such instances the offender might agree to some specific restoration project, which might include apology, payment of compensation, and ongoing work to resolve underlying conflicts. The reconciliation proceeding might substitute for trial (if the victim decided not to press charges after an early reconciliation hearing), or might be undertaken after conviction—perhaps initiated by an offender seeking to restore her good standing.

D. Promote Moral Change through Personal Attachments

Is this enough? Retributivists and advocates of moral reform press the point that the offender must be made to feel the weight of his wrongdoing, and that he can only be made to do so through hard treatment. But, because of the lack of an emotional bond between the offender and the state, there is little hope that punishment will accomplish this, even supposing that other objections to these theories could be met. It may be that we simply are not in a position to make him see what we want him to see. In those cases where the offender is not so deeply alienated as to be unreachable, however, our best hope of making the communication effective will be through those to whom he does have some emotional attachment. This is the premise of "reintegrative shaming" programs, which, while not unproblematic, hold out some promise of genuine change.

Police in Wagga Wagga, Australia, developed a diversion program for young offenders, based on family group conferences initiated in New Zealand. These programs, though initiated for pragmatic reasons, turned out to mesh well with John Braithwaite's idea of reintegrative shaming and are now explicitly informed by that model.[16] The program is designed for young offenders arrested for less serious offenses who have admitted to their offense. The conference is held at the police station and facilitated by a police officer, whose role is limited to resolving difficulties that arise during the conference and acting as a witness to the agreement. The offender is accompanied by his family and other supporters, and the victim by his or her supporters. The outcome of the conference is determined by the participants. A follow-up conference with the offender and family is held after four to six weeks.[17]

Braithwaite has argued that, when done appropriately, shaming can result in constructive change, as offenders are forced to drop the various rationalizations that they use to convince themselves that their behavior is permissible. One theory identifies five such rationalizations: "They can afford it," "I didn't really hurt anyone," "They're crooks themselves," and "I had to stick by my mates."[18] The conference is designed to break down these rationalizations, primarily by having the victim recount the effects of the offense in the presence of the offender and people close to him. If things unfold according to plan, the offender will find his own supporters chagrined by his behavior, and will accordingly realize the extent of its wrongfulness, show remorse, and seek to make amends. The literature is replete with touching stories of offenders who break down and cry, victims who decide he is not such a bad fellow after all, and families that vigorously support the offender's new efforts to make amends and turn his life around. This is a lot to ask from a brief hearing, and, unsurprisingly, it happens in only a minority of cases.[19] Critics argue that, contrary to the claims of its proponents, reintegrative shaming is less effective in changing offender behavior than the traditional criminal justice approach.

Preliminary results from a large experimental group in Australia show that those randomly assigned to a Family Group Conference on the reintegrative shaming model have resulting attitudes and outcomes generally comparable to those assigned to court, but notably with a large (38 percent) reduction in recidivism for youthful violent offenders.[20] This is a strength of restorative justice programs, which have overall shown a modest reduction in recidivism as compared to the traditional criminal justice approach.[21] The typical outcome of a conference was more likely to include reparations to the victim or community service and less likely to include a fine. Imprisonment was not an option for the conference group, but only a very small percentage of court-assigned offenders were sentenced to imprisonment. Significantly more conference-assigned offenders than court-assigned controls in the Australian study considered their outcome to be "severe."[22]

There are also a few disturbing stories of "shaming" gone wrong. Braithwaite stresses the distinction between "disintegrative" shaming that stigmatizes the offender and drives a wedge between him and the community, and "reintegrative" shaming that causes him to accept the view that his behavior was wrong while conveying the strong message that he is a worthwhile person who can be welcomed back into the community. But where the shaming process is left up to untrained (or poorly trained) individuals, or where the result of conferencing is heavily influenced by the desires of a vengeful victim, the result can be a horror story such as that of a shoplifter required to parade in front of the store wearing a placard: "I stole from this store" or a sex offender required to post a sign on their house and car, "Dangerous Sex Offender—No Children Allowed."[23] These stories provide a caution to those who seek to leave the conference outcome strictly up to the participants, or worse yet, strictly up to the wishes of possibly vengeful victims.

Importantly for present purposes, offender participation in these conferences is usually coerced, in that the offender who declines to participate or fails to carry out the resulting agreement will be sent to court. Thus, the shaming model is dependent upon the punitive model. Insofar as punishment is ruled out by moral considerations, obtaining cooperation through the threat of punishment is similarly ruled out. Some advocates of restorative justice consider voluntary participation a prerequisite.[24] On a practical level, voluntary participants are likely to provide more fertile soil for desired outcomes than those who are coerced. However, expansion of these programs beyond their current clientele of primarily youthful offenders would also mean that participating offenders would be more likely to be entrenched in their behavior and disinclined to repentance.

E. Protect the Community through Circles of Support

In the Ojibway community of Hollow Water, Manitoba, a widespread pattern of incest and sexual abuse (75 percent of the community of six hundred had been victimized, and 35 percent had offended) was addressed through the traditional method of the Healing Circle. This circle involves everyone who has been or will be touched by the crime or its disclosure.

> They evolved a detailed protocol of 13 steps, from initial disclosure to the Healing Contract to the Cleansing Ceremony. The Healing Contract, designed by people involved in or personally touched by the offence, requires each person to "sign on" to bring certain changes or additions to their relationships with the others. Such contracts are expected to last more than 2 years, given the challenges in bringing true healing. One is still being adhered to 5 years after its creation. If and when the Healing Contract is successfully completed, the Cleansing Ceremony is held to "mark a new beginning for all involved" and to "honour the victimizer for completing the healing contract/process."[25]

Abusers were formally charged with their crimes, and those who pleaded guilty were offered the support of the team. Team members include survivors of abuse and also past victimizers who have completed their "healing work." The team would then request a delay in sentencing as they began their work with the offender and victim(s). They work with the victim to help him or her become strong enough to confront the abuser, as well as with all those who will be affected by disclosure. After the confrontation and initial team efforts to gain the cooperation of the abuser in the healing processs, the team prepares a presentence report indicating the sincerity of the offender's participation and the amount of work that remains to be done. Although at the start of the project the team members held the view that a prison term must be imposed in "serious" cases, they have concluded after long involvement in healing work, first, that there is little correlation between the offender's degree of culpability and the severity of its effects on victims; and second, that the threat of incarceration only serves to impede the healing process:

> In order to break the cycle, we believe that victimizer accountability must be to, and support must come from, those most affected by the

victimization: the victim, the family/ies, and the community. Removal of the victimizer from those who must, and are best able to, hold him/her accountable, and to offer him/her support, adds complexity to already existing dynamics of denial, guilt and shame. The healing process of all parties is therefore at best delayed, and most often actually deterred.[26]

The Healing Circle approach requires the ongoing involvement of all those affected, as well as of medical professionals and team members. Its ultimate goal is to repair the relationships destroyed or impaired by abuse. Holding the offender accountable is an essential part of this process. Team members, informed by their own experience of abuse, work closely with offenders to overcome the psychological barriers to acknowledging responsibility. The Hollow Water approach recognizes the complexity and breadth of the effects of serious crimes, and in turn addresses them in a way that is similarly complex and far reaching.

Use of the Healing Circle is not limited to cases of endemic offending such as that found at Hollow Water, but is used in cases involving individual offenders as well. One published example is the use of a Healing Circle in a case of rape in the Innu community of Sheshahit, Labrador. As in Hollow Water, the process began between conviction and sentencing in a criminal court. After extensive preparatory work, a Healing Circle was held with friends and family of both parties to allow the offender an opportunity to take responsibility for his actions and to allow the victim to present "what needed to happen for her to feel that the situation was being made more right." After the release of much emotion by the participants and the expression of recommendations for sentencing, victim and offender (who had been previously acquainted) were sufficiently reconciled to embrace one another.[27]

The most striking feature of the Healing Circle approach is that, despite rejection of punishment, it is clearly an approach that takes crime seriously—more seriously, indeed, than the typical punitive approach. The emphasis is on restoring damaged relationships—between offender and victim, and between offender and community—rather than on the moral badness of the offender. Offenders are nonetheless made to face the harm done by their behavior and to try to make amends. Their accountability is assured by close monitoring. As with most programs, this one operates in the shadow of the criminal justice system, in that the alternative to participation in the healing circle is traditional sentencing by the court. Moreover, the influence of the group's eventual sentencing recommendation is undoubtedly a factor for many offenders. The desire for restoration would have to replace coercion as a motivation for offenders to participate, which might make it more difficult to secure their participation. It would also mean, however, that the efforts of those who did participate would be more likely to be genuine, and that there would be continued pressure on organizers to assure the meaningfulness of the program.

The approach of the healing circle is similar to that of the reintegrative shaming model, but with the important difference of ongoing participation rather than one or two brief conferences. If the shaming conference is more likely than the traditional formal trial to precipitate moral change, the ongoing involvement of team members, importantly including past offenders, in the life of the offender is more likely yet to make a real difference. The contract that persists over time and the ongoing participation of the team in the life of the offender are the key factors that make it plausible that real change and real healing can occur, even for the repeat sexual offenders in these cases.

The Ojibway approach is, of course, much more suited to a small, closed community than to the typical modern setting. But a somewhat similar approach has been taken by "circle of support" programs in Canada and the United Kingdom. These circles, formed after the offender's release from prison, consist of a group of four to six people who befriend the offender, offering both practical and emotional support for the process of reintegrating with the community. They also help to reassure the community by taking on the responsibility for confronting the offender over any risky behavior. The idea behind these groups is to help even these despised offenders live safely in the community, while also keeping the community safe.[28] Such programs may succeed where the threat of punishment fails, and offenders anxious to soften the social effects of their conviction might readily volunteer to participate.

Whether there has been a reconciliation proceeding or a formal conviction, the offender who finds himself reviled and excluded in various ways may (immediately or eventually) wish to take the steps necessary to restore himself to good standing. The steps required for a particular instance of wrongdoing could be specified at sentencing or at a reconciliation hearing, but if not, it is likely that a common understanding on what kinds of behavior, and how much of it, would count as expiation for a particular type of crime would soon develop. A formal apology and acceptance of responsibility is a likely first step. Property offenses might be considered fully expiated when the victim has been compensated in full—or some further step, such as volunteer service, might be needed as well. Offenders who have done physical harm to others might be more readily forgiven if they volunteered to risk their own physical safety to save others through rescue work, or performed services for the physically disabled. Those who have harmed the community at large through uncivil conduct might restore themselves to general respect by volunteering for cleanup or beautification projects. And many offenders would be able to smooth the path to reacceptance by seeking to remedy any personal failings (impulsiveness, irascibility, avarice, drug dependence, lack of marketable skills) that led them to offend. There might be a place, as well, for a formal restoration proceeding, like the Ojibway Cleansing Ceremony, at which the offender's efforts to redeem herself would be recognized and his restoration to the good graces of the community noted on her public record.

Those guilty of the most serious crimes, such as murder, would appropriately find expiation a lifelong effort. The point, however, is not that the offender should suffer. He should not subject himself to deprivation for its own sake; instead, he should seek to do good, and in that way to change, little by little, the moral quality of his own life. We are all, in moral terms, only the sum of our actions, and some wrongs are so grave that they threaten to define us. Yet it is also true that some exceptional individuals have been able to redefine themselves through later actions and so to escape the shadow of their crimes. Some will never be able to restore themselves fully, no matter what they do; but, because everyone is capable of some good actions, there is no one who cannot at least mitigate the community's judgment of his moral worth.

IV. Conclusion

Looking back at the arguments against punishment, we can see that, while they indicate that radical change is needed, they do not entail surrender to crime or even the abandonment of our entire current approach to criminal justice. There are many other things we can do to secure our safety, and many more appropriate ways to respond to wrongdoing than to impose harm on the wrongdoer. It is time for us to take these alternatives seriously, and to begin as soon as we can to reduce our reliance on punishment to serve purposes which, insofar as they are worthwhile, are better served by measures that do not require us to do wrong ourselves.

Notes

Notes to Chapter 1

1. Robert Johnson and Hans Toch, eds., introduction to *The Pains of Imprisonment* (Beverly Hills, CA: Sage, 1982), 17.

2. Robert Johnson, *Hard Time: Understanding and Reforming the Prison*, 3rd ed. (Belmont, CA: Wadsworth, 2002), 10.

3. Human Rights Watch, "No Escape: Male Rape in U.S. Prisons;" available online at http://www.hrw.org/reports/2001/prison/report.html; Internet; accessed June 11, 2002.

4. The commercial was withdrawn in response to protest, but not before the ad series was nominated for Outstanding Directorial Achievement in Commercials. Sabrina Qutb and Lara Temple, "Selling a Soft Drink, Surviving Hard Time: Just What Part of Prison Rape Do You Find Amusing?" *San Francisco Chronicle*, June 9, 2002. The story also notes that focus groups had reacted favorably to the ad.

5. Roy Walmsley, "World Prison Populations: Facts, Trends and Solutions," presented at the United Nations Programme Network Institutes Technical Assistance Workshop, Vienna, Austria, May 10, 2001.

6. J. H. Abbott, *In the Belly of the Beast: Letters from Prison* (New York: Vintage, 1991), 15. Quoted in Johnson, *Hard Time*, 145–146.

7. Abbott, *Belly of the Beast*, 102. Quoted in Johnson, *Hard Time*, 150.

8. Bruce Jackson, obituary of Jack Abbott, *Buffalo Report*, March 1, 2002.

9. Edward Humes, *No Matter How Loud I Shout: A Year in the Life of the Juvenile Court* (New York: Simon and Schuster, 1996), 34.

10. Homer, *Iliad*, trans. Samuel Butler, Book 6; available online at http://classics.mit.edu/Homer/iliad.html; Internet; accessed January 5, 2004.

11. As Mary Margaret Mackenzie points out, "punishment" as such is not found in Homer. The quoted passage, and other similar passages, refers instead to simple vengeance, in the sense that the retaliatory act is carried out by a private individual rather than by a legal authority. *Plato on Punishment* (Berkeley: University of California Press, 1981), 69. The passage does illustrate the justified infliction of harm, however, and as such is a precursor to the justification of punishment proper.

12. Aeschylus, *Eumenides*, trans. Ian Johnston, lines 649–667; available on-line at http://www.mala.bc.ca/~johnstoi/aeschylus/aeschylus_eumenides.htm; Internet; accessed December 8, 2003. Print version available from Prideaux Street Publications, Nanaimo, BC, Canada.

13. Plato, *Gorgias*, trans. Donald J. Zeyl (Indianapolis: Hackett, 1987), 477.

14. Ibid., 479d.

15. Plato does not, strictly speaking, present the benefit of the wrongdoer as a justification for punishment here, as he relies on the idea that the punishment is just, thereby establishing that it is a benefit to the person who suffers it.

16. Plato, *Gorgias*, 512b.

17. For a detailed treatment of the influence of the Nile on Egypt, see Henri Frankfort and H. A. Gronewegen-Frankfort, *Before Philosophy: The Intellectual Adventure of Ancient Man* (Chicago: University of Chicago Press, 1946).

18. For a discussion of Egyptian beliefs, see Frankfort and Gronewegen-Frankfort, *Before Philosophy*, 92–96, and John Wilson, *The Culture of Ancient Egypt* (Chicago: University of Chicago Press, 1951), 47–51. The ancient Egyptian concept of *ma'at* is quite different from our modern view of justice, requiring more in the way of positive acts of kindness and stressing the preservation of order.

19. Even before the Coffin Texts, the earliest of the pyramids bear curses directed at plunderers. Such curses may, however, be interpreted as a simple attempt on the part of the Pharaoh to protect his own interests, combined with a claim of power to do so, rather than as an indication of the demands of justice.

20. Num. 35:33.

21. William Kelly Simpson, ed., "Teaching for Merikare," in *The Literature of Ancient Egypt*, 2nd ed. (New Haven: Yale University Press, 1973), 183. Aldred interprets this passage as an exhortation to "leave vengeance to God." Cyril Aldred, *The Egyptians* (New York: Praeger, 1961), 106. The Instruction of Amenemope, directed not to kings but to ordinary citizens, suggests:

> Do not expose a widow if you have caught her in the fields,
> Nor fail to give way if she is accused.
> Do not turn a stranger away from your oil jar
> That it may be made double for your family.
> God loves him who cares for the poor
> More than him who respects the wealthy.

Simpson, *Literature of Ancient Egypt*, 264.

22. Lev. 24:17–21. Similar passages are found in Deut. 19:19–21 and Exod. 21:22–25.

23. See Hubert J. Treston, *Poine: A Study in Ancient Greek Blood-Vengeance* (London: Longmans, 1923), 1–3, quoted in "Lex Talionis," chap. 4 in Martin Henberg, *Retribution: Evil for Evil in Ethics, Law, and Literature* (Philadelphia: Temple University Press, 1990), 60–61.

24. Martin Henberg cautions against reading the idea of "progress" into this kind of historical change. As he points out, changes in penalty structures can equally plausibly be construed as resulting from changed circumstances. Ibid.

25. "The Code of Hammurabi," secs. 197–222, trans. Theophile J. Meeks, in *Ancient Near Eastern Texts Relating to the Old Testament*, ed. J. B. Pritchard (Princeton: Princeton University Press, 1969), 163–180.

26. Rom. 12:19.

27. Matt. 7:1.

28. Matt. 5:38–45.

29. Augustine, *Letters*, 91 and 94 (A.D. 408); available online at http://www.newadvent.org/fathers/1102.htm; Internet; accessed October 11, 2003.

30. St. Thomas Aquinas, *Treatise on Law* (*Summa Theologica*, Questions 90–97) (Chicago: Henry Regnery, 1965), 75–76.

31. Augustine, *Letters*, 93 (A.D. 408); available online at http://www.newadvent.org/fathers/1102.htm; Internet; accessed October 11, 2003. Earlier, Augustine had argued that the wicked should be tolerated. Letters 44 (A.D. 398).

32. For a detailed description of medieval thought, see Barbara Tuchman, *A Distant Mirror: The Calamitous Fourteenth Century* (New York: Knopf, 1979).

33. Foucault describes punishment in the premodern period as "an art of unbearable sensations," which was later to give way to "an economy of suspended rights." *Discipline and Punish: The Birth of the Prison*, 2nd ed., trans. Alan Sheridan (New York: Vintage Books, 1995), 11.

34. Thomas Hobbes, "Of the Rights of Sovereigns by Institution," chap. 28 in *Leviathan*, ed. Edwin Curley (Indianapolis: Hackett, 1994), 203. First published in 1651.

35. Hobbes's argument is based on his definition of punishment; he characterizes inflictions of evil falling outside his definition as "acts of hostility." Why the sovereign lacks authority for such acts of hostility is only minimally explained by reference to the law of nature as requiring action only for future good and forbidding ingratitude. This view of punishment also appears contrary to Hobbes's view that the sovereign cannot do injustice to his subjects. Ibid.

36. Ibid.

37. John Locke, *Second Treatise of Government*, ed. Thomas P. Peardon (Indianapolis: Bobbs-Merrill, 1952), 6. First published in 1690.

38. Ibid., 9.

39. Cesare Beccaria, *On Crimes and Punishments*, trans. David Young (Indianapolis: Hackett, 1986), 23. First published in 1764.

40. Jeremy Bentham, "Cases Unmeet for Punishment," chap. 13 in *Introduction to the Principles of Morals and Legislation* (New York: Hafner, 1948). First published in 1781.

41. Randall McGovern, "The Well-Ordered Prison: England, 1780–1865,"

chap. 3 in *The Oxford History of the Prison*, ed. Norval Morris and David J. Rothman (Oxford: Oxford University Press, 1995), 105.

42. Immanuel Kant, *The Metaphysical Elements of Justice*, trans. John Ladd (Indianapolis: Bobbs-Merrill, 1965), 100. First published in 1797.

43. Ibid., 102

44. Ibid., 100.

45. Robert Owen, "A New View of Society: Second Essay," *The Avalon Project at Yale Law School*; (1813); available online at http://www.yale.edu/lawweb/avalon/econ/ow02.htm; Internet; accessed May 15, 2003.

46. J. S. Mill, "An Examination of Sir William Hamilton's Philosophy," in vol. 9 of *Collected Works of John Stuart Mill*, ed. J. M. Robson (Toronto: University of Toronto Press, 1979), 462. Earlier edition quoted in F. H. Bradley, "The Vulgar Notion of Responsibility," in *Ethical Studies*, 2nd ed. (Oxford: Clarendon Press, 1927), 30.

47. David J. Rothman, "Perfecting the Prison: United States, 1789–1865," chap. 4 in Morris and Rothman, *Oxford History*, 121–124.

48. Edgardo Rotman, "The Failure of Reform: United States, 1865–1965," chap. 6 in Morris and Rothman, *Oxford History*, 173.

49. G. W. F. Hegel, *Philosophy of Right*, trans. T. Knox (London: Clarendon Press, 1942), section 99, 69. First published in 1821.

50. F. H. Bradley, *Ethical Studies*, 2nd ed. (Oxford: Clarendon Press, 1927), 27–28. First published in 1876.

51. Ibid., 29.

52. F. H. Bradley, "Some Remarks on Punishment," *International Journal of Ethics* 4, no. 3 (April 1894): 274.

53. Bernard Bosanquet, *Some Suggestions in Ethics* (1918; reprint, New York: Kraus Reprint, 1968), 201–202.

54. Ibid., 191–192.

55. J. D. Mabbott, "Punishment," *Mind*, n.s. 48, no. 190 (April 1939): 152–167.

56. M. R. Glover, "Mr. Mabbott on Punishment," *Mind*, n.s. 48, no. 192 (October 1939): 498–501.

57. Karl Menninger, *The Crime of Punishment* (New York: Viking Press, 1968), 190.

58. See Richard Hawkins and Geoffrey Alpert, "Rehabilitation: Control by Conversion," chap. 6 in *American Prison Systems: Punishment and Justice* (Englewood Cliffs, NJ: Prentice Hall, 1989).

59. John Rawls, "Two Concepts of Rules," *Philosophical Review* 64, no. 1 (January 1955): 3–32. Reprinted in H. B. Acton, ed., *The Philosophy of Punishment* (London: Macmillan, 1969), 105–114.

60. H. L. A. Hart, "Prolegomenon to the Principles of Punishment," chap. 1

in Hart, *Punishment and Responsibility* (New York: Oxford University Press, 1968).

61. In 1974, sociologist Robert Martinson reported the results of an exhaustive study of prison rehabilitation programs, "With few and isolated exceptions, the rehabilitative efforts that have been reported so far have had no appreciable effects on recidivism." Robert Martinson, "What Works? Questions and Answers about Prison Reform," *Public Interest* 35 (Spring 1974): 22–56.

62. See Jeffrie Murphy, "Marxism and Retribution," *Philosophy and Public Affairs* 2, no. 3 (Spring 1973): 217–243.

63. Richard Burgh, "Do the Guilty Deserve Punishment?" *Journal of Philosophy* 79, no. 4 (April 1982): 193–210.

64. See, e.g., Richard Posner, "Criminal Law," chap. 7 in *Economic Analysis of Law*, 5th ed. (New York: Aspen Law and Business, 1998).

65. See, e.g., United States Sentencing Commission, *Federal Sentencing Guidelines Manual*, chap. 1, sec. A (1987).

66. Walter Berns, *For Capital Punishment: Crime and the Morality of the Death Penalty* (New York: Basic Books, 1979); Jeffrie Murphy and Jean Hampton, *Forgiveness and Mercy* (Cambridge: Cambridge University Press, 1988); Michael Moore, "The Moral Worth of Retribution," chap. 8 in *Responsibility, Character and the Emotions*, ed. F. Schoeman (Cambridge: Cambridge University Press, 1987).

67. Herbert Morris, "A Paternalistic Theory of Punishment," *American Philosophical Quarterly* 18, no. 4 (October 1981): 211–263. Robert Nozick, "Retributive Punishment," chap. 4 in *Philosophical Explanations* (Cambridge, MA: Harvard University Press, 1981), 363–388; Jean Hampton, "The Moral Education Theory of Punishment," *Philosophy and Public Affairs* 13, no. 3 (1984): 208–238; R. A. Duff, *Trials and Punishments* (Cambridge: Cambridge University Press, 1986).

68. Philip Montague, *Punishment as Societal-Defense* (Lanham, MD: Rowman and Littlefield, 1995).

69. Daniel M. Farrell, "The Justification of Deterrent Violence," *Ethics* 100, no. 2 (January 1990): 301–317.

NOTES TO CHAPTER 2

1. Steven D. Levitt, "The Effect of Prison Population Size on Crime Rates: Evidence from Prison Overcrowding Litigation," *Quarterly Journal of Economics* 111, no. 2 (May 1996): 319; Thomas Marvell and Carlisle Moody, "Prison Population Growth and Crime Reduction," *Journal of Quantitative Criminology* 10 (1994): 109; William Spelman, *Criminal Incapacitation* (New York: Plenum, 1994). But see William Sabol and James Lynch, *Crime Policy Report:*

Did Getting Tough on Crime Pay? (Washington, DC: Urban Institute, 1997), available online at http://www.urban.org/url.cfm?ID=307337; Internet; accessed January 7, 2004 (evidence that get-tough policies have reduced crime is mixed), and Franklin E. Zimring and Gordon J. Hawkins, *Incapacitation: Penal Confinement and Restraint of Crime* (New York: Oxford University Press, 1995) (no significant incapacitation effect).

2. Occasionally an argument is presented for excluding costs to the offender. For example, Mark A. Cohen argues that only "external" costs should count as social costs of crime and punishment. He defines "external" costs as those involuntarily incurred by third parties. Costs imposed by offenders on victims fall into this category; but Cohen fails to recognize that the costs imposed by society on the offender are also involuntarily incurred (absent an argument that crime counts as consent; see chapter 4), or that the dollar cost of imprisonment to taxpayers (which he counts as the "cost" of punishment) would not count as an "external cost" under his definition because it is a burden voluntarily assumed. Mark A. Cohen, "Measuring the Costs and Benefits of Crime and Justice," in *Criminal Justice 2000* (Washington, DC: U.S. Department of Justice, 2000), 4: 263–315. Others simply note that most people don't care about costs to offenders, which may be charitably interpreted as a suggestion that the justification for imposing these costs is to be found elsewhere.

3. Jeremy Bentham, *Introduction to the Principles of Morals and Legislation* (New York: Hafner, 1948), 170. First published in 1781.

4. Steven Klepper and Daniel Nagin, "Tax Compliance and Perceptions of the Risks of Detection and Criminal Prosecution," *Law and Society Review* 23, no. 2 (1989): 204–240. Study cited in Daniel S. Nagin, "Criminal Deterrence Research at the Outset of the 21st Century," in *Crime and Justice: A Review of Research*, ed. Michael Tonry (Chicago: University of Chicago Press, 1998), 23: 16–17.

5. Nagin, "Criminal Deterrence Research," 21.

6. Jack P. Gibbs, *Crime, Punishment and Deterrence* (New York: Elsevier, 1975).

7. Nagin, "Criminal Deterrence Research," 10.

8. David McDowell, Colin Loftin, and Brian Wiersema, "A Comparative Study of the Preventive Effects of Mandatory Sentencing Laws for Gun Crimes," *Journal of Criminal Law and Criminology* 83, no. 2 (Summer 1992): 378–394, cited in Nagin, "Criminal Deterrence Research," 33.

9. M. W. Lipsey, "What Do We Learn from 400 Research Studies on the Effectiveness of Treatment with Juvenile Delinquents?" in *What Works: Reducing Reoffending*, ed. J. McGuire (New York: John Wiley and Sons, 1995) (boot camps and "Scared Straight" programs increased recidivism among juveniles).

10. Klepper and Nagin, "Tax Compliance and Perceptions," 209, and Steven Klepper and Daniel Nagin, "The Deterrent Effect of Perceived Certainty and

Severity of Punishment Revisited," *Criminology* 27 (1989): 721, cited in Nagin, "Criminal Deterrence Research," 20.

11. Nagin argues that perception-based studies of deterrence "suggest that the deterrent effect of formal sanctions arises principally from fear of the social stigma that their imposition triggers"; see "Criminal Deterrence Research," 4. A number of scholars have argued that the collateral effects of conviction, such as unemployment and social stigma, may prove more effective deterrents than the punishment itself. Franklin E. Zimring and Gordon J. Hawkins, *Deterrence: The Legal Threat in Crime Control* (Chicago: University of Chicago Press, 1973), 4; Johannes Andenaes, *Punishment and Deterrence* (Ann Arbor: University of Michigan Press, 1974); Gibbs, *Crime, Punishment and Deterrence*; Alfred Blumstein and Daniel Nagin, "The Deterrent Effect of Legal Sanctions on Draft Evasion," *Stanford Law Review* 29 (1976): 241–275, cited in Nagin, "Criminal Deterrence Research," 19.

12. Graeme Newman advocates corporal punishment (through electric shocks) in *Just and Painful* (New York: Macmillan, 1983).

13. David Friedman, *Law's Order: What Economics Has to Do with Law and Why It Matters* (Princeton: Princeton University Press, 2000), 237. Friedman ultimately argues that maximally efficient punishments are not desirable because they create too much of an incentive for false prosecution. Ibid., 240–241.

14. Efforts to measure empirically the crime-preventive effects of punishment face a number of significant obstacles. Changes in the rate of reported crime can be observed and correlated with changes in sentencing practices, but we need to be sure that an increase in reported crimes reflects a higher crime rate rather than, e.g., increased police activity or changes in reporting procedures, and that a correlation between harsher sentences and decreased crime, for example, does not result from the effects of some third variable such as a rise in the employment rate. It is also possible for a rise in the rate of reported crime itself to cause a drop in average sentences as prosecutors, faced with more new cases than they can practically take to trial, offer plea agreements to a larger proportion of defendants. Nagin, "Criminal Deterrence Research," 24–25.

15. About 50 percent of prisoners do not recidivate after release. Gerald G. Gaes et al., "Adult Correctional Treatment," in Michael Tonry and Joan Petersilia, *Crime and Justice: A Review of Research*, vol. 26: *Prisons* (Chicago: University of Chicago Press, 1999), 1–16.

16. The scope of the potential effectiveness of incapacitation could be expanded by including preventive detention, discussed below, or by increased effectiveness of policing. However, the potential of punishment to prevent crime by incapacitating offenders is limited to prevention of crimes by those who have been convicted—not by those who have never committed a previous crime or have avoided arrest, prosecution, or conviction for their previous crimes. That the latter is not a negligible number is indicated by the fact that about 75 percent

of arrestees in one study were first offenders. Jacqueline Cohen, "Incapacitation as a Strategy for Crime Control: Possibilities and Pitfalls," in Michael Tonry and Norval Morris, eds., *Crime and Justice*, vol. 5 (Chicago: University of Chicago Press, 1983), 28. Some 33 percent of those entering prison have never been imprisoned before. Sabol and Lynch, "Did Getting Tough on Crime Pay?"

17. Peter W. Greenwood, *Selective Incapacitation* (Santa Monica, CA: Rand, 1982). See detailed criticism in Christy A. Visher, "The Rand Inmate Survey: A Reanalysis," in *Criminal Careers and "Career Criminals,"* ed. Alfred Blumstein, Jacqueline Cohen, Jeffrey A. Roth, and Christy Visher (Washington, DC: National Academy Press, 1986), vol. 2: 161–211. The study has recently been replicated by Kathleen Auerhahn, who found that it performed poorly in both validity and reliability. "Selective Incapacitation and the Problem of Prediction," *Criminology* 37, no. 4 (November 1999): 703–734.

18. Levitt, "The Effect of Prison Population Size on Crime Rates." Levitt's results show a correlation between lower incarceration rates and the rate of reported crime. He applies a multiplier to the increase in reported crime to allow for unreported crimes.

19. Visher, "The Rand Inmate Survey" (doubling of prison population reduced crime 10–30 percent); Thomas Marvell and Carlisle Moody, "Prison Population Growth and Crime Reduction," *Journal of Quantitative Criminology* 10 (1994): 109–140; Greenwood, *Selective Incapacitation*, 78–80. Cohen and Canela-Cacho estimate that incapacitation effects are high at low incarceration rates but decline sharply as the prison population grows (because of the increased percentage of low-rate offenders). Jacqueline Cohen and Jose A. Canela-Cacho, "Incarceration and Violent Crime, 1965–1988," in *Understanding and Preventing Violence: Consequence and Control*, ed. Albert J. Reiss, Jr., and Jeffrey A. Roth, vol. 4 (Washington, DC: National Academy Press, 1994). Zimring and Hawkins find the effects of increased incarceration rates on the crime rate to be negligible. Franklin E. Zimring and Gordon J. Hawkins, *Incapacitation: Penal Confinement and Restraint of Crime* (New York: Oxford University Press, 1995).

20. Blumstein et al., *Criminal Careers and "Career Criminals,"* 92. Blumstein suggests that the average length of a criminal career is less than six years.

21. Nagin, "Criminal Deterrence Research," 28–29.

22. This estimate has a standard error of ±$30,000 because of the imprecision of the figures for murder. Leaving murder out of the calculation produces a figure of $43,000, with a standard error of ±$12,000. Levitt, "The Effect of Prison Population Size on Crime Rates," 346 n.34.

23. Ibid., 347. The assignment of dollar costs to intangible losses is controversial, and I do not mean to endorse it here. In order to use a utilitarian calculus, some method of comparing costs and benefits in commensurable terms is necessary.

24. Levitt estimates the intangible (nonmonetary) social cost of an assault at $10,200. Levitt, "Estimated Impact on Crime from Adding One Additional Prisoner," table 8, 345.

25. Angela S. Maitland and Richard D. Sluder, "Victimization in Prisons: A Study of Factors Related to the General Well-Being of Youthful Inmates," *Federal Probation* 60, no. 2 (June 1996): 24–31. Cited in Anthony E. Bottoms, "Interpersonal Violence and Social Order in Prisons," in *Prisons*, ed. Michael Tonry and Joan Petersilia, 222 n.20. Because some communities have much higher victimization rates than others, however, the differential between risks of victimization inside and outside prison may well be much less for the actual prison population, much of which is drawn from neighborhoods with high crime rates.

26. These effects are discussed in John Hagan and Ronit Dinovitzer, "Collateral Consequences of Imprisonment for Children, Communities and Prisoners," in Tonry and Petersilia, *Prisons*, 121–162.

27. See, e.g., Greenwood, *Selective Incapacitation* 19–26 (California, Texas, and Michigan); John DiIulio and Anne Morrison Piehl, "'Does Prison Pay?' Revisited: Returning to the Crime Scene," in *Brookings Review* (Madison: Brookings Institution, 1995).

28. Levitt, "Effect of Prison Population Size on Crime Rates."

29. See William Spelman, *Criminal Incapacitation* (New York: Plenum Press, 1994), cited in Levitt, "Effect of Prison Population Size," 321 n.3. Levitt notes that, in view of these criticisms, "the median may be a more reliable estimator than the mean." Ibid.

30. Blumstein et al., *Criminal Careers and "Career Criminals,"* 92.

31. Nagin, "Criminal Deterrence Research."

32. Marvin Wolfgang, Robert M. Figlio, and Thorsten Sellin, *Delinquency in a Birth Cohort* (Chicago: University of Chicago Press, 1972). Wolfgang's long-term study of all males born in Philadelphia in 1945, followed from age six to eighteen, showed that 6 percent of the individuals were responsible for 52 percent of the crimes committed by the group. The Rand study of selective incapacitation, based on self-reports of prison inmates, showed 10 percent of the offenders reported robbery rates seventeen times the median for all inmates surveyed. Greenwood, *Selective Incapacitation*, 16–26, 56–60. The data reported by Wolfgang et al. should not be confused with cross-sectional data. That is, the 6 percent of the cohort who committed 52 percent of the crimes committed *by the group* did not commit 52 percent of the crimes in Philadelphia during that time period. Later analysis of Wolfgang's data showed that if the youths in the cohort committing serious crimes had not been incarcerated for their offenses, there would have been only a 1 to 4 percent increase in crime in Philadelphia during the period. S. H. Clarke, "Getting 'Em Out of Circulation: Does Incarceration of Juvenile Offenders Reduce Crime?" *Journal of Criminal Law and Criminology* 65, no. 4 (1974): 528–535.

33. Greenwood, *Selective Incapacitation*, 26. Also Stephen D. Gottfredson and Don M. Gottfredson, "Behavioral Prediction and the Problem of Incapacitation," *Criminology* 32, no. 3 (1994): 441–474.

34. In one such study, 52 subjects were accurately predicted violent, 404 were incorrectly predicted violent, and 52 were incorrectly predicted nonviolent. In other words, for every true positive there were eight false positives and one false negative. Ernst A. Wenk, James O. Robison, and Gerald W. Smith, "Can Violence Be Predicted?" *Crime and Delinquency* 18 (October 1972): 393–402.

35. Ibid.

36. Peter R. Jones, Philip W. Harris, Jamie Fader, "Identifying Chronic Offenders," Research Paper for the Council of Juvenile Correctional Administrators Conference (Crime and Justice Research Institute, Philadelphia, January 1999).

37. The study also showed that interventions such as family services and school programs were most effective in reducing the proportion of chronic offenders in the group. Ibid., 19.

38. Martinson's assessment of 231 rehabilitative programs from 1945 to 1967 concluded that "with few and isolated exceptions the rehabilitative efforts that have been reported so far have had no appreciable effect on recidivism." Robert Martinson, "What Works? Questions and Answers about Prison Reform," *Public Interest* 35 (Spring 1974): 22–56. This conclusion was challenged by others who suggested that both the research methodology and program implementation were so weak that no conclusions could be drawn about the effectiveness of rehabilitation. Peter Greenwood and Franklin Zimring, *One More Chance: The Pursuit of Promising Intervention Strategies for Chronic Juvenile Offenders* (Santa Monica, CA: Rand, 1985).

39. Gerald G. Gaes et al., "Adult Correctional Treatment," in Tonry and Petersilia, *Prisons*, 371; Doris L. MacKenzie, "Criminal Justice and Crime Prevention," in Lawrence W. Sherman et al., *Preventing Crime: What Works, What Doesn't, What's Promising: A Report to the United States Congress* (Washington, DC: National Institute of Justice, 1997); available online at http://www.ncjrs.org/works/; Internet; accessed June 20, 2002.

40. Gerald G. Gaes et al., "Adult Correctional Treatment," 369, citing Lipsey, "Effectiveness of Treatment."

41. Elliott Currie, "Crime and Punishment in the United States: Myths, Realities, and Possibilities," in David Kairys, ed., *The Politics of Law: A Progressive Critique* (New York: Basic Books, 1998).

42. Caroline Wolf Harlow, *Prior Abuse Reported by Inmates and Probationers*, (Washington, DC: U.S. Department of Justice, Bureau of Justice Statistics April 1999).

43. Currie, "Crime and Punishment in the United States," citing Cathy Spatz Widom, *The Cycle of Violence Revisited* (Washington, DC: National Institute of

Justice, 1996); Carolyn Smith and Terence Thornberry, "The Relationship between Childhood Maltreatment and Adolescent Involvement in Delinquency," *Criminology* 33, no. 4 (1995): 451–477; and Center on Child Abuse Prevention Research, *Intensive Home Visitation: A Randomized Trial, Follow-up, and Risk Assessment Study of Hawaii's Healthy Start Program* (Chicago: National Committee to Prevent Child Abuse, 1996).

44. See Currie, "Crime and Punishment in the United States: Myths, Realities, and Possibilities."

45. Robert J. Sampson and William Julius Wilson, "Toward a Theory of Race, Crime, and Urban Inequality," in *Crime and Inequality*, ed. John Hagan and Ruth D. Peterson (Stanford, CA: Stanford University Press, 1995).

46. Steven F. Messner and Richard Rosenfeld, *Crime and the American Dream*, 3rd ed. (Belmont, CA: Wadsworth, 2001).

47. Ibid., 9.

48. James Lynch, "Crime in International Perspective," in *Crime: Public Policies for Crime Control*, ed. James Q. Wilson and Joan Petersilia (Oakland, CA: Institute for Contemporary Studies, 2002), 10–12. Lynch points out the pitfalls of crude comparisons of cross-national crime rates, which would show even wider disparities. See Messner and Rosenfeld, *American Dream*, 18–23 (using Interpol statistics). The rates quoted in the text represent homicides, for which figures are reliable, and victim reports of violence, which are more similar across nations than police reports. Police reports also show that other comparable countries have much higher rates of property crime than the United States; these differences narrow when data from victimization surveys are used. Lynch, "Crime in International Perspective," 12.

49. Messner and Rosenfeld, *American Dream*, 19–20 (1997 figures).

50. C. Hsieh and M. D. Pugh, "Poverty, Income Inequality, and Violent Crime: A Meta-Analysis of Recent Aggregate Data Studies," *Criminal Justice Review* 18, no. 2 (1993): 182–202; B. P. Kennedy et al., "Social Capital, Income Inequality, and Firearm Violent Crime," *Social Science and Medicine* 47, no. 1 (1998): 7–17. François Bourguignon, "Crime as a Social Cost of Poverty and Inequality: A Review Focusing on Developing Countries," in *Facets of Globalization*, ed. Shahid Yusuf, Simon Evenett, and Weiping Wu (Washington, DC: World Bank, October 2001), 171–191; Morgan Kelly, "Inequality and Crime," *Review of Economics and Statistics* 82, no. 4 (November 2000): 530–539.

51. Some would argue that, although utility can be increased by shifting material goods or buying power from rich to poor, any comprehensive redistributive scheme would itself have such significant negative effects on the total available for redistribution as to swamp the positive effects on social cohesion. See, e.g., Friedrich Hayek, "'Social' or Distributive Justice," chap. 9 in *Law, Legislation, and Liberty: The Mirage of Social Justice* (Chicago: University of Chicago

Press, 1990), first published in 1973. Such negative effects, if demonstrated, would also have to be taken into account in the utilitarian's comparative assessment of crime-prevention strategies; I shall not pursue here the question of whether it is likely that such effects will prevail.

52. Accidents are the leading cause of death at ages 1–34, giving way thereafter to cancer and heart disease. Homicide is number 2 at 15–24 and number 3 at 25–34. Overall, accidents are the fifth highest cause of death, suicide is eighth, and homicide is thirteenth; the remainder of the top twenty are diseases or medical conditions. (Homicide figures include "legal intervention.") National Center for Injury Prevention and Control, "Leading Causes of Death" (1998 figures); available online at http://webapp.cdc.gov/sasweb/ncipc/leadcaus.html; Internet; accessed August 10, 2001.

53. Although it is difficult to estimate the benefit gained from a dollar spent on medical research, which by its nature has unknown outcomes, it is worth noting that advances in medical knowledge provide benefits extending indefinitely into the future. Perhaps as good utilitarians we would spend money on the immediate prevention of crime, suicide, or accidents only after we had fully funded all promising medical research. The apparent necessity, under utilitarianism, of sacrificing the present to the future in this way is just a special case of the general feature of utilitarianism that it may require sacrifice of the interests of the few to serve the interests of the many.

54. It is also possible that the optimal utilitarian approach would be a combination of punishment and other approaches. This would be the case if there are some crimes that can only be prevented by deterrence or incapacitation, and are also sufficiently costly to outweigh costs of punishment to the offender.

55. If predictions became increasingly accurate (contrary to my argument above), incapacitation would at some point become a utility-maximizing strategy: more harm would be prevented per man-year of incarceration. But at whatever level we set the threshold of "dangerousness" as warranting incapacitation, if the prediction of dangerousness is based on factors other than prior conviction, there will be some individuals who meet that criterion despite having committed no crimes so far.

56. John Rawls, "Two Concepts of Rules," *Philosophical Review* 64, no. 1 (1955): 3–13. Reprinted in *Philosophy of Punishment*, ed. Robert M. Baird and Stuart Rosenbaum (Buffalo, NY: Prometheus Books, 1988), 37–45.

57. Jeffrie Murphy, "Marxism and Retribution," part 2 in *Retribution, Justice, and Therapy* (Dordrecht, Holland; Boston: D. Reidel, 1979), 94.

58. A detailed argument for this point is found in Richard Wasserstrom, "Why Punish the Guilty?" *Princeton University Magazine* 20 (Spring 1964): 14–19.

59. For an illuminating discussion of the doctrine of double effect and its relationship to the Kantian injunction never to use persons merely as means, see

Warren Quinn, "Actions, Intentions, and Consequences: The Doctrine of Double Effect," *Philosophy and Public Affairs* 18, no. 4 (Autumn 1989): 334–351.

60. See, e.g., R. M. Hare, *Moral Thinking* (Oxford: Oxford University Press, 1982).

61. For a discussion of this point, see J. L. Mackie, "Rights, Utility, and Universalization," in R. G. Frey, ed., *Utility and Rights* (Minneapolis: University of Minnesota Press, 1984).

62. Robert Nozick, *Anarchy, State, and Utopia* (New York: Basic Books, 1974), 28–30.

63. See note 34.

64. Howard Markel, *Quarantine! East European Jewish Immigrants and the New York City Epidemics of 1892* (Baltimore: Johns Hopkins University Press, 1999).

NOTES TO CHAPTER 3

1. G. W. F. Hegel, *Philosophy of Right*, trans. T. Knox (London: Oxford University Press, 1942), sec. 99, 69–70; first published in 1821.

2. Ibid., 69.

3. J. L. Mackie, "Morality and the Retributive Emotions," *Criminal Justice Ethics* (1982): 3–9, 4.

4. It would be consistent with Hegel's linking of rights to the legitimate use of coercion to treat punishment as preventing rights violations. But Hegel, like Kant, rejects any consequentialist view of punishment. See *Philosophy of Right*, sec. 100, 71.

5. Ibid., sec. 92, 67.

6. Note that the scope of justified punishment is immediately restricted to acts that are morally wrong. Simple violations of law would not justify punishment unless it can also be shown that one has a moral duty to obey the law, independent of its content.

7. Jean Hampton, "The Retributive Idea," chap. 4 in Jeffrie Murphy and Jean Hampton, *Forgiveness and Mercy* (Cambridge: Cambridge University Press, 1988).

8. Jack Katz, *Seductions of Crime: Moral and Sensual Attractions in Doing Evil* (New York: Basic Books, 1988), 36.

9. Alternatively, he may be seen as claiming that the victims have no such rights (for example, he may see them as enemies to whom one owes nothing). I ignore this complication.

10. Another way of putting the same point is to say that Heiress has no rights (or not this particular right) when her rights conflict with Badman's desires. In an absolute monarchy, for example, subjects might have a right to their property as long as that right does not conflict with the wishes of the king.

11. The average kidnapping for ransom may cause more harm to the victim than the average term of imprisonment (e.g., the kidnapping may put the victim in fear of her life). For purposes of this example, though, we may assume that harm done by the kidnapping in question is exactly comparable to the harm done to the offender by the term of imprisonment that is his punishment. Such a kidnapping would clearly be a crime.

12. Jeffrie Murphy, "Getting Even: The Role of the Victim," in *Crime, Culpability, and Remedy*, ed. Ellen Frankel Paul, Fred D. Miller, and Jeffrey Paul (Oxford: Basil Blackwell, 1990).

13. The punishment then must be taken to make the statement that the wrongdoer is lower in value than the rest of the citizenry (all those who have not committed comparable crimes). This presents some further difficulties. If Badman's original act states that he is more valuable than Heiress, while the punishment states that Badman is less valuable than the rest of the citizenry, Badman's original statement is not refuted, unless we make some further assumptions about the content of the statement made by punishment. We might say, for example, that the punishment states that Badman is less valuable than the rest of the citizenry just because of his original (false) statement about Heiress. This is less than satisfying in that it more closely resembles an ad hominem attack on the speaker than a refutation of his claims.

14. On this model, the difference between the civil and the criminal law is essentially that civil wrongs do not reduce the offender's value, while criminal wrongs do.

15. Jeffrie Murphy and Jules Coleman, *The Philosophy of Law: An Introduction to Jurisprudence* (Boulder, CO: Westview Press, 1990), 115.

16. Walter Berns, *For Capital Punishment: Crime and the Morality of the Death Penalty* (New York: Basic Books, 1979).

17. Ibid., 156.

18. On the structure of emotions generally, see Justin Oakley, *Morality and the Emotions* (London: Routledge, 1992), and William Lyons, *Emotions* (Cambridge: Cambridge University Press, 1980). A selection of historical readings is found in *What Is an Emotion?* ed. Cheshire Calhoun and Robert C. Solomon (New York: Oxford University Press, 1984). The idea that emotions are founded on beliefs dates back to Aristotle, but has recently received new attention, as these sources make clear.

19. Dan M. Kahan and Martha C. Nussbaum, "Two Conceptions of Emotion in Criminal Law," *Columbia Law Review* 96 (1996): 269–374.

20. One interesting study of expressions of anger in seventeenth and eighteenth century American diaries found that diarists seldom admitted to anger of their own, particularly appearing to view it as inappropriate to be angry with their social superiors. An apprentice poorly treated by his Scrooge-like master, for example, indicated only that he was "grieved" by his master's behavior.

Carol Z. Stearns, "Lord Help Me Walk Humbly: Anger and Sadness in England and America, 1570–1750," chap. 2 in *Emotion and Social Change: Toward a New Psychohistory*, ed. Carol Z. Stearns and Peter N. Stearns (New York: Holmes and Meier, 1988).

21. Aristotle, *Rhetoric* 1378ª20–1380ª4, trans. Jon D. Solomon, in Calhoun and Solomon, *What Is an Emotion?* 44. This view is shared by many, if not most, contemporary writers.

22. The suggestion that the object of anger is a proposition rather than a person is Solomon's.

23. Experimental programs have consistently demonstrated a reduction in anger and anxiety for crime victims who had the opportunity to meet with offenders, discuss their motivations, and in some cases, obtain an apology. See, e.g., Caren Flaten, "Victim-Offender Mediation," in *Restorative Justice: International Perspectives*, ed. Burt Galaway and Joe Hudson (Monsey, NY: Criminal Justice Press, 1996).

24. Compare Jeffrie Murphy's notion of "retributive hatred" in "Hatred: A Qualified Defense," chap. 3 in *Forgiveness and Mercy*. I take hatred to be a disposition to take harm to its object as a good for oneself; unlike anger, it requires a personal object. One can hate without being angry, and be angry without hating. Anger accompanied by hatred will take the form of vindictive anger; anger accompanied by retributive hatred will be retributive anger.

25. Jeffrie Murphy, "Getting Even: The Role of the Victim."

26. Catherine Lutz, *Unnatural Emotions* (Chicago: University of Chicago Press, 1988), 176.

NOTES TO CHAPTER 4

1. See Immanuel Kant, *Foundations of the Metaphysics of Morals*, trans. Lewis White Beck (Macmillan, 1959). First published in 1785.

2. Herbert Morris, "Persons and Punishment," *Monist* 52, no. 4 (October 1968): 476–501. Reprinted in Jeffrie Murphy, ed., *Punishment and Rehabilitation*, 3rd ed. (Belmont, CA: Wadsworth, 1995).

3. See, e.g., George Sher, "Deserved Punishment," chap. 5 in *Desert* (Princeton: Princeton University Press, 1987); Morris, "Persons and Punishment."

4. Immanuel Kant, *Metaphysics of Morals*, trans. Mary Gregor (Cambridge: Cambridge University Press, 1991). First published in 1797.

5. Jeffrie Murphy, "Marxism and Retribution," in *Retribution, Justice and Therapy* (Boston: D. Reidel, 1979), 93–115.

6. Murphy, "Marxism and Retribution," 107.

7. Bureau of Justice Statistics, *Homicide Trends in the U.S.*; available online at http://www.ojp.usdoj.gov/bjs/homicide/homtrnd.htm; Internet; accessed November 8, 2003.

8. John van Kesteren, P. Mayhew, and P. Nieuwbeerta, *Criminal Victimisation in Seventeen Industrialised Countries: Key Findings from the 2000 International Crime Victims Survey* (The Hague, Netherlands: Wetenschappelijk Onderzoeken Documentatiecentrum, 2001).

9. Homicide rates are generally considered a better comparative statistic than rates for other types of crime because there are fewer sources of variation in detection and reporting of homicide.

10. See, e.g., S. Messner and R. Rosenfeld, *Crime and the American Dream* (Belmont, CA: Wadsworth, 1997).

11. See Ezzat A. Fattah, *Criminology: Past, Present and Future* (London: Macmillan, 1997), 231–234 (discussing views of Gabriel Tarde).

12. Cohen and Felson have postulated that there are three necessary conditions for predatory crimes: a motivated offender, a suitable target, and an absence of capable guardianship. They thus attribute the increase in crime after World War II to structural changes in society that moved potential targets to public places and reduced guardianship. L. E. Cohen and M. Felson, "Social Change and Crime Rate Trends: A Routine Activity Approach," *American Sociological Review* 44, no. 4 (August 1979): 588–608.

13. R. Sampson and W. J. Wilson, "Toward a Theory of Race, Crime, and Urban Inequality," in *Crime and Inequality*, ed. John Hagan and Ruth Peterson (Stanford, CA: Stanford University Press, 1995), 37–54.

14. Retributivism does not necessarily imply that the punishment for killing will be death (though many retributivists, including Kant, have adhered to that position), but the point here holds regardless of the specific penalty.

15. As Jeffrie Murphy has noted in this connection, "given the rarity of an intense sense of abstract justice, classical retributivism seems unmotivated within liberal theory." See "Getting Even: The Role of the Victim," in *Crime, Culpability and Remedy*, ed. Ellen Frankel Paul (Oxford: Basil Blackwell, 1990), 224. Murphy suggests in this essay that the appropriate motivation can be found in victims' desire for revenge. See my discussion of vindictive anger in chapter 3.

16. See Herbert Fingarette, "Punishment and Suffering," Presidential Address, Eastern Division of the American Philosophical Association, *Proceedings of the American Philosophical Association*, 1977; J. D. Mabbott, "Punishment," *Mind* 48 (April 1939): 152–167.

17. Kant, *Metaphysics of Morals*.

18. See David Dolinko's argument for a similar point in "Some Thoughts about Retributivism," *Ethics* 101, no. 3 (April 1991): 537–559.

19. W. D. Ross, *The Right and the Good* (Oxford: Clarendon Press, 1930), 58–59.

20. Elizabeth Wolgast, *The Grammar of Justice* (Ithaca, NY: Cornell University Press, 1987), 160–166.

21. Ibid., 161.

22. H. L. A. Hart, "Are There Any Natural Rights?" *Philosophical Review* 64 (1955): 155. See Rawls's discussion of the principle in *A Theory of Justice* (Cambridge, MA: Harvard University Press, 1971), 112.

23. Morris, "Persons and Punishment," 477.

24. Murphy, "Marxism and Retribution," 114

25. Morris, "Persons and Punishment," 478.

26. Burgh, "Do the Guilty Deserve Punishment?" *Journal of Philosophy* 79 (April 1982): 193–210.

27. Richard Dagger, "Playing Fair with Punishment," *Ethics* 103 (1993): 473–488.

28. Sher, *Desert*, 81–82.

29. Ibid., 88.

30. It also seems that the proper balance on this view would be achieved by exposing the wrongdoer to crime, rather than to punishment.

31. Matt Matravers, *Justice and Punishment: The Rationale of Coercion* (Oxford: Oxford University Press, 2000), 178–180.

32. Ibid., chap. 9.

33. Ibid., chap. 7.

34. Ibid., 222–223.

35. Ibid., 223–229.

36. Ibid., 256.

37. Susan Dimock, "Retributivism and Trust," *Law and Philosophy* 16 (1997): 37–62.

38. Morris, "Persons and Punishment," 487.

Notes to Chapter 5

1. This principle was first suggested by Philip Montague in "Self-Defense and Choosing between Lives," *Philosophical Studies* (1981): 40, and is adopted by Daniel M. Farrell, "The Justification of General Deterrence," *Philosophical Review* 94, no. 3 (July 1985), reprinted in *Punishment and Rehabilitation*, 3rd ed., ed. Jeffrie Murphy (Belmont, CA: Wadsworth, 1995), 38–60.

2. I am indebted to William Wilcox for this point.

3. See Warren Quinn, "The Right to Threaten and the Right to Punish," *Philosophy and Public Affairs* 14, no. 4 (Fall 1985): 327–373.

4. Ibid., 364.

5. Ibid., 340.

6. Ibid. Emphasis added.

7. Philip Montague, "Societal Defense," chap. 3 in *Punishment as Societal-Defense* (Lanham, MD: Rowman and Littlefield, 1995).

8. Ibid., 63.

Notes to Chapter 6

1. See discussion of rehabilitation in chapter 2.

2. Aversion therapy is dramatically depicted in *A Clockwork Orange*, prod. and dir. Stanley Kubrick, 137 min., Warner Brothers, 1991, in which the protagonist is conditioned to become violently ill at any display of violence. Even more extreme methods were used in the Vacaville Medical Facility in California, where prisoners were given anectine, a curare derivative that induces respiratory paralysis, simulating the experience of dying. Peter Schrag, *Mind Control* (New York: Random House, 1978), 7–8. In the 1960's and 1970's, some writers advocated the use of more precise brain surgery targeted at the amygdala in place of the discredited prefrontal lobotomy to calm violent behavior. Vernon H. Mark and Frank R. Ervin, *Violence and the Brain* (New York: Harper and Row, 1970). It was in fact suggested at the time that such surgery might be used on urban rioters. Peter R. Breggin, "Campaigns against Racist Federal Programs by the Center for the Study of Psychiatry and Psychology," *Journal of African American Men* 1, no. 3 (Winter 1995–96): 3–22.

3. Herbert Morris, "Persons and Punishment," *Monist* 52, no. 4 (October 1968): 475–501. Reprinted in Jeffrie G. Murphy, ed., *Punishment and Rehabilitation*, 3rd ed. (Belmont, CA: Wadsworth, 1995), 74–93.

4. Herbert Morris, "A Paternalistic Theory of Punishment," *American Philosophical Quarterly* 18, no. 4 (October 1981): 211–263; reprinted in Murphy, *Punishment and Rehabilitation*, 154–168 (page references are to the reprinted version). R. A. Duff, *Trials and Punishments* (Cambridge: Cambridge University Press, 1986). Jean Hampton, "The Moral Education Theory of Punishment," *Philosophy and Public Affairs* 13, no. 3 (Summer 1984): 208–238. Robert Nozick makes a related argument in "Free Will," chap. 4 in *Philosophical Explanations* (Cambridge, MA: Harvard University Press, 1981), but, although he suggests that punishment can serve to link the offender up with correct values, he declines to rest its justification on that possibility.

5. Duff, *Trials and Punishments*, 236–238.

6. Ibid., 246.

7. Ibid., 239.

8. See Plato, *Crito*, in *The Trial and Death of Socrates*, trans. G.M.A. Grube (Indianpolis: Hackett, 1975), and Plato, *Gorgias*, trans. Donald J. Zeyl (Indianapolis: Hackett, 1987).

9. In this section I loosely follow the general approach to paternalism spelled out by Joel Feinberg in *Harm to Self*, vol. 3 of *The Moral Limits of the Criminal Law* (New York: Oxford University Press, 1986).

10. This claim recalls a haunting passage from Kafka's story, "In the Penal Colony," in which an exhortation to good behavior is inscribed on the body of the wrongdoer with needles. After several hours of this bloody treatment,

Enlightenment comes to the most dull-witted. It begins around the eyes. From there it radiates. A moment that might tempt one to get under the Harrow oneself. Nothing more happens than that the man begins to understand the inscription, he purses his mouth as if he were listening. You have seen how difficult it is to decipher the script with one's eyes; but our man deciphers it with his wounds. To be sure, that is a hard task; he needs six hours to accomplish it. By that time the Harrow has pierced him quite through.

From *In the Penal Colony: Stories and Short Pieces*, trans. Willa and Edwin Muir (New York: Schocken Books, 1995), 204. We are dubious of the moral benefit, as well as of the price paid to get it; certainly, we would not characterize the preference not to be enlightened in this way as unreasonable.

11. Morris bases his argument on the centrality of this identity as a "morally autonomous person attached to the good" to the good of the person. If we are at all concerned for our fellow citizens, he argues, we cannot permit them to give up this good. This good—which is the good of the offender to be aimed at by punishment—includes an appreciation of the nature of the evil involved in one's wrongdoing; feeling guilt over wrongdoing; rejecting the disposition to do wrong; and possessing a conception of oneself as an individual worthy of respect; see "Paternalistic Theory," 157–158.

12. As in Duff's version, the offender is left free to reject the moral message, but as we can't know in advance who will in fact reject it, we must impose punishment on all. Unlike Duff, Hampton emphasizes that even if the moral message is rejected, the punishment still serves as a deterrent.

13. Hampton, "Moral Education," 213.

14. Ibid.

15. To justify the use of hard treatment to communicate with hardened offenders who are unlikely to repent, we would have to think that, of all the options available, punishment has the best chance of working, even though we set that chance at near zero. Perhaps more significantly, we would also have to believe that punishment presents an even more negligible chance of retarding moral development than it does of advancing it. A similar point can be made with respect to the already-repentant offender: we must believe that punishment is the best way of reinforcing repentance, and especially that punishment will not instead produce resentment and banish remorse.

16. If the man does not know the effect of his words, then his conduct may be excusable, rather than justifiable. The same may be said of our efforts at morally reforming punishment, at least to the extent that we may plausibly be said not to know that the message is seldom received as sent.

17. I am indebted here to Laurence Thomas's account of good moral character in "Persons of Good Moral Character," chap. 1 in *Living Morally* (Philadelphia: Temple University Press, 1989), 3–25.

18. Willard Van Orman Quine, "Two Dogmas of Empiricism," chap. 2 in *From a Logical Point of View*, 2nd ed. (Cambridge, MA: Harvard University Press, 1961), 20–46.

19. This is not the same as sacrificing one value in a particular situation. I might, for example, have to choose between going to work today and staying home with my family; my choice of one does not mean I give up my attachment to the other. Rather, attachments are (painfully) sacrificed when they cannot be sustained; for example, to preserve my self-esteem, I assign less weight to my professional ambitions; to protect myself from the ongoing pain of separation, I reduce the level of my attachment to an absent friend. This is typically not a matter of conscious decision.

20. Jonathan Bennett provides a compelling account of such a case in "The Conscience of Huckleberry Finn," *Philosophy* 49 (April 1974): 123–134.

21. Frank McCourt, *Angela's Ashes* (New York: Scribner, 1996), 80.

22. Hampton, "Moral Education," 227.

23. Duff, *Trials and Punishments*, 273.

24. While self-interest provides the most obvious example, the point does not depend on the rather controversial proposition that children are naturally attached to their own self-interest. As long as the natural attachments of the child vary from the attachments the parents wish them to have, the transferring of values will occur in the same way.

25. Haim G. Ginott, *Between Parent and Child: New Solutions to Old Problems* (New York: Macmillan, 1965).

26. J. Braithwaite and H. Strang, "Connecting Philosophy and Practice," in *Restorative Justice: Philosophy to Practice*, ed. H. Strang and J. Braithwaite (Aldershot, UK: Ashgate/Dartmouth, 2000), 215. Cited in Gerry Johnstone, *Restorative Justice: Ideas, Values, Debates* (Cullompton, Devon, UK: Willan, 2002), 101–102.

27. William Styron, *Sophie's Choice* (New York: Modern Library, 1998).

28. Nozick, *Philosophical Explanations*, 387. Note, however, that Nozick does not argue that this justifies punishment.

29. Barbara Tuchman notes that the flagellants attracted popular attention just for this reason. *A Distant Mirror: The Calamitous Fourteenth Century* (New York: Knopf, 1979), 114–115.

30. Nozick argues that hard treatment is necessary to erase the gladness that the offender feels about his wrong act. He ought not to be glad that he has done wrong; by punishing him, we will make him regret doing wrong, even if he feels no remorse. Nozick, *Philosophical Explanations*, 379, 386. As Duff's analysis of relevant versus prudential reasons for avoiding wrongdoing reveals, however, mere regret is no more an appropriate response to one's own wrongdoing than is gladness. An appropriate response requires that one's sorriness be based on the suffering one has caused to others, not on incidental inconvenience to oneself.

31. Duff, *Trials and Punishments*, 254–257.

32. Morris, "Paternalistic Theory," 165.

33. Duff, *Trials and Punishments*, 292.

NOTES TO CHAPTER 8

1. Bruce Western et al., "Crime, Punishment, and American Inequality," unpublished manuscript, June 2003. Available online at http://www.princeton.edu/~western/ineq2.pdf; Internet; accessed November 4, 2003.

2. Income inequality in a population can be measured by the Lorenz curve, which maps the percentage of households, from lowest to highest income, against the percentage of total income they have. On this curve, perfect equality would be represented by a 45-degree line. A sag in the Lorenz curve below the 45-degree line represents inequality. The Gini coefficient captures this sag numerically by comparing the area under the Lorenz curve for a population to the total area under the line of perfect equality. A Gini coefficient of 0 thus represents perfect equality, while a Gini coefficient of 1 would be perfect inequality (top 1 percent have all the income). The Gini coefficient for the United States in 1998 was .456. U.S. Census, *The Changing Shape of the Nation's Income Distribution, 1947–1998*, June 2000, fig. 2. Available online at http://www.census .gov/prod/2000pubs/p60-204.pdf; Internet; accessed January 5, 2004. Worldwide, the most unequal countries (e.g., Sierra Leone, Brazil, South Africa) have coefficients of around .6 and the most equal (e.g., Slovak Republic, Sweden, Norway) around .25. Data from Luxembourg Income Study, available online at http://www.lisproject.org/; Internet; accessed January 11, 2004.

3. See, e.g., C. Hsieh and M. D. Pugh, "Poverty, Income Inequality, and Violent Crime: A Meta-Analysis of Recent Aggregate Data Studies," *Criminal Justice Review* 18(2): 182–202 (1993), concluding that both poverty and income inequality were associated with violent crime; B. P. Kennedy, I. Kawachi, D. Prothrow-Stisth, K. Lochner, and B. Gibbs, "Social Capital, Income Inequality, and Firearm Violent Crime," *Social Science and Medicine* 47, no. 1 (1998): 7–17, concluding that both income inequality and lack of social capital were highly correlated with firearm violent crime rates in the United States. Western et al. found that correlations were weaker at the county level. "Inequality," 31.

4. S. Messner and R. Rosenfeld, *Crime and the American Dream*, 3rd ed. (Belmont, CA: Wadsworth, 2000), 7–10.

5. Western et al., "Inequality," 36.

6. Robert J. Sampson and William Julius Wilson, "Toward a Theory of Race, Crime, and Urban Inequality," in *Crime and Inequality*, ed. John Hagan and Ruth D. Peterson (Stanford, CA: Stanford University Press, 1995).

7. William Julius Wilson, *The Truly Disadvantaged: The Inner City, the Underclass, and Public Policy* (Chicago: University of Chicago Press, 1987).

8. National Low Income Housing Coalition, *2003 Advocates' Guide to Housing and Community Development Policy*, 87–90. Available online at http://www.nlihc.org/advocates/2003ag.pdf; Internet; accessed December 18, 2003.

9. Sampson and Wilson, "Race, Crime, and Inequality," 42–43.

10. Messner and Rosenfeld, *Crime and the American Dream*, 7–8, 101–104.

11. Kathleen Daly, "Restorative Justice: The Real Story," *Punishment and Society* 4, no. 1 (2002): 55–79. Available online at http://www.gu.edu.au/school/ccj/kdaly_docs/kdpaper12.pdf; Internet; accessed January 11, 2004. Page references are to Web version.

12. Gerry Johnstone, *Restorative Justice* (Cullompton, Devon, U.K.: Willan 2002), 80.

13. Daly, "Real Story," 26.

14. Friedrich Nietzsche, "'Guilt,' 'Bad Conscience,' and the Like," second essay in *On the Genealogy of Morals* in *On the Genealogy of Morals and Ecce Homo*, trans. Walter Kaufman (New York: Vintage Books, 1967).

15. Roger Wertheimer, "Understanding Retribution," *Criminal Justice Ethics* 3 (Summer/Fall 1983): 22–23.

16. Terry O'Connell, "From Wagga Wagga to Minnesota," paper presented at the First North American Conference on Conferencing, Minneapolis, August 6–8, 1998. Available online at http://www.restorativepractices.org/Pages/nacc/nacc_oco.html; Internet; accessed November 15, 2003; John Braithwaite, *Crime, Shame and Reintegration* (Cambridge: Cambridge University Press, 1989).

17. New South Wales Law Reform Commission, "Community Based Sentences," chap. 9 in *Discussion Paper 33: Sentencing* (April 1996). Available online at http://www.austlii.edu.au/au/other/nswlrc/dp33/9_78.html; Internet; accessed January 10, 2004.

18. Johnstone, *Restorative Justice*, 97, citing John Braithwaite, "Restorative Justice: Assessing Optimistic and Pessimistic Accounts," in *Crime and Justice: A Review of Research*, vol. 25, ed. Michael Tonry (Chicago: University of Chicago Press, 1999), 47.

19. Daly, "Real Story," 24–25.

20. Heather Strang, Geoffrey C. Barnes, John Braithwaite, and Lawrence W. Sherman, *Experiments in Restorative Policing: A Progress Report on the Canberra Reintegrative Shaming Experiments (RISE) July 1999*. Available online at http://www.aic.gov.au/rjustice/rise/progress/1999-6.pdf; Internet; accessed January 5, 2004. The leader of the Wagga Wagga effort, Terry O'Connell, reports that recently the police coordinators have been replaced by outside facilitators. O'Connell, "From Wagga Wagga to Minnesota."

21. John Braithwaite, *Restorative Justice and Responsive Regulation* (Oxford: Oxford University Press, 2002), 54–66. Braithwaite reviews the results of a

large number of empirical studies, most of which showed some improvement over traditional practices, and some of which showed dramatic improvement.

22. Strang et al., *Experiments in Restorative Policing.*

23. Johnstone, *Restorative Justice,* 124.

24. Jeff Latimer, Craig Dowden, and Danielle Muise, *The Effectiveness of Restorative Justice Practices: A Meta-Analysis* (Ottawa: Department of Justice, Canada, 2001), 5.

25. Rupert Ross, "Duelling Paradigms? Western Criminal Justice versus Aboriginal Community Healing," in *Justice as Healing: A Newsletter on Aboriginal Concepts of Justice.* Native Law Centre of Canada, Spring 1995. Excerpt available online at http://www.usask.ca/nativelaw/jah_ross.html; Internet; accessed October 20, 2003. See also Berma Bushie, "Community Holistic Circle Healing: A Community Approach," available online at http://www.iirp.org/Pages/vt/vt_bushie.html; accessed November 15, 2003.

26. Ross, "Duelling Paradigms?"

27. "A Healing Circle in the Innu Community of Sheshashit," *Justice as Healing* 2, no. 2 (Spring 1997). Also available online at http://www.usask.ca/nativelaw/jah_sellon.html; Internet; accessed October 20, 2003.

28. Johnstone, *Restorative Justice,* 106.

Bibliography

Abbott, J. H. *In the Belly of the Beast: Letters from Prison*. New York: Vintage, 1991.

Abel, Charles F., and Frank H. Marsh. *Punishment and Restitution*. Westport, CT: Greenwood Press, 1984.

Acton, H. B., ed. *The Philosophy of Punishment*. New York: St. Martin's Press, 1969.

Aeschylus. *The Eumenides*. Translated by Ian Johnston. Available online at http://www.mala.bc.ca/~johnstoi/aeschylus/aeschylus_eumenides.htm; Internet; accessed December 8, 2003. Print version available from Prideaux Street Publications, Nanaimo, BC, Canada.

Aldred, Cyril. *The Egyptians*. New York: Praeger, 1961.

Andenaes, Johannes. *Punishment and Deterrence*. Ann Arbor: University of Michigan Press, 1974.

Aquinas, St. Thomas. *Treatise on Law (Summa Theologica, Questions 90–97)*. Chicago: Regnery, 1965.

Aristotle. *De Anima*. Translated by Hugh Lawson-Tancred. New York: Penguin Books, 1987.

———. *The Art of Rhetoric*. Translated by Hugh Lawson-Tancred. New York: Penguin Books, 1992.

Armstrong, K. G. "The Retributivist Hits Back." *Mind* 70 (1961): 471–490.

Attenborough, F. L. *Laws of the Earliest English Kings*. New York: AMS Press, 1974.

Augustine. *Letters* 91, 93, 94, A.D. 408; 44, A.D. 398; available online at http://www.newadvent.org/fathers/1102.htm; Internet; accessed October 11, 2003.

Baird, Robert M., and Stuart Rosenbaum, eds. *Philosophy of Punishment*. Buffalo, NY: Prometheus Books, 1988.

Beccaria, Cesare. *On Crimes and Punishments*. Translated by David Young. Indianapolis: Hackett, 1986. First published in 1764.

Bedau, Hugo. "Retribution and the Theory of Punishment." *Journal of Philosophy* 75 (1978): 601–625.

Bennett, Jonathan. "The Conscience of Huckleberry Finn." *Philosophy* 49 (April 1974): 123–134.

Bentham, Jeremy. *Introduction to the Principles of Morals and Legislation*. New York: Hafner, 1948. First published in 1781.

Berns, Walter. *For Capital Punishment: Crime and the Morality of the Death Penalty*. New York: Basic Books, 1979.

Blom-Cooper, Louis. "The Penalty of Imprisonment." Tanner Lectures on Human Values, Cambridge University, 1987. Available online at http://www.tannerlectures.utah.edu/lectures/Blom-Cooper88.pdf; accessed May 15, 2003.

Blumstein, Alfred, and Daniel Nagin. "The Deterrent Effect of Legal Sanctions on Draft Evasion." *Stanford Law Review* 29 (1976): 241–275.

Blumstein, Alfred, Jacqueline Cohen, Jeffrey A. Roth, and Christy Visher, eds. *Criminal Careers and "Career Criminals,"* vol. 2. Washington, DC: National Academy Press, 1986.

Bosanquet, Bernard. *The Philosophical Theory of the State and Related Essays*. London: Macmillan; New York: St. Martin's Press, 1965. First published in 1923.

———. *Some Suggestions in Ethics*. 1918. Reprint, New York: Kraus Reprint, 1968.

Bottoms, Anthony E. "Interpersonal Violence and Social Order in Prisons." In *Prisons*, ed. Michael Tonry and Joan Petersilia. Vol. 26 of *Crime and Justice: A Review of Research*. Chicago: University of Chicago Press, 1999.

Bourguignon, François. "Crime as a Social Cost of Poverty and Inequality: A Review Focusing on Developing Countries." In *Facets of Globalization*, 171–191. Edited by Shahid Yusuf, Simon Evenett, and Weiping Wu. Washington, DC: World Bank, October 2001.

Box, Steven. *Power, Crime, and Mystification*. London: Tavistock Publications, 1983.

Bradley, F. H. "The Vulgar Notion of Responsibility." In *Ethical Studies*. 2nd ed. Oxford: Clarendon Press, 1927. First published in 1876.

———. "Some Remarks on Punishment." *International Journal of Ethics* 4, no. 3 (April 1894): 269–284.

Braithwaite, John. *Crime, Shame, and Reintegration*. Cambridge: Cambridge University Press, 1989.

———. *Restorative Justice and Responsive Regulation*. Oxford: Oxford University Press, 2002.

Brandt, Richard. *Ethical Theory*. Englewood Cliffs, NJ: Prentice Hall, 1959.

Breggin, Peter R. "Campaigns against Racist Federal Programs by the Center for the Study of Psychiatry and Psychology." *Journal of African American Men* 1, no. 3 (Winter 1995–96): 3–22.

Buffalo Report, March 1, 2002.

Bureau of Justice Statistics. *Bulletin*, April 1997.

Burgh, Richard. "Do the Guilty Deserve Punishment?" *Journal of Philosophy* 79, no. 4 (April 1982): 193–210.

Bushie, Berma. "Community Holistic Circle Healing: A Community Approach." Available online at http://www.iirp.org/Pages/vt/vt_bushie.html; accessed November 15, 2003.

Butler, Samuel. *Erewhon*. New York: Modern Library, 1927. First published in 1872.

Calhoun, Cheshire, and Robert C. Solomon, eds. *What Is an Emotion?* New York: Oxford University Press, 1984.

Center on Child Abuse Prevention Research. *Intensive Home Visitation: A Randomized Trial, Follow-up, and Risk Assessment Study of Hawaii's Healthy Start Program*. Chicago: National Committee to Prevent Child Abuse, 1996.

Clarke, S. H. "Getting 'Em Out of Circulation: Does Incarceration of Juvenile Offenders Reduce Crime?" *Journal of Criminal Law and Criminology* 65, no. 4 (1974): 528–535.

Clockwork Orange, A. Produced and directed by Stanley Kubrick. 137 min. Warner Brothers, 1991. Videocassette.

Code of Hammurabi, The. Translated by Theophile J. Meeks. In *Ancient Near Eastern Texts Relating to the Old Testament*. Edited by J. B. Pritchard. Princeton: Princeton University Press, 1969.

Cohen, Jacqueline, and Jose A. Canela-Cacho. "Incarceration and Violent Crime, 1965–1988." In *Understanding and Preventing Violence: Consequence and Control*, vol. 4. Edited by Albert J. Reiss, Jr., and Jeffrey A. Roth. Washington, DC: National Academy Press, 1994.

Cohen, L. E., and M. Felson. "Social Change and Crime Rate Trends: A Routine Activity Approach." *American Sociological Review* 44 (1979): 588–608.

Cohen, Mark A. "Measuring the Costs and Benefits of Crime and Justice." In *Criminal Justice 2000*, vol. 4: *Measurement and Analysis of Crime and Justice*, 263–315. Washington, DC: National Institute of Justice, 2000.

Corlett, J. Angelo. "Foundations of a Kantian Theory of Punishment." *Southern Journal of Philosophy* 31 (1993): 263–283.

Currie, Elliott. "Crime and Punishment in the United States: Myths, Realities, and Possibilities." In *The Politics of Law: A Progressive Critique*. 3rd ed. Edited by David Kairys. New York: Basic Books, 1998.

Dagger, Richard. "Playing Fair with Punishment." *Ethics* 103 (1993): 473–488.

Daly, Kathleen. "Restorative Justice: The Real Story." *Punishment and Society* 4, no. 1 (2002): 55–79 . Also available online at http://www.gu.edu.au/school/ccj/kdaly_docs/kdpaper12.pdf; Internet; accessed January 11, 2004.

De Haan, Willem. *The Politics of Redress*. London: Unwin Hyman, 1990.

De Sousa, Ronald. *The Rationality of Emotion*. Cambridge, MA: MIT Press, 1987.

Descartes, René. *The Passions of the Soul*. Indianapolis: Hackett, 1989. First published in 1649.

DiIulio, John, and Anne Morrison Piehl. "'Does Prison Pay?' Revisited: Returning to the Crime Scene." *Brookings Review* (Spring 1995).

Dimock, Susan. "Retributivism and Trust." *Law and Philosophy* 16 (1997): 37–62.

Dolinko, David. "Thoughts about Retributivism." *Ethics* 101 (April 1991): 537–559.

Doyle, James. "A Radical Critique of Punishment." Presented at AMINTAPHIL, Allentown, Pennsylvania, 1992.

Duff, R. A. *Trials and Punishments*. Cambridge: Cambridge University Press, 1986.

———. *Punishment, Communication, and Culture*. New York: Oxford University Press, 2001.

Duff, R. A., and David Garland, eds. *A Reader on Punishment*. Oxford: Oxford University Press, 1994.

Durham, Alexis M., III. *Crisis and Reform: Current Issues in American Punishment*. Boston: Little, Brown, 1994.

Durkheim, Emile. *The Division of Labor in Society*. New York: Macmillan, 1933.

Ewing, A. C. *The Morality of Punishment*. Montclair, NJ: Patterson Smith, 1970. First published in 1929.

Farrell, Daniel M. "The Justification of Deterrent Violence." *Ethics* 100, no. 2 (1990): 301–317.

———. "The Justification of General Deterrence." *Philosophical Review* 94, no. 3 (July 1985): 367–394.

———. "On Threats and Punishments." *Social Theory and Practice* 15 (1989): 125–154.

Fattah, Ezzat A. *Criminology: Past, Present and Future*. London: Macmillan, 1997.

Feeney, Floyd. *German and American Prosecutions: An Approach to Statistical Comparison*. Washington, DC: Bureau of Justice Statistics, 1998.

Feinberg, Joel. *Doing and Deserving*. Princeton: Princeton University Press, 1970.

———. *Harm to Self*. Vol. 3 of *The Moral Limits of the Criminal Law*. New York: Oxford University Press, 1986.

Fields, Charles B., and Richard H. Moore, Jr., eds. *Comparative Criminal Justice: Traditional and Nontraditional Systems of Law and Control*. Prospect Heights, IL: Waveland Press, 1996.

Fingarette, Herbert. "Punishment and Suffering." Presidential Address, Eastern Division of the American Philosophical Association. *Proceedings of the American Philosophical Association*, 1977.

Finnis, J. "The Restoration of Retribution." *Analysis* 32 (1971–72): 131–135.

Flaten, Caren. "Victim-Offender Mediation." In *Restorative Justice: International Perspectives*. Edited by Burt Galaway and Joe Hudson. Monsey, NY: Criminal Justice Press, 1996.

Fletcher, George P. *Rethinking Criminal Law*. Boston: Little, Brown, 1978.

Foucault, Michel. *Histoire de la Sexualité*. Vol. 1: *La Volonté de Savoir*. Paris: Gallimard, 1976.

———. *Discipline and Punish: The Birth of the Prison*. Translated by Alan Sheridan. New York: Vintage Books, 1995.

Frankfort, Henri, and H. A. Gronewegen-Frankfort. *Before Philosophy: The Intellectual Adventure of Ancient Man*. Chicago: University of Chicago Press, 1946.

Frase, Richard S. "Sentencing in Germany and the United States: Comparing Aepfel with Apples." Freiburg, Germany: Max Planck Institute, 2001. Available online at http://www.iuscrim.mpg.de/verlag/Forschaktuell/Frase-Endausdruck.pdf; accessed November 4, 2003.

Friedman, David. *Law's Order: What Economics Has to Do with Law and Why It Matters*. Princeton: Princeton University Press, 2000.

Gaes, Gerald G., Timothy J. Flanagan, Larry Motiuk, and Lynn Stewart. "Adult Correctional Treatment." In *Prisons*, ed. Michael Tonry and Joan Petersilia. Vol. 26 in *Crime and Justice: A Review of Research*. Chicago: University of Chicago Press, 1999.

Galaway, Burt, and Joe Hudson, eds. *Restorative Justice: International Perspectives*. Monsey, NY: Criminal Justice Press, 1996.

Garland, David. *Punishment and Modern Society*. Oxford: Clarendon Press, 1985.

Garland, David, and Peter Young. *The Power to Punish*. London: Heinemann Educational Books, 1983.

Gibbs, Jack P. *Crime, Punishment and Deterrence*. New York: Elsevier, 1975.

Ginott, Haim G. *Between Parent and Child: New Solutions to Old Problems*. New York: Macmillan, 1965.

Glover, M. R. "Mr. Mabbott on Punishment." *Mind*, n.s. 48, no. 192 (October 1939): 498–501.

Goldman, Alan. "The Paradox of Punishment." *Philosophy and Public Affairs* 9 (1979): 42–58.

———. "Toward a New Theory of Punishment." *Law and Philosophy* 1 (1982): 57–76.

Gorczyk, John F. "If We Were Serious about Public Safety, What Would It Look Like?" Paper presented at Building Strong Partnerships for Restorative Practices Conference, August 5–7, 1999, Burlington, Vermont. Available online at http://www.iirp.org/Pages/vt/vt_gorczyk.html; accessed November 15, 2003.

Gottfredson, Stephen D., and Don M. Gottfredson. "Behavioral Prediction and the Problem of Incapacitation." *Criminology* 32, no. 3 (1994): 441–474.

Green, T. H. *Lectures on the Principles of Political Obligation*. London, New York: Longmans, Green, 1931. First published in 1882.

Greenberg, David, and Ronald C. Kessler. "The Effects of Arrest on Crime: A Multivariate Panel Analysis." *Social Forces* 60 (1982): 771–790.

Greenwood, Peter W. *Selective Incapacitation*. Santa Monica, CA: Rand, 1982.

Greenwood, Peter W., Karyn E. Model, C. Peter Rydell, and James Chiesa. *Diverting Children from a Life of Crime: Measuring Costs and Benefits*. Santa Monica, CA: Rand, 1996.

Gross, Hyman. *A Theory of Criminal Justice*. New York: Oxford University Press, 1979.

Habermas, Jürgen. *Between Facts and Norms*. Translated by William Rehg. Cambridge, MA: MIT Press, 1996.

Hagan, John, and Ronit Dinovitzer. "Collateral Consequences of Imprisonment for Children, Communities and Prisoners." In *Prisons*, ed. Michael Tonry and Joan Petersilia. Vol. 26 of *Crime and Justice: A Review of Research*. Chicago: University of Chicago Press, 1999.

Hagan, John, and Ruth D. Peterson, eds. *Crime and Inequality*. Stanford, CA: Stanford University Press, 1995.

Hampton, Jean. "The Moral Education Theory of Punishment." *Philosophy and Public Affairs* 13, no. 3 (Summer 1984): 208–238.

Harlow, Caroline Wolf. *Prior Abuse Reported by Inmates and Probationers*. Washington, DC: Bureau of Justice Statistics, April 1999.

Hart, H. L. A. *Punishment and Responsibility*. New York: Oxford University Press, 1968.

Hawkins, Richard, and Geoffrey Alpert. *American Prison Systems: Punishment and Justice*. Englewood Cliffs, NJ: Prentice Hall, 1989.

Hayek, Friedrich. *Law, Legislation, and Liberty*. Chicago: University of Chicago Press, 1990. First published in 1973.

"A Healing Circle in the Innu Community of Sheshashit." *Justice as Healing* 2, no. 2 (Spring 1997). Available online at http://www.usask.ca/nativelaw/jah _sellon.html; Internet; accessed October 20, 2003.

Hegel, G. W. F. *Philosophy of Right*. Translated by T. M. Knox. London: Clarendon Press, 1942. First published in 1821.

Henberg, Martin. *Retribution: Evil for Evil in Ethics, Law, and Literature*. Philadelphia: Temple University Press, 1990.

Hobbes, Thomas. *Leviathan*. Edited by Edwin Curley. New York: Washington Square Press, 1964. First published in 1651.

Homer. *Iliad*, Book 6. Quoted in *What Is Justice?* ed. Robert J. Solomon and Mark C. Murphy. Oxford: Oxford University Press, 1990.

Honderich, Ted. *Punishment: The Supposed Justifications*. Harmondsworth, Middlesex, UK: Penguin, 1971.

Hsieh, C., and Pugh, M. D. "Poverty, Income Inequality, and Violent Crime: A

Meta-Analysis of Recent Aggregate Data Studies." *Criminal Justice Review* 18, no. 2 (1993): 182–202.

Hudson, Barbara A. "Restorative Justice: The Challenge of Racial and Sexual Violence." Presented at Law and Society Association annual meeting, St. Louis, Missouri, May 1997.

Human Rights Watch. "No Escape: Male Rape in U.S. Prisons." Available online at http://www.hrw.org/reports/2001/prison/report.html; Internet; accessed June 11, 2002.

Hume, David. *Treatise of Human Nature.* Book 2. Oxford: Clarendon Press, 1888.

Ignatieff, Michael. *A Just Measure of Pain: The Penitentiary in the Industrial Revolution, 1750–1780.* New York: Pantheon Books, 1978.

James, William. *What Is an Emotion?* Excerpted in Calhoun and Solomon, *What Is an Emotion?* 127–141. First published in 1890.

Johnson, Robert. *Hard Time: Understanding and Reforming the Prison.* 3rd ed. Belmont, CA: Wadsworth, 2002.

Johnson, Robert, and Hans Toch, eds. Introduction to *The Pains of Imprisonment.* Beverly Hills, CA: Sage, 1982.

Johnstone, Gerry. *Restorative Justice: Ideas, Values, Debates.* Cullompton, Devon, UK: Willan, 2002.

Jones, Peter R., Philip W. Harris, and Jamie Fader. "Identifying Chronic Offenders." Research Paper for the Council of Juvenile Correctional Administrators Conference, Crime and Justice Research Institute, Philadelphia. Philadelphia Department of Human Services, January 1999.

Justice as Healing: A Newsletter on Aboriginal Concepts of Justice. Native Law Centre of Canada. Available online at http://www.usask.ca/nativelaw/jah ross.html; Internet; accessed October 20, 2003.

Kafka, Franz. *In the Penal Colony: Stories and Short Pieces.* Translated by Willa and Edwin Muir. New York: Schocken Books, 1995.

Kahan, Dan M., and Martha C. Nussbaum. "Two Conceptions of Emotion in Criminal Law." *Columbia Law Review* 96 (1996): 269–374.

Kairys, David, ed. *The Politics of Law: A Progressive Critique.* 3rd ed. New York: Basic Books, 1998.

Kant, Immanuel. *Foundations of the Metaphysics of Morals.* Translated by Lewis White Beck. Indianapolis: Bobbs-Merrill, 1959. First published in 1785.

———. *The Metaphysical Elements of Justice.* Translated by John Ladd. New York: Macmillan, 1965. First published in 1797.

Katz, Jack. *Seductions of Crime: Moral and Sensual Attractions in Doing Evil.* New York: Basic Books, 1988.

Kelly, Morgan. "Inequality and Crime." *Review of Economics and Statistics* 82, no. 4 (November 2000): 530–539.

Kennedy, B. P., I. Kawachi, D. Prothrow-Stith, K. Lochner, and B. Gibbs. "Social Capital, Income Inequality, and Firearm Violent Crime." *Social Science and Medicine* 47, no. 1 (1998): 7–17.

Klepper, Steven, and Daniel Nagin. "Tax Compliance and Perceptions of the Risks of Detection and Criminal Prosecution." *Law and Society Review* 23, no. 2 (1989): 204–240.

———. "The Deterrent Effect of Perceived Certainty and Severity of Punishment Revisited." *Criminology* 27 (1989): 721.

Kübler-Ross, Elizabeth. *Living with Death and Dying*. New York: Macmillan, 1981.

Latimer, Jeff, Craig Dowden, and Danielle Muise. *The Effectiveness of Restorative Justice Practices: A Meta-Analysis*. Ottowa: Department of Justice, Canada, 2001. Available online at http://canada.justice.gc.ca/en/ps/rs/rep/meta-e.pdf; Internet; accessed November 15, 2003.

"Laws of the Twelve Tables." Translated by S. P. Scott. In *The Civil Law*. Edited by S. P. Scott, 57–77. New York: AMS Press, 1973.

Levitt, Steven D. "The Effect of Prison Population Size on Crime Rates: Evidence from Prison Overcrowding Litigation." *Quarterly Journal of Economics* 111, no. 2 (May 1996): 319–351.

Lipsey, M. W. "What Do We Learn from 400 Research Studies on the Effectiveness of Treatment with Juvenile Delinquents?" In *What Works: Reducing Reoffending*. Edited by J. McGuire. New York: John Wiley and Sons, 1995.

Locke, John. *Second Treatise of Government*. Edited by Thomas P. Peardon. Indianapolis: Bobbs-Merrill, 1952. First published in 1690.

Lutz, Catherine. *Unnatural Emotions*. Chicago: University of Chicago Press, 1988.

Lynch, James P. "Does Punishment Pay?" Washington, DC: Urban Institute, 1997.

———. "Crime in International Perspective." In *Crime: Public Policies for Crime Control*. Edited by James Q. Wilson and Joan Petersilia, 5–42. Oakland, CA: Institute for Contemporary Studies, 2002.

Lyons, William. *Emotions*. Cambridge: Cambridge University Press, 1980.

Mabbott, J. D. "Punishment." *Mind*, n.s. 48, no. 190 (April 1939): 152–167.

MacKenzie, Doris L. "Criminal Justice and Crime Prevention." In Lawrence W. Sherman et al., *Preventing Crime: What Works, What Doesn't, What's Promising: A Report to the United States Congress*. Washington, DC: National Institute of Justice, 1997. Available online at http://www.ncjrs.org/works/htm; Internet; accessed June 20, 2002.

Mackenzie, Mary Margaret. *Plato on Punishment*. Berkeley: University of California Press, 1981.

Maitland, Angela S., and Richard D. Sluder. "Victimization in Prisons: A Study of Factors Related to the General Well-Being of Youthful Inmates." *Federal Probation* 60, no. 2 (June 1996) 24–31.

Mariner, Joanne. *No Escape: Male Rape in U.S. Prisons.* New York: Human Rights Watch, April 2001.

Mark, Vernon H., and Frank R. Ervin. *Violence and the Brain.* New York: Harper and Row, 1970.

Martinson, Robert. "What Works? Questions and Answers about Prison Reform." *Public Interest* 35 (Spring 1974): 22–56.

Marvell, Thomas, and Carlisle Moody. "Prison Population Growth and Crime Reduction." *Journal of Quantitative Criminology* 10 (1994): 109–140.

Matravers, Matt. *Justice and Punishment: The Rationale of Coercion.* Oxford: Oxford University Press, 2000.

McCloskey, H. J. "The Complexity of the Concepts of Punishment." *Philosophy* 37 (1962): 307–325.

———. "Utilitarian and Retributive Punishment." *Journal of Philosophy* 64 (1967): 91–110.

———. "A Non-Utilitarian Approach to Punishment." In *Contemporary Utilitarianism.* Edited by Michael D. Bayles, 239–259. Garden City, NY: Anchor Books, 1968.

McCourt, Frank. *Angela's Ashes.* New York: Scribner, 1996.

McGuire, J., ed. *What Works: Reducing Reoffending.* New York: John Wiley and Sons, 1995.

Menninger, Karl. *The Crime of Punishment.* New York: Viking Press, 1968.

Messner, S., and R. Rosenfeld. *Crime and the American Dream.* 3rd ed. Belmont, CA: Wadsworth, 2000.

Mill, J. S. "An Examination of Sir William Hamilton's Philosophy." Vol. 9 of *Collected Works of John Stuart Mill.* Edited by J. M. Robson. Toronto: University of Toronto Press, 1979.

———. *Utilitarianism.* Edited by George Sher. Indianapolis: Hackett, 1979. First published in 1861.

Montague, Philip. *Punishment as Societal-Defense.* Lanham, MD: Rowman and Littlefield, 1995.

Moore, Michael. "The Moral Worth of Retribution." In *Responsibility, Character and the Emotions.* Edited by F. Schoeman. Cambridge: Cambridge University Press, 1987.

Morris, Herbert. "Persons and Punishment." *Monist* 52, no. 4 (October 1968): 475–501.

———. "A Paternalistic Theory of Punishment." *American Philosophical Quarterly* 18 (October 1981): 211–263.

Morris, Norval, and David J. Rothman, eds. *The Oxford History of the Prison.* Oxford: Oxford University Press, 1995.

———. "Marxism and Retribution." *Philosophy and Public Affairs* 2, no. 3 (Spring 1973): 217–243.

———. *Retribution, Justice, and Therapy.* Dordrecht, Holland; Boston: D. Reidel, 1979.

———. "Getting Even: The Role of the Victim." In *Crime, Culpability and Remedy.* Edited by Ellen Frankel Paul et al., 209–225. Oxford: Basil Blackwell, 1990. Originally published in Jeffrie Murphy and Jean Hampton, *Forgiveness and Mercy.* Cambridge: Cambridge University Press, 1988.

———. "Retributivism and the State's Interest in Punishment." In *Nomos 28: Criminal Justice.* Edited by J. R. Pennock and J. Chapman, 156–164. New York: NYU Press, 1985.

Murphy, Jeffrie, ed. *Punishment and Rehabilitation.* 3rd ed. Belmont, CA: Wadsworth, 1995.

Murphy, Jeffrie, and Jules Coleman. *The Philosophy of Law: An Introduction to Jurisprudence.* Boulder, CO: Westview Press, 1990.

Murphy, Jeffrie, and Jean Hampton. *Forgiveness and Mercy.* Cambridge: Cambridge University Press, 1988.

Nagin, Daniel. "Criminal Deterrence Research at the Outset of the 21st Century." In *Crime and Justice: A Review of Research*, vol. 23. Edited by Michael Tonry, 1–42. Chicago: University of Chicago Press, 1998.

Narayan, Uma. "Appropriate Responses and Preventive Benefits: Justifying Censure and Hard Treatment in Legal Punishment." *Oxford Journal of Legal Studies* 13 (1993): 166–181.

Nathanson, Stephen. "Is the Death Penalty What Murderers Deserve?" In *Living Well: Introductory Readings in Ethics.* Edited by Steven Luper, 543–553. New York: Harcourt Brace, 2000.

National Center for Injury Prevention and Control. "Leading Causes of Death." Available online at http://webapp.cdc.gov/sasweb/ncipc/leadcaus.html; Internet; accessed August 10, 2001.

Newman, Graeme. *Just and Painful.* New York: Macmillan, 1983.

Nietzsche, Friedrich. *On the Genealogy of Morals.* Translated by Walter Kaufman. New York: Vintage Books, 1967. First published in 1887.

Nino, C. S. "A Consensual Theory of Punishment." *Philosophy and Public Affairs* 12 (1983): 289–306.

Nozick, Robert. *Philosophical Explanations.* Cambridge, MA: Harvard University Press, 1981.

Oakley, Justin. *Morality and the Emotions.* London: Routledge, 1992.

O'Connell, Terry. "From Wagga Wagga to Minnesota." Paper presented at the First North American Conference on Conferencing, Minneapolis, August 6–8, 1998. Available online at http://www.restorativepractices.org/Pages/nacc/nacc_oco.html; Internet; accessed November 15, 2003.

Oldenquist, Andrew. "An Explanation of Retribution." *Journal of Philosophy* 85 (1988): 464–478.

O'Neill, Onora. *Constructions of Reason: Explorations of Kant's Practical Philosophy.* Cambridge: Cambridge University Press, 1989.

Owen, Robert. "A New View of Society: Second Essay." *The Avalon Project at Yale Law School* (1813). Available online at http://www.yale.edu/lawweb/Avalon/econ/ow02.htm; Internet; accessed May 15, 2003.

Packer, Herbert. *The Limits of the Criminal Sanction.* Stanford: Stanford University Press, 1968.

Paul, Ellen Frankel, Fred D. Miller, Jr., and Jeffrey Paul, eds. *Crime, Culpability and Remedy.* Oxford: Basil Blackwell, 1990.

Pepinsky, Harold E. *The Geometry of Violence and Democracy.* Bloomington: Indiana University Press, 1991.

Pincoffs, Edmund. *The Rationale of Legal Punishment.* New York: Humanities Press, 1966.

Plato. *Protageras.* Translated by Stanley Lombardo and Karen Bell. Indianapolis: Hackett, 1992.

———. *The Trial and Death of Socrates.* Translated by G. M. A. Grube. Indianapolis: Hackett, 1975.

———. *Gorgias.* Translated by Donald J. Zeyl. Indianapolis: Hackett, 1987.

Posner, Richard. "Criminal Law." Chap. 7 in *Economic Analysis of Law.* New York: Aspen Law and Business, 1998.

Quine, Willard Van Orman. "Two Dogmas of Empiricism." In *From a Logical Point of View.* 2nd ed. Cambridge, MA: Harvard University Press, 1961.

Quinn, Warren. "The Right to Threaten and the Right to Punish." *Philosophy and Public Affairs* 14, no. 4 (Fall 1985): 327–373.

———. "Actions, Intentions, and Consequences: The Doctrine of Double Effect." *Philosophy and Public Affairs* 18, no. 4 (Autumn 1989): 334–351.

Radin, Margaret. "Capital Punishment and Respect for Persons: Super Due Process for Death." *Southern California Law Review* 55 (1980): 1143–1189.

Rawls, John. "Two Concepts of Rules." *Philosophical Review* 64, no. 1 (January 1955): 3–32. Reprinted in *The Philosophy of Punishment.* Edited by H. B. Acton, 105–114. London: Macmillan, 1969.

———. *A Theory of Justice.* Cambridge, MA: Harvard University Press, 1971.

Reiss, Jr., Albert J., and Jeffrey Roth, eds. *Understanding and Preventing Violence,* vol. 4: *Consequence and Control.* Washington, DC: National Academy Press, 1994.

Rorty, Amelie, ed. *Explaining Emotions.* Berkeley: University of California Press, 1980.

Ross, Rupert. "Duelling Paradigms? Western Criminal Justice versus Aboriginal

Community Healing." In *Justice as Healing: A Newsletter on Aboriginal Concepts of Justice*. Native Law Centre of Canada, Spring 1995. Excerpt available online at http://www.usask.ca/nativelaw/jah_ross.html; Internet; accessed October 20, 2003.

Ross, W. D. *The Right and the Good*. Oxford: Clarendon Press, 1930.

Rotman, Edgardo. *Beyond Punishment*. New York: Greenwood Press, 1990.

Rubin, Edward L., ed. *Minimizing Harm: A New Crime Policy for Modern America*. Boulder, CO: Westview Press, 1999.

Rusche, Georg, and Otto Kirchheimer. *Punishment and Social Structure*. New York: Columbia University Press, 1968. First published in 1939.

Rutherford, Andrew. *Prisons and the Process of Justice*. London: Heinemann Educational Books, 1984.

Ryle, Gilbert. *The Concept of Mind*. New York: Barnes and Noble, 1969. First published in 1949.

Sabol, William, and James Lynch. *Crime Policy Report: Did Getting Tough on Crime Pay?* Washington, DC: Urban Institute, 1997.

Sadurski, Wojciech. "Theory of Punishment, Social Justice, and Liberal Neutrality." *Law and Philosophy* 7 (1989): 351–373.

Sampson, Robert J., and William Julius Wilson. "Toward a Theory of Race, Crime, and Urban Inequality." In *Crime and Inequality*. Edited by John Hagan and Ruth D. Peterson. Stanford, CA: Stanford University Press, 1995.

Sayre-McCord, Geoffrey. "Criminal Justice and Legal Reparations as an Alternative to Punishment." *Philosophical Issues* 11 (2001): 502–529.

Schachter, Stanley. "The Interaction of Cognitive, Social, and Physiological Determinants of Emotional State." *Psychological Review* 69 (1962): 379–399.

Schlick, Moritz. "When Is a Man Responsible?" In *Problems of Ethics*. Translated by David Rynin, 143–156. Englewood Cliffs, NJ: Prentice Hall, 1939.

Schoemann, Frederick, ed. *Responsibility, Character and the Emotions*. Cambridge: Cambridge University Press, 1987.

Scull, Andrew. "Community Corrections: Panacea, Progress, or Pretence?" In *The Power to Punish*. Edited by David Garland and Peter Young, 146–169. Atlantic Highlands, NJ: Humanities Press, 1983.

Sher, George. *Desert*. Princeton: Princeton University Press, 1987.

———. "An Unsolved Problem about Punishment." *Social Theory and Practice* 4 (1977): 149–165.

Sherman, Lawrence W., Denise Gottfredson, Doris MacKenzie, John Eck, Peter Reuter, and Shawn Bushway. *Preventing Crime: What Works, What Doesn't, What's Promising: A Report to the United States Congress*. Washington, DC: National Institute of Justice, 1997. Available online at http://www.ncjrs.org/works/; Internet; accessed June 20, 2002.

Simpson, William Kelly, ed. *The Literature of Ancient Egypt*. 2nd ed. New Haven: Yale University Press, 1973.

Smith, Carolyn, and Terence Thornberry. "The Relationship between Childhood Maltreatment and Adolescent Involvement in Delinquency." *Criminology* 33, no. 4 (1995): 451–477.

Solomon, Robert J., and Mark C. Murphy, eds. *What Is Justice?* Oxford: Oxford University Press, 1990.

Spelman, William. *Criminal Incapacitation*. New York: Plenum, 1994.

Sprigge, T. L. S. "A Utilitarian Reply to Dr. McCloskey." In *Contemporary Utilitarianism*. Edited by M. D. Bayles, 261–299. Garden City, NY: Anchor Books, 1968.

Stearns, Carol Z., and Peter N. Stearns, eds. *Emotion and Social Change: Toward a New Psychohistory*. New York: Holmes and Meier, 1988.

Stephen, James Fitzjames. *A History of the Criminal Law in England*. 1883. Reprint, Buffalo, New York: Wm. S. Hein, 1993.

Strang, Heather, and John Braithwaite, eds. *Restorative Justice: Philosophy to Practice*. Aldershot, UK: Ashgate/Dartmouth, 2000.

Strang, Heather, Geoffrey C. Barnes, John Braithwaite, and Lawrence W. Sherman. "Long-Term Effects of Court and Conference." Chap. 6 in *Experiments in Restorative Policing: A Progress Report on the Canberra Reintegrative Shaming Experiments (RISE)*. July 1999. Available online at http://www.aic .gov.au/rjustice/rise/progress/1999-6.pdf; Internet; accessed December 4, 2003.

Styron, William. *Sophie's Choice*. New York: Modern Library, 1998.

Ten, C. L. "Positive Retributivism." In *Crime, Culpability and Remedy*. Cambridge, MA: Basil Blackwell, 1990.

Thomas, Laurence. *Living Morally*. Philadelphia: Temple University Press, 1989.

Tonry, Michael, ed. *Crime and Justice: A Review of Research*. Vol. 23. Chicago: University of Chicago Press, 1998.

Tonry, Michael, and Joan Petersilia. "Prisons Research at the Beginning of the 21st Century." In *Prisons*. Vol. 26 of *Crime and Justice: A Review of Research*. Edited by Tonry and Petersilia, 1–16. Chicago: University of Chicago Press, 1999. Available online at http://www.ncjrs.org/pdffiles1/nij/184478 .pdf; Internet; accessed October 16, 2003.

Treston, Hubert J. *Poine: A Study in Ancient Greek Blood-Vengeance*. London: Longmans, 1923

Tuchman, Barbara. *A Distant Mirror: The Calamitous Fourteenth Century*. New York: Knopf, 1979.

Tyler, Tom R., and Fay Lenore Cook. "The Mass Media and Judgments of Risk: Distinguishing Impact on Personal and Societal Level Judgments." *Journal of Personality and Social Psychology* 47: 693–708.

United States Sentencing Commission. *Federal Sentencing Guidelines Manual*. Washington, DC, 1987.

Visher, Christy A. "The Rand Inmate Survey: A Reanalysis." In *Criminal Careers and "Career Criminals."* Edited by Alfred Blumstein, Jacqueline Cohen, Jeffrey A. Roth, and Christy Visher, 2: 161–211. Washington, DC: National Academy Press, 1986.

Walker, Samuel. *Sense and Nonsense about Crime and Drugs*, 4th. ed. Belmont, CA: Wadsworth, 1948.

———. *Why Punish?* Oxford: Basil Blackwell, 1991.

Walmsley, Roy. "World Prison Populations: Facts, Trends and Solutions." Presented at the United Nations Programme Network Institutes Technical Assistance Workshop, Vienna, Austria, May 10, 2001.

Warner, Sue. *Making Amends: Justice for Victims and Offenders.* Aldershot, UK: Avebury, 1992.

Wasserstrom, Richard. "Why Punish the Guilty?" *Princeton University Magazine* 20 (Spring 1964): 14–19.

Wenk, Ernst A., James O. Robison, and Gerald W. Smith. "Can Violence Be Predicted?" *Crime and Delinquency* 18 (October 1972): 393–402.

Wertheimer, Roger. "Understanding Retribution." *Criminal Justice Ethics* 3 (Summer/Fall 1983): 19–38.

Western, Bruce, Meredith Kleykamp, and Jake Rosenfeld. "Crime, Punishment and American Inequality." Unpublished manuscript, June 2003. Available online at http://www.princeton.edu/~western/ineq2.pdf; Internet; accessed November 4, 2003.

Widom, Cathy Spatz. *The Cycle of Violence Revisited.* Washington, DC: National Institute of Justice, 1996.

Wilson, James Q. *Thinking about Crime.* New York: Basic Books, 1975.

Wilson, James Q., and Joan Petersilia, eds. *Crime: Public Policies for Crime Control.* Oakland, CA: Institute for Contemporary Studies, 2002.

Wilson, John. *The Culture of Ancient Egypt.* Chicago: University of Chicago Press, 1951.

Wilson, William Julius. *The Truly Disadvantaged: The Inner City, the Underclass, and Public Policy.* Chicago: University of Chicago Press, 1987.

Wolfgang, Marvin, Robert M. Figlio, and Thorsten Sellin. *Delinquency in a Birth Cohort.* Chicago: University of Chicago Press, 1972.

Wolgast, Elizabeth. *The Grammar of Justice.* Ithaca, NY: Cornell University Press, 1987.

Zimring, Franklin E., and Gordon J. Hawkins. *Deterrence: The Legal Threat in Crime Control.* Chicago: University of Chicago Press, 1973.

———. *Incapacitation: Penal Confinement and Restraint of Crime.* New York: Oxford University Press, 1995.

Index

Abbott, Jack, 3
Abolition of punishment, 14, 149
Aeschylus, 6
Agamemnon, 6
Alternatives to punishment, 92,
155–172; utilitarian analysis of,
38–43
Anger, 62–71; and attachment to values, 62–63; contribution of subject to, 68, 70; cultural glorification of, 69; defined, 65; and demand for harm to offender,
65–66; distinguished from fear,
63, 63–64; and judgment of undeserved harm, 62, 62–63; distinguished from sorrow, 63; as foundation of moral community, 61;
as justification for punishment,
154; justification of, 64–65; pride
in, 69–71; punishment as expressing, 60–71; recognition of, 68–69;
retributive, 67; and self-respect,
61, 69; of victims, punishment as
satisfying, 20; vindictive, 65,
65–67, 151
Annulling of crime, 16, 17, 50–52,
147, 150–151, 154, 164; through
restitution, 93
Anomie, 40; institutional-anomie,
158. See also Institutional-anomie

theory of crime; Messner, S., and
R. Rosenfeld
Apology, 153, 162, 163, 171
Aquinas, St. Thomas, 11
Attachments, conflicting, 136–137
Auerhahn, Kathleen, 180n. 17
Augustine, 11
Automatic retaliation device,
106–107, 115
Autonomy: respect for, 14, 19, 125,
127, 130; of offender, 118, 119,
123
Aversion therapy, 190n. 2

Beccaria, Cesare, 12
Beliefs, and values, 132–133, 137
Benefit. See Good of offender; Good
of society
Benefits and burdens, punishment as
correcting balance of, 19–20, 81,
81–85
Bentham, Jeremy, 13, 23
Berns, Walter, 50, 65, 68
Blood feud, 6, 9
Blood guilt, 8, 9, 78
Blumstein, Alfred, 179n. 11, 180n. 20
Bosanquet, Bernard, 17
Bradley, F. H., 16–17
Braithwaite, John, 167
Burgh, Richard, 83

About the Author

Deirdre Golash is Associate Professor in the Department of Justice, Law and Society at American University in Washington, D.C.